BOXING

THE UNITED STATES NAVAL INSTITUTE, publisher of the Naval Aviation Physical Training Manuals, is a nationwide organization of military and civilian members and affiliations. The Institute was founded, not for profit, but for the advancement of professional, literary, and scientific knowledge in the Navy and among military and civilian contemporaries.

THE INSTITUTE has assumed the responsibility of keeping the Naval Aviation Physical Training Manuals revised and up-to-date in every respect for use by the military services in event of national emergency. Maintenance of high standards of physical fitness in the youth of our nation is considered a prerequisite to national preparedness. With this in mind every effort has been made to insure revisions, through the V-Five Association of America, that are compatible with civilian educational interests.

The Naval Aviation Physical Training Manuals

Revised by the

V-Five Association of America

BOARD OF DIRECTORS

OFFICERS AND BOARD MEMBERS

REVISION STAFF

Supervising Editor

Harold E. Lowe, Chairman

Department of Physical Education—Columbia University

Cartoonist; and Illustrators

Ensign Elizabeth Bunker, W-VS, USNR

Martin A. Topper, District Supervisor
of Health and Physical Education
Chicago Board of Education

Robert C. Osborn
(The Dilbert Series)
Salsbury, Connecticut

REVISION COMMITTEES

BASKETBALL

Co-Chairman

Gordon H. Ridings

Coach of Basketball—Columbia University

Co-Chairman

LCDR. Kenneth A. Hashagen, USNR

Coach of Basketball

U. S. Naval Air Station, Memphis

Advisory Member

Justin M. Barry

Coach of Basketball—University of Southern California

BOXING

Chairman

Roy D. Simmons

Coach of Boxing—Syracuse University

Advisory Member

Ike F. Deeter

Coach of Boxing

Washington State College

Advisory Member

LCDR. Anthony J. Rubino, USNR

Instructor in Physical Training

U. S. Naval Academy

CONDITIONING EXERCISES, GAMES, TESTS

Co-chairman

Karl C. H. Oermann, Director of Teacher
Education in Physical Education for Men
University of Pittsburgh

Co-Chairman

Carl H. Young, Chairman
Department of Physical Education
University of California Los Angeles

Advisory Member

Mitchell J. Gary

Director of Athletics and Physical Education—Western Michigan College

FOOTBALL

Chairman

Don B. Faurot

Coach of Football—University of Missouri

Advisory Member

W. Madison Bell

Coach of Football—Southern Methodist
University

Advisory Member

Bernard W. Bierman

Coach of Football—University of Minnesota

GYMNASTICS AND TUMBLING

Chairman

Hartley D. Price

Coach of Gymnastics—Florida State University

Advisory Member

Joseph M. Hewlett

Coach of Gymnastics—Ohio State University

Advisory Member

Newton C. Loken

Coach of Gymnastics—University of Michigan

HAND-TO-HAND COMBAT

Chairman
LCDR. Wesley Brown, Jr., USNR
Director of Athletics
U. S. Naval Air Station, Memphis

Advisory Member
Joseph W. Begala
Coach of Wrestling
Kent State University

INTRAMURAL PROGRAMS

Chairman
Lloyd H. Lux, Director of Athletics and Physical Education—Bates College

Advisory Member
Allen B. Klingel
Director of Recreational Sports
University of Illinois

Advisory Member
Charles F. Kerr
State Supervisor of Physical Education
Tennessee State Department of Education

SOCCER

Chairman
Earle C. Waters
Coach of Soccer—State Teachers College
West Chester, Pennsylvania

Advisory Member
John R. Eiler
Coach of Soccer
State Teachers College
Slippery Rock, Pennsylvania

Advisory Member
A. E. Florio
Assistant Professor of
Physical Education
University of Illinois

SWIMMING AND DIVING

Chairman
Alfred R. Barr
Coach of Swimming—Southern Methodist University

Advisory Member
Ben F. Grady
Coach of Swimming
University of Pittsburgh

Advisory Member
LCDR. John H. Higgins, USNR
Senior Swimming Instructor
Naval School Pre-Flight
U. S. Naval Air Station, Pensacola

TRACK AND FIELD

Co-Chairman
Charles D. Werner
Coach of Track
Pennsylvania State College

Co-Chairman
Frank J. Ryan
Assistant Coach of Track
Yale University

Advisory Member
Laurence N. Snyder
Coach of Track—Ohio State University

WRESTLING

Chairman
Clifford P. Keen
Coach of Wrestling—University of Michigan

Advisory Member
David C. Bartelma
Coach of Wrestling
University of Minnesota

Advisory Member
Charles M. Speidel
Coach of Wrestling
Pennsylvania State College

BOXING

Revision Staff

Chairman
Roy D. Simmons
Coach of Boxing
Syracuse University

Advisory Member
Ike F. Deeter
Coach of Boxing
Washington State College

Advisory Member
LCDR. Anthony J. Rubino, USNR
Instructor in Physical Training
U. S. Naval Academy

Supervising Editor
Harold E. Lowe, Chairman
Department of Physical Education
Columbia University

Executive Director
M. Budd Cox
V-Five Association
Annapolis, Maryland

First Edition Staff
(Please see Preface)

Directors

RADM. Thomas Hamilton, USN (Ret.)

CDR. Frank H. Wickhorst, USNR

Compiler-Writer
LCDR. Edwin L. Haislet, USNR

Editorial Staff

CDR. Harold E. Lowe, USNR

LCDR. Gordon H. Ridings, USNR

BOXING

Revised Edition

**PREPARED BY THE
V-FIVE ASSOCIATION OF AMERICA**

First Edition

PREPARED BY OFFICERS OF THE

**AVIATION TRAINING DIVISION
OFFICE OF THE CHIEF OF NAVAL OPERATIONS**

UNITED STATES NAVY

Annapolis, Maryland

UNITED STATES NAVAL INSTITUTE

First Edition Published 1943

Revised Edition Published 1950

PREFACE

The Naval Aviation V-5 Physical Training Manuals were prepared and published during World War II to provide the best standardized instruction in the sports selected to give the youth, training to be combat Naval pilots, the maximum physical and psychological benefits. It was the first time that intensive athletic training was used militarily, not only for conditioning and recreation, but to develop and intensify desired qualities, such as quick reaction, coordination, accurate timing, tool judgment, aggressiveness, and determination. It was, without question, the most rigorous mass program conducted in this country utilizing a large group of different sports. Each cadet was required to spend four to six hours a day in intense athletic training for eight months, the time diminishing in later months as other elements of flight and ground training were added. The results were highly successful as proven by the testimony of the high performance of this group of pilots, and the acclaim given them and the training methods by all who observed.

Over two thousand of the nation's leading physical educators and coaches of all sports participated in the planning and operation of this program as Reserve Officers, and most of them actually contributed in the preparation of these Manuals in their own specialty. While in some instances only one author did the final writing, it may in truth be said that the project was conceived and carried out as a group enterprise. The names of those officers who originally compiled and wrote the manuals now appear with the committees of revisions opposite the title page, and we deeply regret that space does not permit acknowledgment of the contribution of literally hundreds of others whose assistance was substantial. The original edition of these manuals was completed in 1943 under the direction of Commander Frank H. Wickhorst, USNR, Head of the Naval Aviation V-5 Physical Training Program at that time.

These books have found a wide usage in the civilian field of instruction in sports and have been adopted as text books and coaching manuals throughout the country. The Navy, recognizing the valuable service the manuals perform, authorized the V-Five Association, a peace time non-profit organization, whose nucleus is the above group of officers, to revise the books. The revisions are aimed to make the volumes fully up-to-date, with added material to treat with new techniques and emphasis, and to adapt the experience and lessons learned for instruction in proper gradations at the college and high school level.

It is increasingly evident that participation in a well-rounded physical training and sports program integrated with academic and spiritual elements is highly desirable in a youth's training. Different sports can be increasingly effective in developing many splendid qualities, and contribute to the well-being of the individual and the nation. It is hoped this V-5 Sports Series will continue to contribute to the general welfare of our youth.

T. J. Hamilton
Rear Admiral, USN (Ret.)
Director of Athletics
University of Pittsburgh

INTRODUCTION TO FIRST EDITION

BOXING is the essence of the fighting man. Through time immemorial it has been used to train, harden and discipline men for military purposes. For that reason boxing was given a prominent place in the list of those sports chosen by Naval Aviation to help produce fighting flyers.

The value of boxing is not in the skill that is acquired, although that too has real value for hand-to-hand combat, but because it quickly acclimates the body and mind to the violence and shock so foreign to modern day youth, yet so absolutely essential to fighting men.

Fighting men and especially fighting flyers must deal in violence and shock. They must be geared to it both physiologically and psychologically; they must accept it as a part of their stock in trade.

Boxing most easily helps the cadet make that transition. It teaches the ability to take a punch, and with the head reeling and the body staggering, to fight back viciously, calmly and with deadly purpose. It teaches disregard for hurts, that the body can endure terrific punishment and still come back for more. It teaches quick aggressive action with no quarter being asked or given, to follow every opening, to make every blow count. It teaches a disregard for violence and pain, safe in the knowledge that the impact of a blow does not hurt, that a knockout is not felt. It teaches amazing confidence in the ability of one's self to do the job that has to be done.

The book has been prepared for all Naval Aviation physical training ofiicers, keeping in mind that at any time such officers may be assigned to instruct in boxing. For that officer the book will not only tell him all about the different techniques and drills that go to make up boxing, but will give him a day by day lesson plan including the exact drills to follow and the percentage of time allotted to each.

The body of the book deals with technique and coaching hints. It should be read first and action simulated through the help of the illustrations.

In the appendix of the book are the drills for the teaching of mass boxing. They comprise the actual material that goes to form the lesson plans.

Also in the appendix is a section containing the lesson plans that go to form the Naval Aviation Boxing Program. Lesson plans to be followed will be indicated by special directives for each stage of training.

The directive will indicate which lesson plans comprise the syllabus for the stage of training in question. The drills included in the lesson plans should then be studied before actually taking over a class. Lesson plans should be followed exactly so that at any particular stage of training the content and method will be the same.

INTRODUCTION TO REVISED EDITION

At the start of World War II a representative of Naval Aviation, speaking to a group of officers who were formerly leading coaches and physical educators, offered to place boxing in the program of training for naval flyers if they could meet two challenges. One, they were told, was to devise an effective means or method of mass instruction; the other, was to present a complete and technically sound training in such a manner as to assure against injury to the participants.

The ultimate answer of the officers to this challenge to provide sound and safe instruction in boxing is the essence of this book. So well have these criteria been met that a fitting title for the manual might have been "a new plan for mass instruction in boxing under controlled conditions."

The book was also originally intended to better coordinate the program of boxing at the various stages of the Naval Aviation physical training program. The lesson plans and drills have proved to be sound not only in teaching cadets during World War II but since have proved equally useful for civilians in many high schools and colleges.

Institutions where boxing is a prominent sport, such as Louisiana State University, Syracuse, Washington State, San Jose State and others, have successfully followed the drills given in the appendix as the fundamental plan of instruction.

The aim of the committee in this revision has been to: bring the book up-to-date with the current rules; add further instructions on safeguarding the student; and adapt the material where possible to make it more useful for civilian programs of instruction.

The experienced coach or instructor in physical education, even though not a specialist in boxing, should experience little difficulty in adapting the lesson plans herein described for class work in physical education, either in high school or college.

The day by day lesson plans showing the sequence of drills to be used, together with the amount of time allotted to each, have proved to be most helpful to the inexperienced teacher.

Many coaches of varsity boxing teams also have found the pictures on the techniques a valuable individual teaching aid when given to the team candidates for study and analysis.

The Revision Committee
R.D.S.
A.J.R.
I.F.D.

TABLE OF CONTENTS

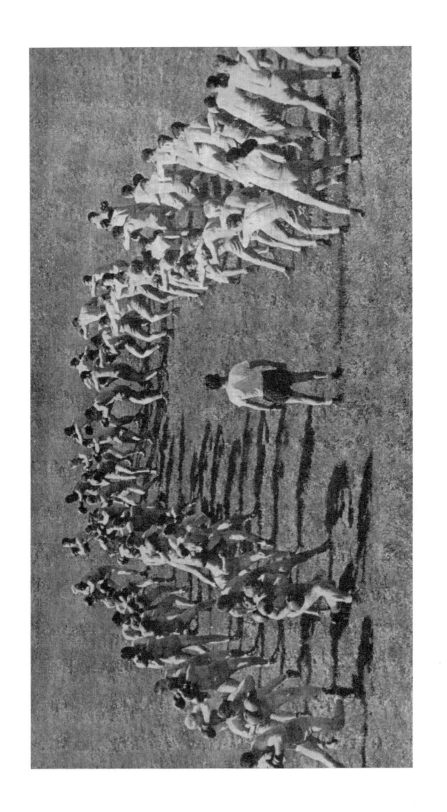

CHAPTER 1
The History of Boxing

The history of boxing is essentially the story of the molding of the combative or fighting instinct of man into a moral substitute for war.

This development presupposes an antiquity which can only be guessed. During the excavation of Cnossus by Sir Arthur Evans in 1900, a fragment of a relief picturing a boxer was discovered. Cnossus was the most important center of civilization from 2500 B.C., to 1500 B.C. Thus there is evidence that the antiquity of boxing in all probability goes back to the early Aegean civilization of 3000 to 4000 B.C.

EARLY HISTORY

Early man lived only by avoiding combat at close quarters. Such fighting meant death or injury. It was a fight for life. Sometime, somewhere, somehow, early man learned that damage could be wrought with the human fist. It probably first occurred during a "close in" where to survive meant fighting with every faculty. Perhaps the first blow with the fist was accidental. Any advantage gained was quickly used to help preserve the balance of life. It was used as a weapon of defense and only then as the last resort.

As the ages rolled by and some of the fierce struggle for existence was lessened, when men lived in groups for protection, perhaps it was then that boxing as a sport was born.

The strongest man was the chief and remained so only as long as he was strongest. Thus contests for physical supremacy developed. It is easy to imagine the types of activity which lent themselves to contests, strength contests in the lifting and carrying of heavy stones, and physical supremacy either by wrestling or by striking a man down.

Such a picture is a mere hypothesis, and yet, in some such manner boxing must have slowly evolved. Certainly it did not begin at the stage of development found during the Greek era.

THE AGE THAT WAS GREECE

Greek boxing is best divided into three periods. The first period is the Homeric age, from 900 B.C. to 600 B.C. During this period soft thongs,* ten

---

* This handwrapping was called Himantes and later Melichai.

1

to twelve feet in length, were wrapped around the hands and up to the elbow. Because the hand coverings were soft and used to protect the hand rather than to injure the opponent, boxing was conducted on a high level. Rules were few, but fair play, strength, courage and some skill were portrayed.

Boxing was introduced to the Olympic games during the 23rd Olympiad, 688 B.C., or near the end of this first period of Greek boxing. Boxing for boys was added during the 41st Olympics and brought to a close the greatest boxing era in the history of the Greek Age.

During the next period, the classic period of Greece, from 600 B.C., to 400 B.C., boxing changed but little. There was a tendency to make the hand covering harder and heavier, but the purpose of the covering was still hand protection, and not injury of the opponent. The covering was now called Spairai.

Boxing was one of the most popular sports of this age, as is indicated by referring to the Catalogue of Sports, in which boxing is listed second only to horse racing.

Only those contestants who were able to survive nine months of training at the place of the contest were allowed to participate in the Olympic games. Drawings were made for opponents, even as today, after which the fighting began. Boxing usually came on the third day at high noon, the middle day of the festival. It was the custom of the time to have boxing when the sun was the hottest in order to further test the fortitude and endurance of the athletes. The ring, such as it was, was formed by the spectators. Actually a ring was unnecessary because to "give ground" was a sign of cowardice. Footwork as used later, was unknown. Each boxer was allowed one "second" whose duty was to bind the hands and render advice. Unlike today, advice could be given any time during the bout. When the two men were ready to box they advanced toward each other, manoeuvered for position,* then commenced to fight. Each bout was fought to a finish. The boxers fought until either one or both were exhausted, or defeat was acknowledged. There were no weight divisions although the boxers were usually heavyweights.

The boxing position was more square than today. The left arm was held folded tight to the body and was used principally as a guard, while the right

---

* This manoeuvering was made necessary because of the uneven ground as well as the position of the sun.

arm was usually swung in an arc over and downward. No clinching or wrestling was allowed. Rules were enforced and order maintained.

The third period in Greek history as determined by the type of hand wrappings used for boxing purposes, extended from the fourth century B.C. until the rise of the Roman Empire. The handwrapping was now called "caestus."* They were no longer mere hand protectors but had become weapons of great weight and force. Using such weapons boxing lost its identity as a sport. Instead, it was a battle to death. Science had given way to brute force. The Olympic games lost their national character and became professionalized. Theodocius abolished the games entirely in 394 A.D. During the days of the Roman Empire boxing was not a sport, but a spectacle. Slaves, using the caestus as their only weapon fought to death for the amusement of populace.

Thus ends the first great age of boxing as a science, as a sport, and as an expression of the life of the time.

BOXING DURING THE MIDDLE AGES

Boxing seems to have declined with the fall of the Roman Empire. It did not disappear altogether as some writers seem to think. It is true that it did not have a prominent place in the life of the people nor was it written about extensively, but this was characteristic of the age, not of boxing.

With the conquest of Britain by the legions of Rome, it is entirely probable that boxing found its way to these island people.

It is recorded that St. Bernard established boxing in Italy in the year 1200 in order to stamp out the many fatal abuses of the deadly weapons of that time. Boxing was one of the sports used in the training of pages for knighthood during the feudal age.

There is an occasional reference to the word "box" in the literature of the sixteenth and seventeenth centuries, which reveals that boxing did survive during the Middle Ages.

BOXING IN ENGLAND

England is regarded as the birthplace of modern boxing.

---

* The caestus was also known as the Myrmex. It was strictly a weapon and was so regarded. It is thought to have an early pre-classic origin. Daniel J. Brinton suggests that its purpose was to kill the object of the sacrifice before the ceremony.

In any discussion of boxing in England it is well to remember that there are three distinct periods, the early days of the Prize Ring, the great age of the Prize Ring, when boxing was a natural expression of English life, and the decline of the Prize Ring.

THE EARLY DAYS OF THE PRIZE RING

The first period of the Prize Ring might be said to extend from 1698 to 1790. During this period a certain order was developed. Many of the evils of the ring were done away with.

The practice of sword play and the use of the cudgel was perhaps directly responsible for the beginning of boxing at this time. John Figg, master of the sword and stick, was the founder of boxing, and the Prize Ring. Evidently through his knowledge of fencing with its stops and parries, Figg worked out a system of fencing with the bare fist. However, Figg was famous more for his sword and stick play than for his boxing skill.

Figg was England's first boxing champion, fighting Ned Sutton in the first championship prize fight ever held. He was champion of England from 1719 until he died in 1734. While too much credit cannot be given Figg for what he did for the Prize Ring, yet it remained for one of his students to be the real benefactor.

Jack Broughton was also a swordsman and an expert with the cudgel. Like his teacher, he too opened a school, but with more emphasis on teaching boxing. In order to attract the public to his school, he advertised the use of "muffles"* for sparring purposes. Because of this, Broughton is credited with the origin of the modern boxing glove.

His second great contribution to boxing was a set of rules called "Broughton's Code." These rules like the gloves were an attempt to regulate boxing in order to attract the nobility to the sport, and to create a greater all-around interest in boxing. A system of rules was needed at this time. Because there were no rules, boxing was a very brutal affair attracting the worst type of ruffians. Consequently the better classes were not attracted, and Broughton had difficulty in finding patrons for his school.

While his rules were concerned mainly with the regulation of the audience and obtaining fair play for the boxer, they succeeded remarkedly well in

---

* Broughton evidently received his idea of gloves from the Greek "muffles," which were used for training purposes only.

restoring order to the ring. Standards of a sort as well as fair play were introduced.

THE GREAT AGE OF THE PRIZE RING

From the time of Mendoza in 1790, to Tom Spring in 1824, is chronicled a period of boxing that might be paralleled to the classic age of Greece. At this time the ring was crowded with great fighters[*] and the greatest names in England[†] were associated with the Prize Ring. Amateur boxing was practiced as a sport. Mendoza was the first champion to study boxing as an art. He attained the greatest degree of skill of any fighter up to his time. Thereafter the emphasis on skill grew greater and because of this, it may be said that Mendoza started a new idea of boxing.

In the year 1795 Mendoza was defeated by John Jackson. Jackson retired after this one fight and started a school of boxing. Here he gained his greatest fame because of his remarkable ability as a teacher. His school became the meeting place of the gentry, and due to their recognition and enthusiasm boxing soon gained a place in the life of that day. Boxing became a part of the education of the sons of the nobility and gentry and was taught in the public schools of Westminster and Cambridge.

THE DECLINE OF THE PRIZE RING

As in the days of Greece, boxing deteriorated and declined with the advent of monetary prizes and awards. The minute that large sums of money became possible through the Prize Ring, its patronage was rapidly taken over by professional promoters who were concerned primarily with pecuniary gains.

The practice of "fighting a cross" or as it is now called "throwing a fight," soon became prevalent. As a result boxing clubs closed their doors and patrons and public alike refused to be connected in any manner with the Prize Ring. The force of public sentiment became so strong that the police were obliged to carry out the law, which prohibited prize fighting. Thereafter prize fights were conducted in great secrecy. Naturally, rules and regulations were relaxed and the prize fight degenerated into a brutal contest which resulted in many severe injuries and a few deaths.

---

[*] Such men as Mendoza, Belcher and Spring.
[†] The Prince of Wales; the Dukes of Clarence, Queensbury and Blaufort; the Marquesses of Tweedale and Worcestor; Lords Sifton_ Wilton, Yarmouth, Berkley, etc.

This corruption continued until the death of Brighton "Bill" in 1838. Then in an effort to save the Prize Ring, the New Rules of the London Prize Ring were formulated and adopted. The damage had been done however and only the quick action of the Marquis of Queensbury in 1866 saved boxing from complete disrepute.

EVOLUTION OF RULES GOVERNING BOXING

The first recorded rules were not formulated to improve boxing itself, but to keep the spectators from interfering or preventing a fight from reaching its natural conclusion. It was an attempt to gain the interest of the better classes, not only as spectators and patrons of prize fighting, but as students of boxing. The boxers were given a fair deal because the prize money was divided on the stage and the umpires were chosen by the fighters from among the crowd.

The rules did not provide for a ring of any certain size or for a referee. A round of fighting lasted until one or both of the contestants were knocked or wrestled down. Thirty seconds were allowed in which to return to the center of the ring, or to "scratch," as it was known. Only two fouls were listed, hitting when down, and obtaining wrestling holds below the waist. Holding, butting, gouging, kicking, tripping and wrestling were all common practices.

These rules, sketchy as they were, brought a certain order to the ring in comparison to the savage brutality that characterized the beginnings of prize fighting in England. They were introduced by Jack Broughton in 1743, and are referred to as Broughton's Code. These rules were the only regulation of the Prize Ring for over ninety-five years.

In 1838, due to the many irregularities in the ring, and to the death of Brighton Bill, a new set of rules was drawn up and known as "The Rules of the London Prize Ring." While these rules were definitely superior to the first code, they came too late. Public opinion was definitely opposed to the Prize Ring. These rules were revised again in 1853.

These new rules are interesting for several reasons. They were made to govern prize fighting out-of-doors. Therefore, they included many rules and regulations that are used today. The tossing of a coin to decide the choice of corners was practiced. Spiked shoes were allowed in order to give a better footing on the turf. Biting, gouging, kicking or deliberately falling down were eliminated.

A twenty-four foot ring was required. For the first time a watch was used by the referee to enforce the "eight second" rule.* The referee became the arbitrator between the umpires and seconds. He was chosen by the two umpires, who in turn were chosen by the two seconds or backers.

By the year 1866, the Prize Ring had so declined that in order to save boxing the Marquis of Queensbury started amateur competition. He had W. Chambers draw up rules to control this amateur competition. In substance these rules contained practically all that is included in our present day rules. All wrestling and holding were eliminated. The length of the bout was limited to three rounds, two rounds being of three minutes each, with the last round of four minutes' duration. In case of disagreement between the judges, the referee was required either to cast the deciding vote, or to order another two minute round to be fought. Ten seconds time was allowed to "come to scratch" after a knockdown. Inability to finish a round gave the match to the other contestant. Cleats were not allowed on the shoes. Gloves had to be used in all bouts. The referee was the only man allowed in the ring with the boxers.

These rules were later modified for professional boxers, but the changes made were trivial, except the one which allowed an unlimited number of rounds to be fought during a match.

In 1881 because of the difficulty encountered in judging under the Queensbury Rules, the Amateur Boxing Association Rules were introduced. On the whole, these new rules were the very same as the Queensbury Rules, but with emphasis placed on a method of scoring and judging.

THE AGE OE THE GLOVE

The use of gloves in boxing was given a tremendous impetus with the advent of the Queensbury rules. The transition from the knuckle to the glove was slow, but with it came the greater possibility for boxing as an art. The glove made possible free hitting because of the greater hand protection. This resulted in a greater development of speed, skill and boxing technique. Better physical condition was necessary to stand the strenuous pace. Because faster hitting was possible without fear of hand injury, more openings could be taken advantage of. Thus the "knockout" blow was born.

The sole aim in the old prize fighting days was to conserve energy as long as possible. With no limit as to the number of rounds to be fought, the one

---

* The "eight second" rule merely stated that eight seconds beyond the customary thirty would be allowed "to come to scratch" before the match would be declared forfeited.

constant need was endurance. The matches were all fought out-of-doors where the elements were a limiting factor to skill. Because of the turf, footing was insecure and movement was limited. "Hooks and swings" of various types was the chief manner of attack. Because such blows are easily blocked, it was necessary to wear the opponent down by force rather than finesse.

BOXING IN THE UNITED STATES

There are no definite records available as to when boxing actually started in the United States. It has been suggested that it was brought about by the custom of the southern aristocrats of sending their sons abroad for a part of their education. No doubt a phase of their education in England consisted of learning the "manly art of self-defense." On their return, it is easy to imagine the introduction of boxing to the negro slaves on the southern plantations.

Early boxing in America never had a chance. Introduced by the same men who had caused its downfall in England, the early bare knuckle days in America were scenes of brutal brawls. As a result, prize fighting was outlawed in every State of the Union. The last bare knuckle fight in America, under the Rules of the London Prize Ring, took place during July, 1889, at Richburg, Mississippi, between John L. Sullivan and Jack Kilrain.

Thereafter, Sullivan issued a statement to the effect that he would never again fight with bare knuckles, although his opponents might do so if they desired. Because of Sullivan's evident preference for glove fighting the Rules of the London Prize Ring were barred in America.

THE STATUS OR BOXING BEFORE 1915

Before 1915 there was very little legalized boxing. At the turn of the Century, boxing, or as it was then called, prize fighting, was legalized in only five states—New York, California, Louisiana, Nevada and Florida.

In New York State the old "Horton Boxing Law" was in effect before 1900 but was outlawed in that year until 1915.

Between 1900 and 1915, although illegal, prize fights were still being held in New York under the guise of club fights. While some clubs actually had an honest membership with a gymnasium, the purpose in most cases was to hold prize fights. Fighters were given membership in the club and announced as being from the Club. Tickets were sold on a membership basis for one night. All the big name fighters fought in such bouts. In 1908, ten round, no decision bouts were held in the open although boxing was still illegal.

Finish fights were held in the mid-west prior to 1890, although boxing was not legalized. Because there was no law against boxing, it flourished openly in those states where the Governors lent their approval.

On the west coast twenty round fights to a finish were held before 1914, but in that year such fights were declared illegal.

The four round era in California started in 1815. Such bouts were called amateur, but all the great fighters of that time, including most of the world's champions fought on the cards.

BOXING AFTER 1915

The greatest era of boxing the world has ever seen came between 1915 and 1930. There are several reasons for the sudden expansion. About 1915 boxing finally found its way into the statute books of the country. It became legalized in New York through the Walker Boxing Law in 1915. In the Midwest the first state to legalize boxing was Wisconsin in 1915. The Wisconsin law provided for ten round, no decision bouts. It became the model for many other states and was widely copied.

In California four round bouts continued until the early twenties, when boxing was again legalized.

Perhaps the greatest impetus to boxing was World War I. The influx of soldier boys from war camps, all trained in boxing, caused a great demand for the sport.

Today boxing is legalized in forty-two states, regulated and controlled by commissions appointed for that purpose.

BOXING DURING WORLD WAR I

During World War I the training division of the army was confronted with the problem of changing the ordinary lay minded individual into a fighting machine. It was necessary to find a means of giving large masses of men "agility of body, quickness of eye, good balance and control in giving a punch or a thrust, and an aggressive fighting spirit." Boxing was selected and did the job then as it is again doing today.

BOXING IN EDUCATIONAL INSTITUTIONS

Boxing first found its way into our educational system through the medium of intramural athletics. Harvard University had intramural boxing as early as 1880. In 1919, after the first World War, many of the service men being released went into our colleges to pick up where they had left off. Their interest in boxing was soon transferred from the camps to the college gymnasiums, and intercollegiate boxing was the direct result. Intercollegiate boxing can be said to have started in 1919, when Penn State College met the University of Pennsylvania. The U. S. Naval Academy started boxing in 1920. By 1923, intercollegiate boxing was a well-developed sport in the eastern states, and in New England. The first intercollegiate boxing tournament was held at Penn State College in 1924.

In 1932, the Eastern Intercollegiate Boxing Conference was formed, consisting of Pittsburgh, Carnegie Tech, Washington and Jefferson, Bucknell, Temple, Duquesne and West Virginia. The University of Virginia introduced boxing to the South in 1922; Louisiana State and the University of Florida introduced boxing to the far south; in the mid-west, Kansas State and the University of Wisconsin have done yeoman work in behalf of intercollegiate boxing. On the west coast boxing has flourished since 1925, and is rapidly expanding. At the present time there are about one hundred colleges in the U. S. that have intercollegiate boxing, and about the same number that have boxing on an intramural basis.

At the present time boxing in high schools is in an era of expansion, and is rapidly finding a place in the sports curriculum. While boxing has been legislated against by many high school athletic associations, yet its growth has been steady, and the demand constant. In such states as Louisiana, Washington and Idaho, state tournaments are conducted each year. In Wisconsin and Oregon the sport is rapidly developing, sectional and district meets being held.

AMATEUR BOXING

If boxing existed at all during the middle ages, it existed as an amateur sport. In England the history of the sport indicates that it was first amateur, then professional. Later both existed side by side.

As early as 1860 there were a few amateur boxing clubs in England. In 1867, under the sponsorship of the Marquis of Queensbury, the first amateur tournament was staged. Championships were held in only three weights, light, middle and heavy.

In 188O, the Amateur Boxing Association of England was formed on the belief that boxing was too good to be used solely as a means of financial gain.

In the United States, the Amateur Athletic Union was formed in 1888. It has exercised jurisdiction over amateur boxing since that time. Annual amateur championships have been held without interruption since that date. There are approximately 16,500 registered boxers in the thirty-nine district associations of the Union. Amateur boxers representing the United States, competed in the Olympic Games of 1904, 1920, 1924, 1928, 1932 and 1956.

THE GOLDEN GLOVES

Previous to 1923, amateur boxing in the true sense of the word was non-existent. Aware of this deplorable state, knowing that amateur boxing was nothing more than commercial exploitation of our youth by unscrupulous men, but believing that amateur boxing had much to offer to growing youth if conducted under responsible auspices, the *Chicago Tribune* presented what was called the *Chicago Tribune* Amateur Boxing Meet. Due to the fact that boxing was illegal at this time in the State of Illinois, it was necessary to hold the event under an injunction which prohibited the state from interfering with the conduct of the event.

The *Chicago Tribune* did not again sponsor a Golden Gloves boxing tournament until 1928, the year boxing was legalized in Illinois. In 1927, the *New York Daily News* introduced a huge amateur boxing tournament to New York City, patterning it after the one held in Chicago in 1924, but calling it the Golden Gloves. The *Chicago Tribune* returned to the field again in 1928, sponsoring thereafter a yearly Golden Gloves tournament.

Intercity competition between the winners of the *New York Daily News* Tournament and the *Chicago Tribune* Tournament was started in 1928. Intercity bouts have been conducted annually without interruption since that time.

In 1931 international competition was initiated. Each year the champions of some foreign country were brought over to fight the *Chicago Tribune* team. After five years of such matches it was apparent that the talent in the Chicago area was too strong for the Champions of any one particular European country. Instead, the champions of an all-European tournament were sent over to compete against Chicago.

This continued until the war interrupted the series.

BOXING IN THE ARMY IN WORLD WAR II

There is no doubt that the use of boxing by the army during the first world war gave boxing the chance to develop in our colleges and schools, and in our communities.

Today the army "gives boxing an important place in their athletic program, not only because it teaches aggressiveness and a fighting spirit, but because boxing is still the best training for bayonet fighting. Nearly every block and punch in boxing has its counterpoint in bayoneting . . . the *long point* in bayonet work corresponds to the left lead in boxing, while the blow with a butt of a gun is similar to the right hand counter. The position of the legs in executing a chop with the bayonet is similar to the leg work in the "Fitzsimmons shift." The army still believes that the soldier trained in boxing generally becomes the expert with a bayonet.

In all army camps boxing is one of the preferred sports, not only because of its spectator and morale building qualities, but because of its definite contributions in the making of a better fighting soldier.

BOXING IN THE NAVY IN WORLD WAR II

Boxing has always been the "number one" sport of the Navy. On board ship where space is at a premium, sports must of a necessity be selected because they require little in the way of space. Boxing not only answers this purpose, but is a method of instilling high morale, not only in the fighter and his backers, but for a whole division, a whole ship—and sometimes even a whole fleet. Before the war, each ship would have its own team. They would compete in regular scheduled tournaments against champions of other ships. Each fleet would eventually determine its own Champions. Naturally, during war this cannot be followed but wherever you find the Navy you will always find boxing gloves.

Boxing is a part of the physical training at all Naval Training Stations, and one of the core sports in the Naval Aviation Physical Training Program.

CHAPTER II
The Place of Boxing in the Naval Aviation Physical Training Program

One of the greatest problems facing Naval Aviation is to match its modern combat planes with men who not only can fly them, *but with men who can and will fight them.* Such is the underlying aim of the entire physical training program of Naval Aviation, and therefore of each sport in the program.

Boxing, a sport as old as war itself, because it is a substitute for personal combat, closely parallels the actual battle situation of the pilot. The feint, the dodge, the quick counter attack, together with the final finishing blow is as much a part of modern combat flying as it is of boxing. The ultimate aim of the boxing program is to develop better naval aviators, aviators who are not only better mechanical flyers, but fighting pilots who are eager to contact and destroy the enemy.

There are certain qualities inherent in boxing which tend to make better mechanical flyers. They are:

Endurance and Stamina makes possible continued effort over a long period of time without loss of efficiency; means the ability to direct a steady flow of energy over a specified period of time, allowing for occasional spurts as the situation demands. A flyer if he is to survive, must maintain peak efficiency all the time he is in the plane. He must have endurance, and the ability to continue the same pace until the objective is reached, and the job is accomplished. He must have the endurance of the trained boxer.

A highly trained nervous system, capable of instant reflexive action—Boxing requires faster action of learned movements in less time than any other sport. The boxer must make a choice of possible action, and then react correctly, all in a fraction of a second. It demands the same reflexive action that is required of the combat flyer.

The ability to constantly maintain effective body balance and therefore a body position capable of greatest efficiency—Balance is the key to efficient movement, power and speed in boxing. The expert boxer is always on balance, ready to defend or attack. He automatically assumes the balanced position in order to function. This is equally true of the good flyer.

The ability to make quick and accurate judgments—Intelligence and judgment are prime essentials to boxing. A boxer literally boxes with his head and heart, rather than with his hands and feet. The boxer must out-think, out-smart and out-manoeuver his opponent. He must act quickly and correctly, or be instantly penalized. *Combat flying demands the same qualities of judgment.*

The development of a sense of "body feel"—The ability to always know body position, feet, trunk, hands and head in relation to the opponent, no matter what the technique employed, and at the same time have knowledge of correct action in relation to openings created, is developed only through experience in competitive boxing. Such kinesthetic sense, or body feel, is the same that enables the flyer to always know body position in relation to the normal upright position and to know the correct "feel" of the many drills, formations and manoeuvers of modern combat flying.

The ability to relax, to keep calm and poised thus allaying the possibility of emotional block, is one of the greatest contributions of boxing—To the flyer such ability means the difference between victory or defeat, life or death.

Traits accruing from participation in boxing which make for a fighting flyer are:

Aggressiveness—Boxing teaches one how to make contact with the opponent; to immediately discern weaknesses in the opponent's defense; to instantly take advantage of such weaknesses; and to continuously force the attack until the opponent is defeated. Such aggressiveness is absolutely essential to modern combat flying.

Courage—Boxing gives the ability to face the enemy alone; the willingness to carry the attack in spite of "heavy guns"; to gamble on the ability of the self against all that the enemy can offer. These are the lessons of courage that our fighting flyers must possess.

Self-confidence and self-reliance—Boxing teaches faith in the ability of the self to out-fight, out-smart and to out-game the opponent, no matter what the odds. Such confidence is prerequisite for naval aviators.

THE IMPORTANCE OF BOXING

Boxing is the modern expression of the combative tendency in man. The law of self-preservation is strong in all creatures. Its necessity is readily understood. Without it death is as certain today as in those early days when the inability to fight, to struggle, to adapt or to change, meant death.

Failure to "fight back" successfully causes mental complexes, neuroses and psychoses in one out of every twenty persons. Modern life is characterized by speed. Speed means change and change requires adjustment. Inability to adjust indicates an emotional instability, the incapacity to "take it." Life has always demanded the faculty to "take it," and this is true today more than ever before. It means stamina to successfully control or fight life's battles. There is an indication of growing "softness" in people. Physical "softness" results because there is no longer need for physical hardness, which in turn tends to produce a mental "softness" or emotional instability.

Just as surely as good food is essential to good physical health, so there is a need for the development and expression of the combative spirit for emotional health. The combative spirit finds release in "give and take" sports, but especially in personal contact sports. In games of this type the spirit of "give and take" is developed as part of the game.

BOXING BUILDS POWER

It is agreed that of all activities, boxing is one of the most vigorous. The large muscle groups of the body are used, demanding vigorous action of the heart and lungs. This is a necessity in a power building regime.

Boxing is sustained activity. Not only is the action vigorous, but it is carried on over a period of time. Vigorous action alone is not enough nor is sustained action by itself enough. Acting together, great demands are made of the body, and the body responds by building a greater reserve of power than is required to meet the energy output.

Any person who has boxed at top speed for even one two-minute round knows what is meant by sustained action. As function makes structure, so sustained effort demands and creates more abundant energy.

Boxing makes use of practically every conceivable human movement of the arms, legs and body. There are over six hundred counter-blows in boxing, each requiring different movements. All parts of the body receive attention. Action in boxing is whole-body action, all parts working as one.

Besides the many movements characteristic of boxing, the training procedures are numerous and varied. Pulley work, rope jumping, shadow boxing, light and heavy bag work and calisthenics all give varied types of action. Such diverse forms of exercise give a symmetrical, balanced physical development. The heart, lungs and internal organs are toned and conditioned to peak efficiency. Boxing is varied action.

Boxing then, demands sustained, vigorous and varied big muscle activity. Such activity calls for increased action of the heart, lungs and circulation. Abundant energy is needed.

BOXING BUILDS COORDINATION

Neuro-muscular development means the ability of the body to perform the right action at the right time. It means efficient movement. It means minute control of the body, coordination and graceful action.

Boxing is the most exacting of all sports. It requires faster movement of learned action, in less space of time, than any other sport. In all other sports there is a space of time between attack and defense. In boxing attack and defense are practically one and the same thing. All action must be instantaneous. Between the start of a blow, and its hit (or miss) there is only a fraction of a second's time. In that moment the boxer must decide what to do. This is where intelligence and training enters. If there is such a thing as perfect boxing, four types of blows are used: The straight blows, the wide swings, the short hooks and the uppercuts. Used with both hands to the face or body, the result is sixteen possible combinations. In addition there are eight different modes* of defense: Catching, blocking, guarding, parrying, slipping, ducking, weaving and sidestepping, When it is considered that these techniques can be performed against blows to head or body with either hand, either inside or outside, a possible ninety-four combinations can be worked out. There is a counter possible for each blow, and a defense for each possible counter, resulting in approximately fifteen hundred possible manoeuvers. While this number is really determined by the skill of the performer, it shows the unlimited number of choices that a boxer is forced to make. Naturally, a boxer does not think over each possible action choice. It is more likely to be like this—which hand is the opponent using and what kind of blow? Should a counter be attempted or defensive tactics used? If it is to be a counter, which one should it be? If defense is the proper move, what form should be selected? *All this actually happen: but not in the ring.* Then it would be too late. All possible manoeuvers which occur in the ring must be practiced countless times during training. First, they should be carefully thought out, then slowly tried again and again. Incessant repetition over a long period of time is necessary until the action becomes automatic and instantaneous.

---

* This list does not exhaust the possibilities of defense. Such other techniques as rolling, stopping and stepping out of range could be used.

Any movement or action often repeated becomes habituated and conditioned. Instead of reasoning out what is to be done each time, a stimulus when presented by an opponent becomes directly associated with the correct response and immediate action takes place. It must be understood that such action presupposes long hours of practice in which specific action has been practiced for a specific action situation, until the final action is automatic with the stimuli. Thus, through conditioning, the higher learning centers are left free to think of other things besides the performance of skills and techniques.

Because of the instant penalty resulting from ill-coordinated movements, the necessity for precise skill is great, and highly complex movements are quickly learned. Hours of practice result in efficient handling of the body. Such action indicates a highly developed state of body coordination, promoting grace, ease and confidence.

BOXING DEMANDS INTELLIGENCE

It is sometimes difficult for those people whose experience is outside the field of athletics to understand that boxing requires intelligence. To them, for the most part, boxing is mainly physical prowess.

The baseball pitcher is called "smart" because he outguesses the batter; the quarterback is credited as being the "brains" of the team; the chess player is considered highly intelligent. Yet the element of time does not enter into such situations. The player can study the opposition noticing indications of intention or weakness, and then regulating his next action accordingly. This is not true of boxing. Out of the hundreds of possible choices, one choice must be selected, and it must be right. Will anyone maintain that even the mere acquisition of hundreds of complicated movements does not require intelligence? Does not choice of action need judgment and keen insight?

A skillful boxer must be a master of time-space relationships. The speed of an opponent's blow must be gauged in relation to body position and plan. It is imperative to interpret one's own speed and reaction and judge the possibility of striking the opponent, or adjusting the defense. Interpretation means judgment and judgment implies intelligence. judgment in boxing must be made quickly, accurately and constantly. Because misjudgment brings instant and severe penalty, a premium is placed on correct judgment.

A boxer must interpret the actions of his opponent in order to know whether to attack or defend. Judgment here must be practically simultaneous with action, or the boxer is instantly penalized. He must balance his own abilities against those of his opponents. How well he is able to do this is told on his record sheet.

BOXING DEMANDS ABILITY TO RELAX UNDER PRESSURE

Physical combat is as old as man. It is fraught with emotional change. Boxing is physical combat disciplined, presenting a situation filled with the need for emotional control. Anger is a natural impulse in the heat of battle. Yet in boxing, anger must be controlled because it causes a lack of judgment and the ability to act or think quickly. Boxing teaches cool, easy deliberation, the faculty to think and act under pressure.

Because the rules prescribe certain classes and weight divisions, boxers are fairly evenly matched during bouts. This helps to equalize the chance for either success or failure. A boxer is never so expert as not to be in danger of defeat. One blow can wipe out the greatest lead. One moment the elation of success is experienced the next moment the pangs of defeat. Proper emotional control is the result of a balance between success and failure. Too much of either prevents proper emotional stability to develop and gives rise to many problem cases. Boxing is an activity ripe with the possibilities for emotional development.

CHAPTER III
Facilities, Gear and Safety in Boxing

In the consideration of facilities and gear it is well to remember that no matter how fine or elaborate the facilities, there is value only in direct proportion to the leadership concerned. Poor leadership and good facilities will bring inadequate results. Good leadership and poor facilities will obtain results. The best combination is good facilities and good leadership.

ORGANIZATION OF FACILITIES

Boxing demands less in the way of facilities and gear than the majority of sports. The better and the more specialized facilities are for boxing the better the results to be obtained, leadership remaining the same. Space and leadership are the only absolute requisites of boxing. Actually, beginning boxing can be well taught without the use of gloves.

The All Purpose Boxing Room

This is making use of almost any available space. It can vary from a large drill hall, field house, armory or gymnasium suitable for mass boxing, to a small classroom, hall or stage usable for small group instruction. While the primary purpose of such a room may be other than boxing, all that is required for boxing is unobstructed space, good light and good ventilation.

The Specialized Boxing Room

This is a room built or adapted specifically for boxing purposes. All types of fixed, movable and specialized equipment and gear should be included in its appointments. The room should be divided into the boxing, bag, and exercise sections. It should be well lighted and well ventilated. The floor should be wooden and if possible covered with some type composition board at least an inch thick, over which a heavy canvas covering has been drawn tightly. The following equipment should be found in a specialized boxing room, built to accommodate 250 men at one time.

Boxing Ring Section

4 rings—20X20.
200 pairs of gloves.
2 whistles.
1 bell or buzzer.
1 electric timer.

200 head protectors.

Bag Section

25 striking bag platforms and bags.
25 heavy training or body bags.
50 pairs light bag gloves.

Exercise Section

50 jumping ropes—ball-bearing swivels.
15 medicine balls.
1 20 X 20 mat.
10 sets wall pulleys.
8 section stall bars.

ORGANIZATION OF GEAR

Fixed Equipment

Means equipment which is a part of the room, erected or attached with the idea of permanency.

The Boxing Ring—Regulation boxing rings should be used. They should be placed with regard to natural light, accessibility, and room for bleachers. If possible one of the rings should have bleachers around three sides so that it can be used for team or tournament fighting.

The ring can be either a platform type, built up so that it is about thirty inches off the floor; or a floor type built upon a slightly raised platform laid directly on the floor. The platform type is preferable for actual competition or tournament boxing. For training purposes the floor type is recommended.

The size of the ring can vary from sixteen to twenty feet, inside dimension. The larger sized ring is recommended because more men can use it during practice sessions. Eighteen feet is the standard sized intercollegiate ring, inside measurement.

It is essential that the floor of the ring extend at least thirty inches beyond the lower ropes in order to get away from the possibility of falling or slipping outside of the ring. Over the pad, drawn tightly is a canvas which should completely cover the mat, and extend down over the edge of the ring. Three one-inch ropes encircle the ring, two, three and four feet respectively above the ring floor.

Ropes must be wrapped with cloth to prevent rope burns. Black rubber covered cables, one and one-eighth inches in diameter, can be used instead of ropes and do not have to be covered.

Ring posts should not be nearer to the ring ropes than eighteen inches. Both posts and turnbuckles must be heavily padded. If a platform ring is used steps must be provided. A battery of lights should be dropped from overhead to assure proper lighting for contestants.

Both the platform and floor ring can be of the portable type, quickly taken down, moved and erected at another place.

A portable floor ring with mat and cover can be made up very easily and at little cost. Materials needed are:

Three—1 inch endless ropes 72 feet long.

Four—4″X4″ wooden posts, or 2½″ steel posts equipped with bottom gudgeon, three eye bolts for rope turnbuckles, and two ⅜″ steel guy rods or wires with turnbuckles.

Twelve—Turnbuckles for rope adjustment, Size ½″ X 12¾″ open to 18¾″.

Four—Steel floor plates for corner posts, size 3½″ X 3½″ X 3½″; hole diameter 3/4″.

Eight—Steel floor plates for guy rods or wire. Size 3½″ X 3½″ X ½″.

Striking Bag Platform—Can be either the adjustable or the fixed type. The adjustable type is one easily regulated to proper height by means of a turnwheel and a fixing lever. The mechanism is usually hydraulic. This is perhaps the best, although the most expensive type of platform.

The fixed type can be built in at different heights. Usually the bag is set to the height of a six footer. Low foot platforms should be furnished in order that each individual may regulate the bag to the proper height.

The bag platform itself must be heavy. Often to give added weight, sand bags are placed on the top of the platform. The platform type can be easily built or can be obtained from any sporting goods house.

Training, Body or Heavy Bags—Can be purchased with either leather or canvas covering. The filling should be some resilient material such as a special hair, or hair felt preparation. A body bag can be made up inexpensively by using a duffle or sea bag filled with sawdust, rags or a combination of both.

The bag should be hung securely from the ceiling with a chain attachment. The bags should be spaced so that it will have free action, yet will not interfere with the others. If a long suspension chain is used, a short snub chain should be attached to prevent a free swinging bag.

The training bag can be of any size and shape. The standard bag is 36″ X 14″. However it can be 60″ X 14″, or 40″ X 24″. All sizes should be used if possible.

Stall Bars—A piece of standard gymnasium equipment useful for abdominal work. Must be secured firmly.

Wall Pulleys—Two types are used in boxing gymnasiums. The wall pulley which is a standard piece of gym equipment, operated by use of ropes and adjustable weights and the elastic pulley which needs no explanation. The wall pulley is recommended. Should be found in the exercise section of the room.

Movable Equipment

Refers to that necessary equipment which is neither fixed nor attached to the room but is nevertheless a part of the permanent equipment of the room.

The Bell—Every boxing gymnasium should have a bell used both as a signal for the starting and the stopping of class work, and for indicating the beginning and end of rounds during actual contests.

It should be portable and conveniently placed. A small table is handy for such a purpose making the bell usable for class instruction, the training program, and actual boxing contests.

An electric buzzer, worked either manually or electrically, can be used instead of a bell.

A whistle is an adjunct of the bell. It is necessary for the ten second warning signal.

Mats—Floor mats should be placed in the exercise portion of the boxing room where calisthenics and abdominal work can be taken. One large mat is preferable to several small ones, space permitting.

Boxing Timers—There are time clocks manufactured especially for boxing purposes. They can be set for either two or three minute rounds, one minute rest, a bell ringing or a buzzer sounding at the beginning and end of each round. The timing device can be operated manually or automatically. The clock should be well placed for purposes of vision.

Abdominal Boards—Are merely elevated boards 6' X 24″ with a foot strap at the elevated end under which to place the feet. Used for abdominal exercises. The greater the elevation the more severe the exercise. The board and stand can be built at little cost.

Medicine Ball—Should be the large size ball, 18″ in diameter. Used for calisthenics drills.

Specialized Gear Required for the Boxing Workout

The Striking Bag—Often referred to as a light bag. The speed of the bag varies according to type of leather and lining used. A heavy bag is better for general use as it will stand greater abuse. The speed bag should be used for advanced men only.

Boxing Gloves—Fourteen or sixteen ounce gloves should be used for training purposes. The elastic wristband type is preferable to laced gloves. If gloves with laces are used, instead of tying at wrist, have the cadets place the laces in the palm of the hand and then slip the glove on. Metal tips at end of laces must be cut off.

(a) Front view　　　　　(b) Side view

PLATE 1. NAVY HELMET

Ideally, gloves should be cleaned each time after using. Practically, because of constant use, cleaning once a week will suffice. Use a clean damp cloth and saddle soap, then hang up to dry. After a thorough drying, a solution of 10% carbolic acid and 90% sweet oil should be applied to disinfect and at the same time soften the leather.

Tears and rips should be immediately repaired. Gloves should be discarded or used for body bag work if badly scuffed, or if the padding is either broken or bunched.

Striking Bag Gloves—Should be used to protect the hands while working on the light bag. Gloves should be large enough to wear over bandages. Can be weighted or unweighted.

The Head Protector or Helmet—There are many different types, some giving ear and eye protection, others completely covering the jaw and face.

The new Navy head protector affords complete protection for the ears, eyes, nose and teeth. It fits snugly and is very difficult to displace. A mouthpiece is not necessary when using the head protector. (See Plate 1a, b, page 23)

Jumping Ropes—Should have a ball bearing handle and should be at least seven to eight feet long. A heavy sash cord makes a well weighted rope.

Personal Gear

This is boxing equipment that should be owned by or issued to each trainee.

Mouthpiece—Individually fitted mouthpieces are the only ones that give adequate protection.

Handwraps—The human hand was made for grasping not striking. Bandaging the hand is the method of providing support and therefore protection to the hand and wrist. For training purposes, bandages made of canvas, felt or woven material can be used. In actual competition, one roll of two inch gauze or linen bandage, not to exceed ten yards in length, may be used on each hand. One thickness of adhesive tape one inch wide can be used to hold the bandages at the wrist.

To wrap hands properly, hand anatomy must be known. The hand consists of twenty-seven bones, fourteen forming the fingers and the thumb and called phalanges. The five bones forming the back of the hand are the metacarpal bones. The eight bones of the wrist are the carpal bones. *The purpose of bandaging it to prevent the bones of the hand from spreading, to protect the big knuckle of the thumb and to support the wrist.* Improper bandaging will cause injury as will the use of too much adhesive tape.

The bandage must keep the bones of the hand in place, especially strengthening the metacarpal and carpal bones of the wrist.

In wrapping a hand, the boxer should stand directly in front of the trainer, hand out, palm down, fingers spread. The roll should be held upward, in the palm of the hand. (See Plate 2a, page 26) Start wrapping toward the outside.

1. Anchor the gauze by tearing a loop in one end, and placing over thumb. (See Plate 2b, page 26)

2. Now bring the wrap over the back of the hand to the big knuckle of the wrist.

3. Then underneath wrist to the base of the thumb. (See Plate 2c, page 26)

4. Then diagonally across back of hand to the big knuckle of the little finger. (See Plate 2d page 26)

5. Now encircle completely the big knuckles of the hand, wrapping well up toward the middle joints of the fingers. (See Plate 2e, f, g, page 26)

6. On completion, carry diagonally across back of the hand to outside wrist bone. (See Plate 2h, page 26)

7. Completely encircle the wrist once, angling the wrap slightly upward, stopping at the base of the thumb. (See Plate 2i, j, k, page 26)

8. Completely encircle the thumb once. (See Plate 2l, m, page 26)

9. Then following the normal contour of the hand, bring the wrap over across the back of the hand to the joint of the little finger. (See Plate 2n, page 27)

10. Now again completely encircle the large knuckles of the hand a second time.(See Plate 2o, p, q, page 27)

11. Then carry wrapping down diagonally across the back of the hand (see Plate 2r, page 27), and around to base of thumb. (See Plate 2s, page 27)

12. Then up completely encircling the thumb for a second time. (See Plate 2t, u, page 27)

13. Now bring wrap diagonally over back of hand to wrist. Encircle the wrist once using a small piece of tape to secure it. (See Plate 2v, w, x, page 27)

The above steps are for a standard handwrap. If gauze is used, repeat the above procedure as many times as necessary.

Hints in Wrapping Hands

1. Hand should be held so fingers are spread wide.

2. Do not tape or bandage between fingers because when force is applied the bones of the hand will spread causing injury.

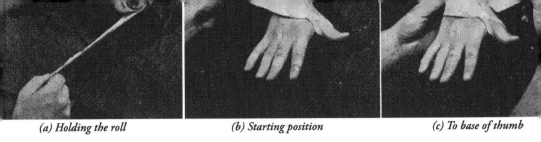

(a) Holding the roll   *(b) Starting position*   *(c) To base of thumb*

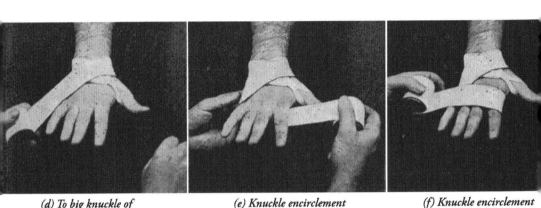

(d) To big knuckle of little finger   *(e) Knuckle encirclement*   *(f) Knuckle encirclement*

PLATE 2. PROPER METHOD OF WRAPPING A HAND

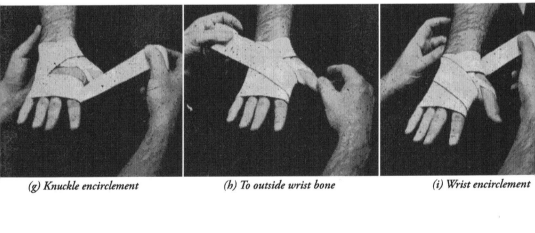

(g) Knuckle encirclement   *(h) To outside wrist bone*   *(i) Wrist encirclement*

(j) Wrist encirclement   *(k) Wrist encirclement*   *(l) Thumb encirclement (on*

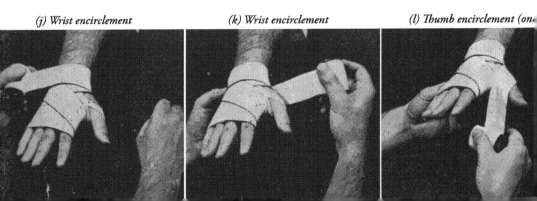

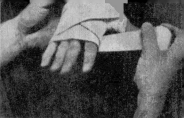

*(m) Thumb encirclement
(one)*

(n) To joint of little finger

*(o) Knuckle encirclement
(2nd time)*

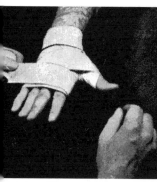
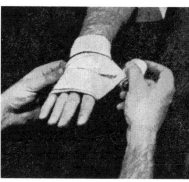
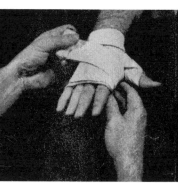

*(p) Knuckle encirclement
(2nd time)*

*(q) Knuckle encirclement
(2nd time)*

*(r) Diagonally across back
of hand*

PLATE 2. PROPER METHOD OF WRAPPING A HAND

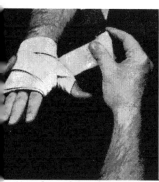
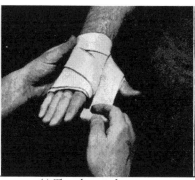
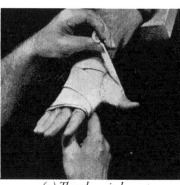

(s) To base of thumb

*(t) Thumb encirclement
(2nd time) (one)*

*(u) Thumb encirclement
(2nd time) (one)*

(v) To wrist

(w) Wrist encirclement

(x) Tape or tie

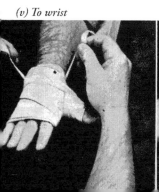
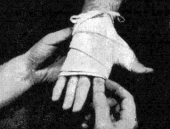
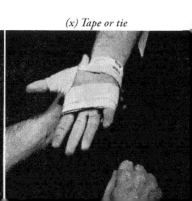

3. In wrapping, always completely encircle the thumb with the pull on the thumb inward toward the hand.

4. Keep a steady pull on the bandage, but do not pull too tight. A tight bandage will shut off circulation.

Protection Cup—The protection cup is a "must" piece of equipment for boxers. In some states it is required to be worn by law.

The cup itself is made out of bakelite or aluminum and should be worn with a pouch supporter. If a pouch supporter is not used it should be slipped in between two regular supporters and then taped in to prevent its slipping out. If it is worn with only one supporter, it should be taped to the supporter to keep it from falling out.

The foul proof cup is one which protects the groin as well as the scrotum and should be used when available.

Shoes—Light fitting, soft soled, high laced shoes should be used if working on a canvas surface. Plenty of resin should be used. Keep away from places where water has spilled on resin as it causes slipperiness.

If boxing on a wooden gym floor, regular sneakers or tennis shoes are best.

Socks—Wear white, wool socks. Should be changed every day.

Trunks—To be legal, trunks should have a three inch minimum inseam and a sixteen inch minimum outseam. They should be elastic waisted and fit snugly about the legs. Rayon-satin, sateen or a cotton material can be used.

Robe—Sleeves should be large enough to allow passage of the glove. Flannel material should be used because it keeps the body warm.

CARE OF FACILITIES AND GEAR

Initial equipment should be the best that money can buy. Such equipment, if cared for properly, will last almost indefinitely, and with but little replacement.

Fixed Equipment

Ring—Ropes—Slack off when not in use. Use sleeve wrappings and launder monthly. Inspect ropes once a year for replacement or repair.

Canvas—Vacuum every day. Scrub monthly with any antiseptic solution which is made commercially for the purpose of washing rugs or upholstery.

Striking Bag Platform—See that bolts are tight. Swivels should be in good working condition. A ball swivel is recommended.

Body Bags—Repair all cracks or tears immediately. Watch so bags do not get too hard. Repair and refill bi-yearly. Check attachments yearly.

Stall Bars—Check installation yearly.

Pulleys—Check ropes yearly.

Movable Equipment

Bell—See that striking mechanism is in workable condition. .

Mats—Vacuum daily, scrub with antiseptic soap monthly. If mat cover is used, wash weekly.

Medicine Ball—Repair all rips and tears immediately.

Specialized Gear

Striking Bags—Repair all tears or rips immediately.

Boxing Gloves—Wash with saddle soap once a week, and dry thoroughly. Gloves should be stowed in open wire racks. Once a week treat gloves with solution of 10% carbolic acid and 90% sweet oil, which will disinfect as well as keep leather soft. Discard all gloves which are scuffed or in which padding has been broken. Repair all rips or tears.

Head Helmets—Repair all harness and straps.

Jumping Ropes—Discard worn out ropes.

Personal Gear

Mouthpieces—Wash thoroughly after using.

Handwraps—Dry out after each use.

Supporter—Change daily.

Boxing Shoes—Keep shoe strings pulled tight.

Robe—Keep laundered.

Socks—Clean pair each day.

CHAPTER IV
Procedure and Method in the Teaching of Boxing

The teaching of boxing is mainly in the field of motor learning. This means habit formation and the development of skill. It is important that the teacher should know which skill should receive emphasis, and at what time the emphasis should be given. Incorrect method based upon an improper teaching sequence definitely limits the possibility of learning.

Automatism of skill and elements of skill in their proper sequence is absolutely essential to the greatest ultimate development.

THE PROPER TEACHING SEQUENCE

Skills and techniques in this book are presented in their actual teaching sequence. In a strictly logical development of a teaching sequence, straight blows to head and body, together with their elementary blocks would be taught first. Later would follow the bent arm blows to head and body, together with their defense. If the teaching was to be carried still further, a few of the fundamental counters would be taught. Finally would come the teaching of the combination blows.

The psychological approach which is herein used, is based upon the development of a more useable technique allowing for greater versatility and movement and the ability to use the left hand completely and effectively from the very beginning,

Complete use of the left hand is taught before the right hand is developed at all. The technique of left hand blows and their defense together with counters to be used for and against each blow, plus teaching the use of the subject blow in effective combination becomes the teaching unit.

Once the effective use of the left has been taught, the same development is followed for the right hand. Defense, counters and combinations are taught as a unit, so that when the student learns how to hit with the right hand, he also becomes conscious of all possible methods of defense, the use of the right hand as a counter blow, the counter blows that will be used by his opponent if he leads with the right hand, and finally effective right hand combinations.

The greatest hindrance to the development of boxing skill is the discovery of right handed hitting power before proper use of the left hand has been taught. Once this discovery is made a very peculiar psychological condition results, which makes skill development practically impossible. If the left hand is developed before the right hand is brought into use, a highly developed pattern of skill results which will always make the use of the left hand primary to that of the right hand.

METHOD IN TEACHING BOXING

Ability to box does not necessarily mean the ability to teach boxing. Teaching is an art, and like any art is perfected only through years of experience. A person may have a complete knowledge of boxing, but unless the particular faculty to translate knowledge into clear analytical description is possessed, successful teaching will not result. It is a difficult task to verbally describe any sensation. Only those teachers who have clearly analyzed each skill, step by step, into action-motivating words will be able to teach effectively.

A teacher may have a complete grasp of subject matter, the ability to describe and know the correct teaching sequence, yet not know how to proceed so that the best results will accrue.

Method is the tool of the teacher, the way to accomplish the desired ends efficiently and economically. It is the guide of the skilled teacher and the "crutch" of the beginner. It is the teacher's formula for insuring educational outcomes.

There is an accepted teaching method in every field of learning. There should be no place for chance or improper method in the teaching of boxing. Both lead to wrong habits, and habits once established are difficult to break and seriously impede proper learning.

In any discussion of method there is always the question of whole or part teaching. The whole method means teaching a unit or an element of a unit as a whole until complete mastery is attained. The part method means breaking down each skill into simple units and learning them, one by one, in proper sequence, until finally the whole movement is being properly performed.

A good boxing teacher makes use of both methods. There are times when either one or both methods should be used. This is a matter for the judgment and experience of the teacher. It is fairly well agreed that teaching should proceed from the psychological to the logical, from the whole to the part. The procedure generally followed is to allow the cadets first to grasp the idea as a whole, then if it is a complicated skill to divide it into more simple learning units.

It should be recognized that the whole method does not mean quite what it implies. It does not mean learning any one sport as a complete whole, but learning each fundamental of the sport as a whole. In boxing, each element is learned through the whole method unless it is too complicated. Then it is better to use the part method.

CLASS ORGANIZATION AND PROCEDURE

Formations for the Teaching of Boxing

The first step in method is the organization of the class for easy and efficient management. The formation used will vary according to the size and shape of the room to be used, the number participating and the type of teaching method being used. It must be easy to supervise, giving the instructor a clear view of all cadets and allowing them to easily keep sight of the instructor.

For Small Groups

There are several formations that can be used for small groups of less than fifty cadets.

The Half-Circle—Means exactly what it implies. Have the men form a half-circle double arms-length apart. The instructor should stand in the center of the open end and in front of the cadets where he can easily be seen and heard. (See Plate 3, Page 33)

Circle Formation—A circle is formed, cadet facing inward, double arm interval apart. The instructor should stand as a part of the circle, where he can see and be seen by everyone in the circle. (See Plate 4, Page 33)

V-Formation—Here again the name implies the formation to be used. From an apex, two lines widen forming a The instructor stands in the center of the open end of the (See Plate 5, Page 33)

The Line Formation—In this formation two files, anywhere from three to twenty feet apart. face inboard toward each other. The instructor stands in the center of the open end of the formation. (See Plate 6, Page 33)

For Medium Sized Groups

For medium sized groups, fifty to one hundred, exactly the same type of formations as listed above can be used except that one cadet always stands arms-length behind the front line or squad. In other words, a double half-circle, a double circle, a double V-formation, or a double line will be formed. (See Plates 7, 8, 9, 10, Page 33)

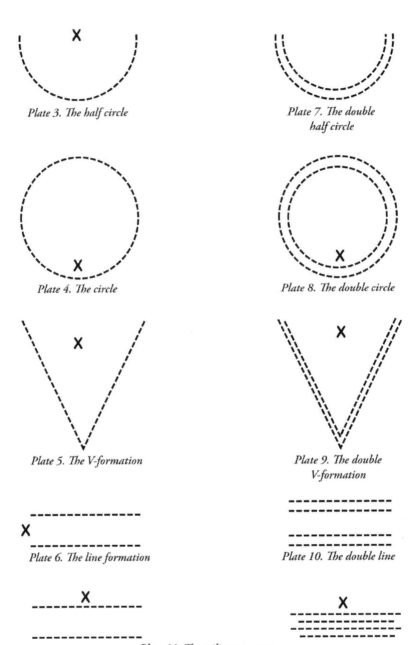

Plate 3. The half circle

Plate 7. The double
half circle

Plate 4. The circle

Plate 8. The double circle

Plate 5. The V-formation

Plate 9. The double
V-formation

Plate 6. The line formation

Plate 10. The double line

Plate 11. The military or open

X = INSTRUCTOR

PLATE 3-11. FORMATION ILLUSTRATED

For Large Groups

For mass teaching purposes, the open or military formation should be used. Form cadets in squads, instructor directly in front. The instructor then gives the command of "double arm order, raise!" All cadets raise both arms, except those on the right end of each file, all giving way to the left. The command of "front" is then given. The Squads are then asked to number off by fours. The next command is, "Odd numbers in first, third and fifth squad, two steps forward, even numbers in second, fourth and' sixth squad, two steps backward." Cadets are now in proper formation for work. (See Plate 11, Page 33)

Commands

Commands are very important when the formal method of teaching is used. The informal method does not require special commands. Boxing is a precision sport, and commands should be used not only to get the class into formation, but to add to the precision and speed of the movements to be performed.

On the first day, the class should be taught what formation will be used and to always "fall in" as soon as they arrive, coming to a double armed interval position and holding that position until command of "front" is given. In this position both arms are raised sidewards so that the fingertips barely touch those of the cadet on either side. The double arm interval is necessary in order to give proper spacing for work. In single line formations, in order to work in pairs have cadets number off by two's, number one's facing number two's. Using the double type formation and working with larger groups, always have the inboard cadet turn and face the outboard cadet, thus forming working units of two.

The tone of command should convey the type of action desired. Slow intonation denotes slow action; a quick command, quick action. All cadets should work in unison and on command. With the whole group performing the movement at the same time, it is easy to ascertain those cadets who are executing the movement improperly, and therefore who need help.

Type of Command—Actually there are only four commands necessary:

To obtain the on-guard position.
To control foot movements.
To control hand movements.
To control special technique.

To obtain the proper boxing position—the command is "On-guard," a preparatory command telling the group to get ready to assume the position, and "Hep!", the command of; execution. The final command is "On guard, hep!"

For all foot movements—the command is as follows: First, an explanatory command, such as *"Left step,"* followed by the preparatory command of *"Ready!"*, followed by the command of execution *"Hep!"*

Examples: *"On guard, hep!"*
              "Advance, ready, hep!"
              "Retreat, ready, hep!"
              "Right step, ready, hep!"
              "Left step, ready, hep!"

The *"Ready!"* always means to prepare for action, the *"Hep!"* means to act. The explanatory command is dropped after the first time, the command being shortened to "Ready, strike!"

For all hand movements, that is striking movements, the command is as follows: First, the explanatory command, followed by the command of execution.

Example: *"Left jab, ready, strike!"*

After the explanatory command has once been given it should be dropped, leaving only the preparatory command, the command of execution, such as "Ready, strike!"

For all special movements or technique the explanatory command is given first, followed by the preparatory and the command of execution.

Example: *"On command, step either to the inside or outside position."*
             "Ready, slip!"
             "Ready, in!" or "Ready, out!"

In all sequence or combination movements, and applying to counters as well, the blows, the blocks, the counters, or the combinations can be numbered, such as 1, 2, 3, 4, 5 etc. When called, the number becomes the command of execution.

Example: *"Ready, one-two!"*

Throughout the drills listed in the body of the book, the proper command for the drill is included. The most difficult part of teaching for the inexperienced is the ability to clearly and concisely incite proper action through the correct command.

Length of Practice Period

No practice of any one boxing skill should be carried on for more than twenty minutes without rest. A frequent change in type of instruction during a period is restful, and tends to keep interest high.

Rest Periods

It is extremely important for the instructor of boxing to understand the importance of rest to learning. Instructors or coaches of skill activities are prone to place *too much emphasis on continued practice.* Usually rest periods are not thought of in terms of learning. Actually, all games allow for certain rest periods and practice should follow the same rule.

Experiments have shown that learning proceeds faster when rest periods are given throughout the whole period of practice. Frequent rest periods eliminate fatigue, thus shortening the learning time. Also numerous rest periods are important because they tend to keep interest at a higher pitch, enabling more to be accomplished.

Practice in boxing should be concentrated and strenuous. A short rest period of twenty or thirty seconds is indicated after each two or three minutes of concentrated attention.

Special work may demand longer periods of continued practice, *but as a rule a series of intensified short practise periods will accomplish the best results.*

Drills

There are five essential teaching drills with which every instructor should be familiar. They are the technique drill, the hitting drill, the blocking drill and the two boxing drills.

In the appendix (page 220) are listed those drills which will enable the instructor to most effectively put his knowledge into action so that skill will result without waste of time or effort.

The Technique Drill—The purpose of this drill is to establish a specific pattern of action. The instructor should first name the skill, then carefully analyze and repeatedly demonstrate it so that the students have a "mind's-eye" picture of correct form. Detailed explanation should be given for each of the elements that go to make up the whole movement. Demonstrate each element as well as the whole movement. The class should then practice or drill on each element until a fair degree of skill is obtained. Elements should be gradually combined until the movement is being executed as a whole.

The drill should be performed by command only. Cadets drill individually while facing inboard. Action should be slow and definite at first, speeding up as the pattern becomes better established.

Common errors should be called to the attention of the entire class, and individual help should be given when necessary.

The Hitting Drill—Once the proper form has been learned, the development of power is next. Such is the purpose of the hitting drill. The whole class should drill in pairs, one using a specific blow on command, his partner holding his glove hand as a target. All blows can be drilled in this manner, either singly or in combination.

The Blocking Drill—Once the proper execution of the blow has been learned, and after power has been developed through hitting drills, a drill designed to teach proper defense is necessary. Defense is best learned by having the men work in pairs. On command, one student practices a slow lead blow, while his partner practices the block as explained and demonstrated by the instructor.

The Boxing Drills—Once form has been learned and defense developed, greater skill is made possible through boxing drills. There are two boxing drills which aid the learning process: The first is defensive boxing, the second is controlled boxing.

Defensive Boxing is used to develop defensive techniques under actual boxing conditions. In this drill, one student is on the defense only. He can defend himself as best he can, using defensive techniques best suited for the opponent's attack. The partner carries the attack as called for by the instructor.

Controlled Boxing is a very valuable drill aiding the development of specific technique, either offensive or defensive, and often both. It means actually limiting the offense to certain specified blows, narrowing attention and concentration, thus facilitating learning. It also requires a defense for the specified blows being practiced, thus aiding in the development of defensive technique.

The Lesson Plan

This means the organization of material for its teaching. The instructor when teaching a class should follow a definite plan. A lesson plan does not involve content material, but how and when content material should be presented so that best results will accrue. The lesson plan consists of the following elements:

Muster—This means taking roll or ascertaining those present for the drill.

Review—A period which serves two purposes, that of "warming up" so the body will be ready for the more strenuous exercise to follow, and as a period of re-learning, a time when skills can be more quickly imprinted into the nervous system. Actually, it is a practice period for the skills learned in previous lessons.

Mass Instruction—Is that part of the lesson in which the new skill is taught. The methods used in mass instruction are technique drills, hitting drills and blocking drills. The drills used vary according to the technique being taught.

Boxing Drills—The next phase of the plan is either defensive or controlled boxing. Occasionally as part of the controlled boxing, actual competitive boxing should be allowed.

Exercise Groups—A period designed to develop special training skills. The class is divided into three or more groups, depending upon equipment and facilities available. One group is assigned to the heavy bags; a second to the striking bags; the third group to rope jumping, and the fourth group to shadow boxing. If more groups are necessary the additional one could work on pulleys, calisthenics and medicine ball work.

Dismissal—The final phase of the plan is the dismissal. The class is brought into proper formation before being dismissed.

A complete series of the lesson plans to be used in Naval Aviation boxing program is listed in the appendix, Page 341. Exact course content will be determined through directives to the various schools and stations concerned with Naval Aviation Flight Training.

Time Allotment—Generally speaking the following time allotment should be used in making out lesson plans (the time scheduled for the lesson plan is based upon a forty-five minute period):

Muster..2 minutes
Review..10 minutes
Mass Instruction..15 minutes
Boxing..12 minutes
Exercise Groups..5 minutes
Dismissal..1 minute

It may be desirable to drop out the exercise group and add more time to both the review and the mass instruction if the period is less than forty-five minutes.

For certain lessons it may be desirable to add more to one, and take away from another.

SAMPLE LESSON PLAN

A sample lesson plan for a forty-five minute period excluding the exercise group is as follows:

		Time Allotment
The Left Jab to the Chin and Blocks	Page 77	
Muster	Page 80	
Review—The on guard position, fundamental foot work, the waist pivot, Drills 1, 2, 3, 5		25%
Mass Instruction		
Drill 6—The left jab to the chin.	Page 227	25%
Drill 7—The stop.	Page 229	25%
Drill 8—The parry.	Page 230	25%
Defensive and Controlled Boxing—Refer to Drills 6,7,8		25%
Dismissal		

Lesson Content

Lesson content means the actual teaching material or subject matter. It changes depending on the group to be taught, the age, experience and objectives. The content of this book is built around the material which is used in the Naval Aviation Boxing Program.

CHAPTER V
Conditioning for Boxing

Training is one of the most neglected phases of athletics. Too much time is given to the development of skill and too little to the development of the individual for participation. The body is treated as if it were an object, subject to definite rules and regulations. Nothing could be further from the truth. Training deals not with an object, but with the human spirit and human emotions. It takes intellect and judgement to handle such important qualities as these.

Training is the psychological and physiological conditioning of an individual preparing for intense neural and muscular action. It implies discipline of the mind, power and endurance of the body. It means skill. It is all these things working together in harmony.

Training means not only knowledge of the things which will build the body, but also knowledge of the things which will tear down or injure the body. Improper training will result in injuries.

PSYCHOLOGICAL CONDITIONING

An individual may have all the physical gifts possible—speed, coordination and power; the body may be ready for extreme exertion, yet the individual may be a poor competitor. It is easy to prepare the body for a contest but it is difficult to prepare the mind. It is necessary to help each individual discipline his thinking, to help him control his emotions, to dispel fear and worry.

Fear is one of the most important considerations in athletic conditioning. It is especially important in boxing. Many are afraid to box because they are timid and shy. They are afraid of any activity in which there is personal contact. In reality, they are only afraid of the idea of being hurt, not of actually being hurt. The task is to get them to prove this fact to themselves.

Be sympathetic. Try to understand the problem of the cadets. Make them feel that they cannot be hurt. Exploit every action. Do everything to make them feel confident. Create situations in which they will be superior.

Mind Discipline

Conditioning of any sort means discipline of the will and through the will, the body. Training rules and habits are most useful for their disciplinary value. In conditioning work, discipline means creating an attitude, a mindset toward a desired end. The end result is the important objective, training only the means to the end. Discipline is the method.

If the end objective is of enough importance, rules and regulations will be followed. It becomes increasingly necessary, then, to stress procedures which not only lead to proficient skill in boxing, but to right attitudes and habits of health and life.

Training must be made a strict disciplinary routine. It must require things which seem difficult, dull and monotonous. It must necessitate giving up many things—ease, comfort and all forms of dissipation. A strong incentive is required in order to be able to enforce such an existence, but in so doing a cadet is given a training in all-out effort toward a goal, and therefore an inkling of the price that is required in such attainment. The end result must be made to loom above all else in the mind of the cadet. If successful, it becomes possible to build into that individual any type of health habit or attitude desired.

The "will to win" is the factor that makes for great competitors. Compare two men of about equal ability and experience. What makes one win and the other lose? Only because one wants to win more badly than the other. There are many instances of men who lack all physical qualifications of great boxers, but who win and continue to win time after time because they are great competitors. They are the best example of the power of psychological conditioning. More than just mechanical skill is necessary for competitive boxing. Beyond a certain point such skill, even when backed by proper physical condition, is not enough to win. Winning is a matter of "a determination to win."

The first step necessary is the winning of the Cadet's confidence by the coach. This is the most important step because it is the basis of the indoctrination to follow. A cadet must have utmost faith in "his" coach. He must believe that his coach is the best coach, and that what he says is right. This can be accomplished only if the coach will make special effort to become acquainted with the cadet in an intimate way. The coach must know the cadet's background, his ambitions and ideals, his hopes and dreams. To the best of his ability the coach must help the cadet accomplish his ambitions. Only by being a real friend can the coach gain the confidence and respect so necessary to the building of correct attitudes.

The second phase of psychological conditioning for competition is the building of self-confidence. Self-confidence is a matter of success and failure. The successful person is the one who is confident in his ability to be further successful. When a person fails something is subtracted from his self-confidence. Applying this to the coaching of boxing means that every cadet must be carefully "nursed" along. Instruction in defense, ordinarily speaking, should precede instruction or coaching of offense. In this manner confidence is built.

Once this has been done the coach must make sure that the first actual experience in competition does not end in disaster. Careful attention, therefore, must be given to match making. Each match made should give the cadet an equal chance to win. It means no one-sided losses. Any loss should be so close that it is easy to convince the cadet that he could have won if he had tried just a little harder, thus establishing the basic attitude that you can win if you want to.

The building of correct attitudes toward competition and winning is the third part of psychological conditioning. The attitudes "that you're really never tired," "that you can win if you want to," "that you can lick anyone who walks," "that you can't be hurt," must be made a part of the boxer's feeling. To this must be added the habit of working up to capacity at all times.

A boxer who believes that "he is only as tired as he feels" or that he is "never tired, but only thinks he is," has learned a very important psychological lesson. Experience shows that an athlete who forces himself to the limit, can keep going as long as necessary. It means that ordinary effort will not tap or release the tremendous store of reserve power latent in the human body. Extraordinary effort, highly emotionalized conditions, or a true determination to win at all costs will release this extra energy. Therefore an athlete is actually as tired as he feels, and if he is determined to win he can keep on almost indefinitely in order to achieve his objective. By driving the cadets at top speed after normal fatigue has set in not only builds a greater reserve of power, but builds an attitude favorable to the maximum release of energy.

The attitude "that you can win if you want to badly enough" means that the will to win is constant and no amount of punishment, no amount of effort, or no condition is too "tough" to take in order to win. Such an attitude can be developed only if winning is closely tied to the cadets' ideals and dreams.

A cadet who has never been defeated can be easily sold on the idea that he can defeat anyone no matter what the size or weight. This, of course, means careful matching and constant talking to by the coach. This feeling is closely allied to the attitude that "you can win if you want to."

The ability to "take a punch" is to some degree actually related to a person's feeling about his ability to do so. A person who is fearful that he will be hurt, defeated, or knocked out, is more easily hurt, or knocked out than the one who feels that he can't be hurt and that he can take anything that comes his way.

Finally, the ability to work close to capacity is directly related to the will to win. Many boxers have the habit of saving themselves; they have a dread of being completely exhausted. Always they compete below their best. The result is that soon they are "psychologically" unable to go "all out." *The real competitor is the one who gives all he has, all the time.* The result is that he works close to his capacity at all times and in so doing forms an attitude of giving all he has. In order to create such a state, the cadet must be driven longer, harder and faster than normally would be required. He must learn to perform at top speed all the time, not to coast with the idea he can "open up" when the times comes. While the habit itself is physiological, the attitude which permits "all-out effort" is psychological. Psychological conditioning creates a state of readiness thus increasing the ability to react and to learn. It narrows the field of stimuli, allowing attention to be concentrated on the task at hand, motivating interest and desire in the objective. This in turn increases the strength of the incoming impulses, generating greater nerve power. The result is an increased capacity and a greater determination to win.

PHYSIOLOGICAL CONDITIONING

Diet

To understand diet is to understand nutrition. Briefly, nutrition means the process of digestion, absorption, assimilation, heat and energy release, the discarding of waste materials, and finally the rebuilding of the cell and the storing of an excess of cell food.

Digestion is the chemical and mechanical breakdown of food. It starts in the mouth through the action of the teeth and salivary juices. It is continued in the stomach by the action of the various gastric juices, the pyloric mill and further aided in the intestine by the pancreatic juices and peristaltic action.

Food is reduced to a state of liquid chyme. In this form it is passed from the intestine into the plasma of the blood through the process of osmosis. As the plasma bathes all the cells of the body, the food is assimilated directly by the cell. The cell stores the food as fuel. In muscle contraction, food is used, heat, water and energy liberated and waste matter thrown off. Then the demand for food is repeated.

Protein, minerals and water are tissue builders and rebuilders. Carbohydrates produce energy and liberate heat. Fat is stored in the body as fat and used only if there is a lack of carbohydrates in the diet. Excessive carbohydrates store in the body as fat. Of all the food elements, protein alone cannot be stored.

Thus a diet for an athlete should be very heavy in proteins and sugar, and low in fats. The carbohydrates should exceed the protein in the diet by almost three to one.

The diet should be so planned that an alkalinity of the tissues results. A diet that produces an excess of acid is incorrect because alkalinity tends to increase wind and endurance. An athlete preparing for competition should eat lean meats, milk, fruit and leafy vegetables. Such rich foods as cream, fried foods, fat meats, rich cake or pastry should be avoided. The sugar content of the diet may be increased during training and just before a contest.

In boxing, orange juice immediately preceding a bout or between contests may be used. Glucose candy is beneficial if it can be obtained.

Water is a most important factor in conditioning. Dehydration results due to profuse perspiration induced by physical exertion. Water should be used freely, both inside and outside, in order to replenish that lost during a workout. However, in all cases, water should be taken sparingly twenty-four hours before a contest.

The pre-contest diet is important. No food is to be taken later than four hours before a contest. Food in the stomach at the time of the contest tends to cause nausea and indigestion. Any food that is eaten should be light but nourishing. A small portion of sirloin steak, or two soft boiled or poached eggs, or two broiled lamb chops, or a small portion of broiled chicken, together with a slice or two of dry toast and a cup of weak tea is all that should be eaten.

Sleep and Relaxation

Sleep and relaxation is as necessary to an athlete as correct diet or special training. Boxing, or any strenuous activity, breaks down the cells, liberates lactic acid and other waste products into the blood, and uses stored-up energy. Sleep is the period when nature replenishes. An athlete needs a great deal of sleep because he is exercising strenuously and because he is usually young and growing.

Sleeplessness may occur before or after a contest. A good book, a quiet movie, congenial company, with light discussion and laughter all help to relieve tension. A hot foot bath, or a warm tub bath of about body temperature for fifteen or twenty minutes are effective methods of relieving insomnia.

After a strenuous contest, a good soaking tub bath not only dispels tension, but will tend to dissipate soreness from the muscles. Fill a tub with water, not more than ninety degrees Fahrenheit. Empty in the tub three to five pounds of Epsom salts.* Bathe for fifteen minutes or longer.

It is important to realize the value of frequent rests during the actual training period. Not only is the interest held, and learning heightened, but efficiency is maintained longer.

Elimination

Proper elimination is essential in the conditioning of athletes. A certain "habit time" is of utmost importance to regularity and should be stressed. The plain simple life of the athlete, wholesome food, plenty of exercise, are controls in themselves. All that is needed is to create a habit. Cathartics are weakening and should not be taken within two days of a contest.

Exercises for Conditioning

The greatest conditioning exercise for boxing is roadwork. If an athlete has time for only a single training activity, that activity should be roadwork. Running strengthens the heart, the lungs and the legs. The heart will be able to adjust to the strenuous exertion, the lungs will be better able to supply more oxygen and the legs will be better able to support the body during a bout.

One method of roadwork is that of "wind sprints." Sprint for a hundred yards and then walk a hundred yards. Start with a quarter mile and gradually increase until a mile can be covered. When sprinting, run with all possible speed.

Another method is to run the same length of time as is to be boxed, resting one minute between runs. For instance, if preparing for three, two minute rounds, run at top speed for two minutes, then walk a minute. Repeat three times.

The aspiring boxer must be made to realize that each part of his body must be exercised and strengthened as much as possible. The extensors of the arms, the abdominal muscles and the neck muscles should receive special attention.

---

* Salt tends to raise the temperature of the water a few degrees. Therefore, do not start with the water too warm.

The arms are used continuously and tire easily unless especially trained. The abdominal region is the "mark" for which all boxers try and therefore well-developed muscles are essential. The neck must be able to absorb the shock of head blows. A strong neck is a protection that should not be overlooked. The following exercises are especially adapted for the boxer:

Neck Exercises

1. *The wrestler's bridge*—Take a supine position on the mat. Fold the arms across the chest. Bring the legs well up underneath the body. Now using the head and legs as supports, raise the body clear of the floor. Roll back on the forehead. Repeat.

2. *The front bridge*—Take a prone position on the mat. Place the top of the head on the mat. Using the head and legs as supports, bend the body forward and up. Repeat.

Stomach Exercises

1. *The sit up*—Assume a supine position, hands outstretched over the head. Raise the trunk to a sitting position, then force it down between the legs. Repeat.

   To increase resistance fold the arms across the chest. For further resistance use a light weight back of the neck. Do as many repetitions as possible.

2. *The leg raise*—Assume a supine position. Raise the legs slowly until they are directly above the eyes. Lower slowly. Repeat as many times as possible.

3. *Knees to chest*—Assume a supine position, arms outstretched over the head. Sit up and bring the arms over in an attempt to touch the toes as they are raised off the floor. Repeat as many times as possible.

4. *The jack knife*—Take the supine position, arms outstretched over the head. Sit up and bring the arms over in an attempt to touch the toes as they are raised off the floor. Repeat as many times as possible.

5. *The alternate leg raise*—Take the supine position. Place the hands under the hips, palms down. Raise the head and pin it to the breast-bone. Raise the legs alternately back and forth as fast as possible. After forty repetitions have been reached, assume a sitting position and repeat.

6. *The double leg circle*—Take the supine position. Holding both legs together, circle them first to the right, then to the left. Make a complete

circle, low and wide. Start five times one way, then five times the other way; practice until the exercise can be performed at least twenty times each way.

7. *The high sit up*—Have a partner hold the heels off the floor about ten inches. With the arms outstretched over the head, swing the trunk up and touch the hands to the toes. Repeat as many times as possible.

8. *The sit up twist*—Have a partner hold the feet to the floor. As the trunk is raised to a sitting position, twist from side to side. Twist down also. Repeat as many times as possible.

9. *The leg whip*—Take the supine position with hands under hips, palms down. Whip both feet up twenty inches, then drop them within two inches of the floor. Then raise them again. Repeat as many times as possible, working for speed.

10. *The scissors*—Take a supine position, hands under the hips. Raise the legs to an angle of forty-five degrees. From this position spread the legs out to the side as far as possible. When crossing the legs over, cross first over, then under. Repeat as many times as possible.

Arm Exercises

1. The triceps muscle is the main extensor of the arm. One of the best development exercises is the "push-up" from the floor. Assume the prone position, hands flat on the floor, shoulder width apart. Keeping the body in a straight line, straighten the arms, and raise the body from the floor. Do not let the body sag. Repeat as many times as possible.

Staleness

Staleness is the result of overwork and neural fatigue. Lack of pep, interest, enthusiasm together with irritability are all evident Signs. Loss of weight is the best objective sign. There is only one remedy; complete rest and change.

SPECIALIZED TRAINING

Specialized training activities are those which deal with the actual process of learning boxing skills, or obtaining boxing condition.

Pulley Weights—Valuable as a physiological "warm-up" exercise and to narrow and concentrate attention. Weights loosen and stretch the different muscle groups of the body. Exercise both while facing and with the back toward the pulleys. Shadow box in both positions. Work fast and smooth so that the weights do not jerk. Work vigorously. Keep the chin down. Work by rounds, with a minute rest between.

Rope Skipping—Is an especially good exercise for the feet, ankles and legs. It is only a fair developer of "wind." Too much rope skipping tends to tense and tighten the shoulder muscles. Jump by rounds.

The Light Bag—Has little use in a boxer's routine. It is impossible to hit a light bag correctly and therefore tends to develop bad hitting habits. It is of little aid in the development of timing as it is almost entirely a matter of rhythm. Work on the light bag will strengthen the hitting muscles of the shoulders and arms and has some value in developing a left jab and in shortening a straight right lead. However, the blows should be practiced individually, not in rhythm.

The Training Bag—Is valuable in the beginning training of a boxer. The primary purpose of the heavy bag is the development of hitting power, and the strengthening of the hands, wrists and arms.

A definite routine of blows should be used. Practice each blow for form, then for power. Perfect one blow at a time before proceeding to another.

The hands should be well protected when using the heavy bag. In the final stages of training the heavy bag should not be used because of the danger of injuring the hands, and because it tends to reduce speed reaction.

Shadow Boxing

Shadow boxing should be used to perfect boxing skill and is the best possible method of acquiring correct form. It teaches ring movement, hitting sequence, speed and relaxation. Each blow should be practiced and perfected before going on to another. If possible shadow box in front of a mirror so that the movements can be watched for correct form. Once form is obtained, work for greater speed and power.

Shadow boxing should be used to habituate each new technique learned. Shadow box according to rounds. Don't loaf. Move deliberately in, out and around. Punch hard all of the time. Plan each round before attempting to shadow box. Then follow the plan. Other than actual boxing, it is the most important technique in the acquisition of boxing skill.

Boxing

The best possible way to learn how to box, is to box. During the boxing drill, always work toward a definite objective. Don't ever box just to be boxing. Never play or "fool around." Stop as soon as fatigue sets in.

Box with all types of individuals, tall, short, slow and fast. Timing and judgment of distance can only be developed through actual boxing.

Box according to a set number of rounds, always resting one minute between rounds. Try to learn something from each man boxed. Box some each day.

Roadwork

A few of the principles of roadwork are:

Run the same number of rounds as will be boxed.

If a three-round bout is being prepared for and the rounds are to be two minutes in length, run two minutes at top speed, then walk a minute. Continue three times.

As wind and endurance improve, increase the distance covered, but keep the time the same. Run into shape by running every day when first starting to train. Once in condition, three times a week is enough, preferably on off-training days.

Dress warmly. Run with the hands high. During the minute of rest, keep moving.

Run in the morning if possible. Do not neglect wind sprints.

Drying Out

Drying out means abstinence from liquids for a period of twenty-four hours before a bout. It is not a method of "making weight." It is used to increase speed and endurance. While a pound or so of weight will be lost in the process that is incidental to, and not the reason. Physiologically, drying means increased ionization of the body, causing increased electric conduction of nervous energy. The body may be likened to a storage battery, it must have water to operate. In the body, as in the battery, there is a certain possible ionization. Up to a degree, the less water the greater the ionization. The result is an increase in endurance, power and speed.

It is advisable for all athletes to abstain from liquids twenty-four hours before a contest. Thirst may be relieved by washing out the mouth, or by sucking on a lemon. No liquid should be taken from the time the drying out process starts until after the contest.

Making weight by the process of dehydration is not a desirable procedure. Each boxer has a natural weight for best performance. This weight can be reached through regular conditioning methods. A weight other than that which is natural is detrimental to health and should not be allowed.

The Workout Procedure

The boxing workout is an individual matter, and should be governed by condition and needs. Endurance should be stressed in training for long bouts. In contests of short duration, speed is of greater importance.

Each workout should be entered into with a purpose. It should be planned ahead of time with a specific idea in mind. Always work at full speed and stop when feeling fresh and desiring more. If fatigued before the scheduled time, stop anyway. Skip a day when feeling low and tired. Fatigue causes careless work, and therefore the formation of bad habits. It is during these times that accidents occur. Always workout according to accurately timed rounds. Relax during the minute rest.

There are two types of general workout procedure. One is where the actual boxing phase comes immediately after the warm-up, the other after several rounds of other activity.

When boxing is placed early in the workout it is with the express purpose of boxing while fresh so that reactions will be sharper and action more vigorous.

When boxing is placed toward the end of the workout it is with the idea that because fatigue has set in over-learning results due to the greater concentration and attention which is required. Thus, later, when going into boxing without previous activity, a greater skill and power results.

A general workout plan when boxing early:

Round 1—Warm up with shadow boxing.
Round 2—Boxing.
Round 3—Work on the heavy bag.
Round 4—Work on the light bag.
Round 5—Pulley work or rope skipping.
Round 6—Calisthenics.

A general workout plan when boxing late:

Round 1—Warm up on the pulley weights.
Round 2—Skip rope.
Round 3—Work on the heavy bag.
Round 4—Boxing.
Round 5—Shadow boxing.
Round 6—Calisthenics.

The total time for the workout in each case is only eighteen minutes. Work at top speed all the time. Take a hot shower while still perspiring.

CHAPTER VI
Position, Movement and Hitting Power

ON GUARD POSITION

The on guard position is that body position which is most favorable to the mechanical execution of the techniques and skills of boxing. This position allows complete relaxation yet at the same time gives a muscle tonus most favorable to quick reaction time. It helps to coordinate hands and feet so that maximum speed and efficiency will result, which in turn permits unlimited possibilities for either attack or defense. It insures the feet being always under the body and therefore, that the body is always in a balanced position.

The primary purpose of boxing is to hit the opponent. Therefore, the on guard position is used to obtain the most favorable position for hitting. To hit effectively it is necessary to shift the weight constantly from one leg to the other. This means perfect control of body balance. *Balance it the most important consideration of the on guard position.*

Balance is achieved only through correct body alignment. The feet, the legs, the trunk and the head are all important in creating and maintaining a balanced position, The arms are important only because they are the vehicles of body force. They give expression to body force only when the body is in proper alignment. A position of the hands and arms which facilitates easy body action is important. The foot position is the most important phase of balance. Keeping the feet in proper relation to each other as well as to the body helps to maintain correct body alignment.

Too wide a stance prevents proper body alignment, destroying balance but obtaining solidarity and power at the cost of speed and efficient movement. A short stance prevents correct balance because it does not allow a firm base upon which to work. Speed results but at a loss of power and balance.

The secret of the proper stance is to keep the feet always directly under the body. This means the feet should be a medium distance apart. The weight is either balanced over both legs or the weight is slightly forward over a straight left leg with the left side of the body forming a straight line from the left heel to the tip of the left shoulder. This position permits relaxation, speed, balance and easy movement, as well as a mechanical advantage from the point of view of body leverage, which makes possible tremendous hitting power to result.

ANALYSIS OF THE ON GUARD POSITION

There are two distinct schools of thought concerning the proper on guard position. One states that the body weight must be carried over the right leg with the front left leg used as a pointer. The body is turned sideward toward the opponent. All defensive work is executed through the use of the high left shoulder with the right hand carried well forward and directly opposite the left shoulder. This is purely a defensive position or one of counter attack. The left jab and left hook are both the main defensive and offensive weapons. Long range, or outfighting is characteristic of this style. All right handed leads or counters require exceptionally fine timing.

(a) Side view—left	*(b) Front*	*(c) Side view—right*

PLATE 12. THE ON GUARD POSITION

The second school favors the square stance, weight well balanced or slightly forward. Such a style is more flexible, allows for more aggressive action and favors slipping, ducking and the use of both hands in the attack. This position allows a boxer to either attack or defend, move in or out, lead or counter. It calls for a command of infighting as well as outfighting and makes possible more versatile and rounded boxing.

The foot stance in either style will vary according to the position of the opponent. Generally speaking, with the body weight shifted over the right foot the right foot is pointed directly sideward with the left foot pointed on about a forty-five degree angle across the body. With the weight forward or balanced, the left foot is on about a twenty-five degree angle and the right foot pointed directly forward toward the opponent.

The Orthodox Position

The on guard position herein described is the one in which the weight is balanced or slightly forward. It is used because it allows greater versatility of attack and defense. (See Plate 12a, b, c)

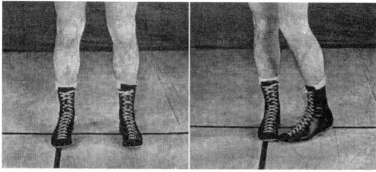

(a) Starting position   (b) Toeing in

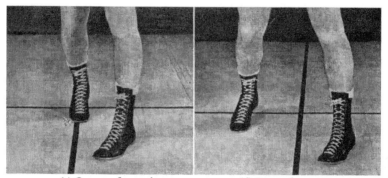

(c) One step forward   (d) Proper foot position

PLATE 13. FUNDAMENTAL FOOT POSITION

The Feet—From an easy standing position (See Plate 13a) shift the weight directly over the right leg until the right side of the body forms a straight line; then raise the left foot slightly off the floor. Rotate the whole left leg inward, and place the left foot on the floor with the left toe touching the toe of the right foot on approximately a forty degree angle. (See Plate 15b) Without altering the relative foot positions, take one natural step forward with the left foot, shifting the weight to the left leg. The left foot is now flat on the deck, rotated inward on about a twenty-five degree angle. The left leg and left side of the body should form a straight line, although the left knee is loose and easy, neither locked nor bent. As the weight is shifted to the left leg, the right heel raises off the floor and the right knee is bent with the toe of the right foot pointing directly forward. (See Plate 13c)

This position without adjustment is too narrow for balanced action. Therefore, to make a wider base, move the right foot six to twelve inches to the right making sure that the foot is moved directly to the right and not backward. (See Plate 15d) In this manner a wide base is obtained without sacrificing speed.

PLATE 14.
PROPER TRUNK POSITION

Note straight left side of body

PLATE 15.
PROPER POSITION,
LEFT ARM AND HAND

Note position of hand

PLATE 16.
PROPER POSITION,
RIGHT ARM AND HAND

Note position of hand

PLATE 17.
PROPER POSITION
OF THE HAND

Note position of hand

The Trunk—The position of the trunk is controlled primarily by the position of the left foot and leg. If the left foot and leg are in the correct position, the trunk automatically assumes the proper position. The one important thing about the trunk to remember is that it should form a straight line with the left leg. (See Plate 14)

As the left foot and leg are turned inward, the body rotates to the right, presenting a narrow target to the opponent. If, however, the left foot and leg are rotated outward, the body is squared toward the opponent presenting a larger target. For defensive purposes the narrow target is advantageous, while the square position lends itself better to attack.

The Left Arm and Hand—Hold the left arm in a folded position, elbow down and in front of the short ribs. Carry the left hand about shoulder height and off the left shoulder to the left as far as possible without raising the left elbow. Place the left hand forward eight to ten inches from the left shoulder, the arm relaxed and may, at rest because of the proximity of the triceps to the latissimus muscle. Turn the hand so that the thumb side is up, knuckles outward, the hand relaxed and open. (Sec Plate 15)

One variation which is very effective is to hold the left hand in the same position, but with the knuckle side of the hand up, thumb side inward.

The Right Arm and Hand—Place the right elbow directly down and in front of the short ribs, holding the right hand open with the palm toward the opponent and directly in front of the right shoulder. Keep the right hand forward in line with the left shoulder. The arm should be relaxed and easy, ready to attack or defend. (See Plate 16)

The Head—In boxing, the head is treated as if it were a part of the trunk with no independent action of its own. It should be carried forward, with the chin held fairly close over the breast-bone. This position must never vary no matter how the body shifts. If the body turns, the head turns.

The chin is not "tucked" behind the left shoulder except in an extreme defensive position. "Tucking" the chin into the left shoulder turns the neck into an unnatural position, takes away the support of the muscles, and prevents straight bone alignment. It also tenses the left shoulder and arm, preventing free action and causing fatigue.

With the chin dropped directly over the breast-bone, not only are the muscles and bone structure in best possible alignment, but the top of the head is the only target presented to the opponent. With the head carried in this manner, it is impossible for a man to be hit on the point of the chin. (See Plate 17)

| *(a) Side left* | *(b) Front* | *(c) Side right* |

PLATE 18. THE UNORTHODOX POSITION

The Unorthodox Position

The left handed boxer, a "southpaw" in the parlance of the ring, should take the exact opposite of the orthodox position described above. Hold the right hand and right foot forward. Do not try to change to the orthodox position until this unorthodox style is mastered. Eventually it is advisable to learn the orthodox form so that both positions can be used. (See Plate 18a, b, c)

COACHING HINTS

Check the following fundamentals. Insist that:

1. The left foot is flat on the floor and turned in at an angle of twenty-five degrees.

2. The left leg is approximately straight but the knee is not locked.

3. The right heel is raised about two inches off the floor, with the right knee bent.

4. The body weight is either balanced between both legs or shifted slightly to the front leg.

5. The left side of the body forms a straight line with the left leg.

6. Both elbows are carried down and in front of the short ribs.

7. The left hand is carried about shoulder height, eight to ten inches in front of the body, and to the left as far as possible without raising the left elbow. The hand is turned so the thumb side is either upward or inward.

8. The right hand is carried so that the palm is open and toward the opponent, shoulder height and directly in front of the right shoulder.

9. The chin is dropped forward to the breast-bone.

FOOTWORK

Fundamental footwork is the ability to move the body easily and efficiently so that balance will not be disturbed. It implies the ability to attack or defend at all times.

The essence of boxing is the art of moving, moving in to attack or defend, moving out to defend or "pull off" balance. The ability to move at the right time is the foundation of great skill in boxing.

Footwork means moving the body so as to be in the best position for attack or defense. It means balance—but movement and balance together. To be on balance but stationary, requires little skill. To maintain balance while constantly shifting body weight is an art few acquire.

Footwork does not mean leg work, it does not mean jumping around. It means moving just enough to make an opponent miss, to deliver a counter blow, or to accomplish the desired objective.

If balance is to be maintained at all times, it is absolutely necessary that the feet always be directly under the body. Any movement of the feet which tends to unbalance the body must be eliminated. The "on guard" position is one of perfect body balance and should always be maintained, especially as regards the feet. Wide steps or leg movements which require a constant shift of weight from one leg to the other cannot be used. While weight is being shifted there is a moment when balance is precarious, rendering attack or defense ineffective.

The greatest phase of footwork is the coordination of the hands and feet. When the feet and hands work together automatically, the art of moving is perfection itself.

There are only four moves possible in footwork—advancing, retreating, circling left and circling right. However, there are important variations of advancing and retreating as well as the necessity of coordinating each fundamental movement with the arms.

The Slow Advance

Is a slow movement forward in such a manner that both feet are on the floor at all times. The body is poised for either sudden attack or a defensive maneuver. Its primary purpose is to create openings and to draw leads.

The Slow Retreat

Is a slow movement backward in such a manner that both feet are on the floor at all times permitting balance to be maintained for attack or defense. It is used to draw leads or to draw the opponent off-balance, thus creating openings.

The Quick Advance

There are times when a slow advance will not suffice, when sudden speed and a quick advance are necessary. Thus the quick advance, which allows sudden movement forward without loss of body balance.

The Quick Retreat

Here, again, is a technique which makes possible sudden retreat. It is a sudden forceful move backward, allowing further retreat if necessary, or a stepping forward to attack if desired.

The Left Step

The ability to move or circle either to left or right is an extremely important part of footwork. In general, it is best to move away from an opponent's strongest blow. In other words, stepping to the left is moving away from a left hook and into the opponent's right. It is essential, then, not only to know how, but when to step or circle left.

Moving to the left may be used to nullify an opponent's left hook. It may be used to get into position for right hand counters, and it can be used to keep the opponent off balance. The important thing to remember is never to step so as to Cross the feet, to move deliberately and without excess motion.

The Right Step

Is used to keep out of the range of right hand blows. It also creates good position for the delivery of a left hook and a left jab. It is more difficult but safer than moving to the left and therefore should be used more often.

The Step Back

Is exactly what the name implies, a quick step out of range with right foot, followed by the left foot to position. This is usually followed with an immediate step in with the left foot, followed by the right foot to position. It is a defensive technique used to move quickly out of range, both feet under the body, making it possible to either attack or retreat.

The Step In-Step Out

Is the start of an offensive maneuver, often used as a feint in order to build up an opening. The foot movement is always combined with the arm movement, The initial movement is directly in, as if to hit, then moving out quickly before the opponent can adjust his defense.

The Quick Shift

Is often referred to as the side step. It is the shifting of the weight and changing the feet without disturbing balance in an effort to quickly gain a more advantageous position from which to carry the attack. It is also used to avoid the straight forward rushes of the opponent and to move quickly out of range of attack. It is a safe, sure Ind valuable defensive movement. By use of the quick shift, the opponent must again get set to hit.

The Drop Shift

Is the same type of movement as the side step. It is used to gain either the outside or inside guard position and therefore a very useful technique in infighting. A vehicle for countering, it requires timing, speed and judgment to properly execute. It may be combined with the left jab, straight right, right and left hooks. The position thus attained is the safest in boxing, head in close and directly beneath the opponent's chest. Here, with the head close, hands carried high and ready to perform a double stop, is an area that is absolutely safe.

The Rear Shift

Using practically the same execution as the drop or quick shift, the rear shift is purely a defensive maneuver which quickly carries the body out of range. It allows time to gather the defense, either to step in to the attack again, or to further step out.

| *(a) Starting position* | *(b) Left foot forward* | *(c) Right foot to position* |

PLATE 19. THE SLOW ADVANCE

ANALYSIS OF FOOTWORK

The Slow Advance

Is a slow advance of the body without disturbing body balance which can be performed only through a series of short steps forward. The steps must be so short that the feet are not lifted, but actually slid along the deck.

With this principle in mind, assume the on guard position. Slide the left foot forward about three inches, followed directly by the right foot three inches to position. The knees are not stiff, nor are they bent, but free and loose with slight movement at all times. Keep the left side of the body in a straight line. The left foot is flat on the deck. The toe of the right foot is placed firmly on the deck. The entire movement is shuffle-like. The feet do not leave the deck. They slide (See Plate 19a, b, c)

Keep moving forward until a "body feel" results. The most important factor is the maintenance of the on guard position while moving slowly forward.

The Slow Retreat

The principle of the slow retreat is the same as that of the slow advance, that is, a slow backward movement without disturbance of the on guard position.

Assume the on guard position. Now slide the right foot backwards three inches, followed by the same movement with the left foot. Continue, maintaining the on guard position at all times. (See Plate 20a, b, c)

PLATE 20. THE SLOW RETREAT

| *(a) Starting position* | *(b) Right foot backward* | *(c) Left foot to position* |

(a) Starting position   *(b) Left step forward*   *(c) Right foot to position*

PLATE 21. THE QUICK ADVANCE

The Quick Advance

There are times when openings appear which can be taken advantage of only through quick action. The ability to step in fast, with both feet under the body, gives the advantage of being able to score, and to follow up.

Assume the on guard position. Push off smartly with the right foot, and at the same time step forward with the left foot. The left foot is carried close to the deck. The right foot is immediately brought forward so that foot positions are essentially those of the fundamental stance. (See Plate 21a, b, c) The body flattens toward the deck rather than leaping into the air. It is not a hop. In all respects it is the same as a long step forward with the left foot, bringing the right foot into position.

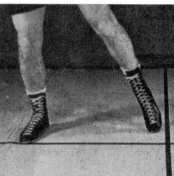

(a) Starting position   *(b) Weight shifting to right foot*   *(c) Left foot as a drag*

PLATE 22. THE QUICK RETREAT

The Quick Retreat

This movement is essentially a long but quick step backward. Assume the on guard position. Push off the left foot, and at the same time step backward with the right, weight shifting to the straight right leg, using the left leg as a drag to maintain balance. (See Plate 22a, b, c, d)

(d) Whole body position

**PLATE 22.
THE QUICK RETREAT**

(a) Starting position   *(b) Left step*   *(c) Right foot to position*

PLATE 23. THE LEFT STEP

The Left Step

The left step is performed by moving the left foot six or eight inches to the left, following immediately with right foot to position. (See Plate 23a, b, c)

In circling, the left leg becomes a movable pivot. Assume the on guard position. Step six to eight inches to the left with the left foot. Then using the left leg as a pivot-point, wheel the whole body to the left until the correct position is resumed. The first step with the left foot may be as short or as long as necessary, the longer the step, the greater the pivot. The on guard position must be maintained at all times. The left hand should be carried higher than ordinary, in readiness for the opponent's right counter.

The Right Step

This is a more precise movement requiring shorter steps. Assume the on guard position. Step from four to six inches to the right with the right foot and immediately follow with the left foot to the fundamental foot position. (See Plate 24a, b, c) The step with the right foot must be short. Carry the right hand high, ready for the opponent's left hook.

(a) Starting position   *(b) The right step*   *(c) Left foot to position*

PLATE 24. THE RIGHT STEP

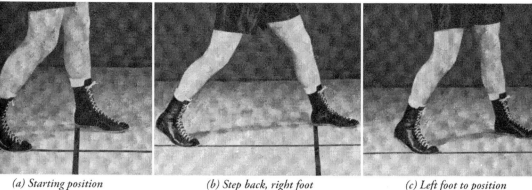

(a) Starting position   *(b) Step back, right foot*   *(c) Left foot to position*

PLATE 25. THE STEP BACK

(a) Whole body position   *(b) Whole body position*

PLATE 26. THE STEP BACK

The Step Back

As the opponent starts the attack, step back smartly with the right foot, following immediately with the left foot. (See Plate 25a, b, c) Then step quickly back to position with left foot, followed immediately by the right.

The whole body moves as a unit, first out and then in, the on guard position being maintained at all times. (See Plate 26a, b)

The Step In-Step Out

Step directly toward the opponent with the left foot, pushing off the right foot as if in the quick advance. Bring the right foot quickly to position. No sooner is that position attained than you move out, shoving off powerfully with the left foot, stepping back with the right, the left then following to position. (See Plate 27a, b, c, d)

The movement can be directly in, then out, or it can be a feint in, but pivoting either to the left or the right, in the stepping out process. The hands must be carried high and if pivoting out to the left, the right hand must be carried high off the left shoulder guarding against an opponent's right hand counter.

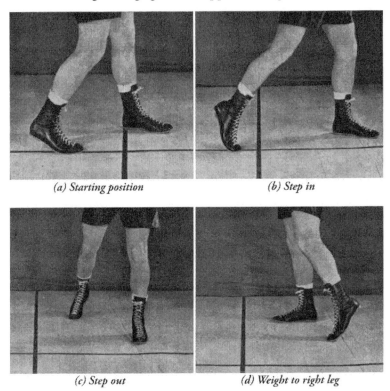

(a) Starting position   (b) Step in

(c) Step out   (d) Weight to right leg

PLATE 27. THE STEP IN-STEP OUT

The Quick Shift

Often referred to as the side step. Assume the on guard position. Slide the left foot backward until the toe is pointing toward the right heel. Move one full step to the right with the right foot, shifting the body weight over the straight right leg. The right foot controls the direction of the step.

To start with, the weight is either forward or distributed between the legs. It is then transferred to the right leg, foot positions now being reversed. The right foot is flat and pointed directly to the side. The heel of the left foot is off the deck and the toe is pointed the same direction as the right foot. Between these stages, when the left foot is dropped back to the right heel, the weight is hardly taken at all on the left foot. It is like stepping on a tack, very little weight is placed on the foot. Once the weight is shifted to the straight right leg, all that is necessary to return to attack is to pivot on the balls of the feet to the left, shifting the weight back to the left leg. (See Plate 28a, b, c, d, e, f)

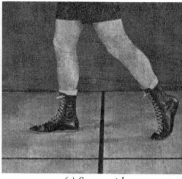

(a) Starting position   *(b) Preliminary movement*   *(c) Step to side*

(d) Pivot back to position   *(e) Starting position,*   *(f) Side step, full body*
                                     full body

PLATE 28. THE QUICK SHIFT

The Drop Shift

The execution is similar to that of the side shift. As the opponent leads a straight left, slide the left foot backward six inches, and at the same time step forward one full step with the right foot. The weight shifts to the right leg. The foot positions are now reversed, the right foot is flat on the deck, and the toe of the left foot is off the deck. As the body shifts forward to avoid the lead, a counter attack may be started. (See Plate 29a, b, c, d, e)

The shift, forward or sideward, may be combined with the left jab, the left hook or the straight right. On the forward shift, as the weight is shifted to the right leg, jab with the left hand, A longer reach and more power will result. On the side or quick shift, as the weight is shifted to the right leg, hook the left hand to the opponent's chin. Tremendous power may be obtained in this way. On the quick shift, after the weight has been shifted to the right leg, turn the body quickly back to position and drive a straight right to the opponent's jaw.

(a) Starting position   *(b) Mid shift*   *(c) Drop shift*

(d) Starting position,   *(e) Drop shift, full body*
        full body

PLATE 29. THE DROP SHIFT

The Rear Shift

Assume the on guard position. Slide the left foot backward until the toe is pointing toward right heel. Now turn the body to the rear and step smartly one full step directly to the rear with the right foot. The left arm drops protecting the left side of the body, while the right hand is carried high to protect the chin (See Plate 30a, b, c, d, e) .After the full step has been taken, either step in to attack or continue moving out of range.

(a) Starting position	(b) Mid shift	(c) Rear shift

PLATE 30. THE REAR SHIFT

(d) Starting position,
full body   (e) Rear shift, full body

PLATE 30. THE REAR SHIFT

COACHING HINTS

The Slow Advance

1. Body weight must not be disturbed.

2. Foot movements should not be more than three inches in length, the right foot following the left.

3. Both feet are on the deck at all times.

4. The on guard position is maintained at all times.

The Slow Retreat

1. As above, except the right foot is moved first.

The Quick Advance

1. Is really a long step forward. It is not a hop.

2. The left foot moves first, followed by the right. One foot is in contact with the deck at all times.

3. Push off with the right foot and step forward with the left.

4. The right foot is brought quickly to the fundamental foot position.

5. The body is flattened toward the deck.

The Quick Retreat

1. It is a sudden long step backward. The right foot moves first, followed by the left.

2. The weight is shifted to a straight right leg.

3. The left foot is used as a drag.

The Left Step

1. Step with the left foot six to eight inches to the left, toe pointed toward the opponent.

2. Move the right foot quickly to position.

3. The left hand is held high in readiness for the Opponent's right counter

The Right Step

1. Move the right foot six to ten inches to the right.

2. The left foot follows to position

3. The right hand is carried high and ready for the opponent's left hook.

The Step Back

1. The movement must be performed as quickly as possible.

2. The body position must not be altered.

3. Move the right foot backward first followed by the left, then step in with left foot followed by the right.

The Step In-Step Out

1. The first movement is directly toward the opponent—both feet recovering the fundamental foot position.

2. The next movement is stepping out—pushing off with the left foot to the right, stepping directly backwards or to the left with the right foot.

3. Hands must be kept high and ready to block.

The Quick Shift

1. Move the left toe back to the right heel, the left toe pointing directly toward the right heel.

2. Take one full step to the right with the right foot shifting the weight to the right leg.

3. The foot positions are now reversed and the body turned directly to the side.

4. From that position step out or,

5. Pivot back to the attack by turning on the balls of the feet to the left and shifting the weight back to the original position.

6. Carry the hands high, in position of guard.

The Forward Shift

1. Move the left foot back six inches and take one full step forward, shifting the weight to the right leg.

The Rear Shift

1. Move the left toe back to the right heel, the left toe pointing directly toward the right heel.

2. Turn the body to the rear and step out smartly with the right leg.

3. Left arm covers the body, right hand is carried high off the left shoulder.

HITTING POWER—THE WAIST PIVOT

The waist pivot is the art of obtaining maximum power in blows with a minimum of effort. Because boxing' is a sport in which one contestant attempts to out-hit the other by means of well-timed and maneuvered blows, hitting is the foundation of boxing.

Hitting is truly an art. It is the systematic study of how to hit straight and fast, using body power rather than mere arm power.

The ability to hit straight from the shoulder is not a natural act. It is not learned by chance, ordinary experience does not teach it. Straight hitting, with body power behind each blow, takes years of study and practice to perfect.

Straight hitting is based upon an understanding of body structure in relation to leverage. It is an attempt to use body weight in every blow, hitting with the body, not the arms. Arms are merely the vehicle of force. Arm action alone is insufficient to give real power to blows. Real power, quick and accurate, can be obtained only by shifting the weight in such a manner that the hip and shoulder precede the arm to the center line of the body. Otherwise, at the moment of impact the body weight will not be behind the blow. There are two methods which accomplish this shift of weight. One is a pivot or quick turn of the waist allowing the hip and shoulder to precede the arm. The other is a full body pivot shifting the weight from one leg to the other. The waist pivot is easier to learn and can be executed more quickly. It should be used as the basis for teaching the art of hitting.

Hitting straight from the shoulder looks very simple, yet it is one of the most difficult lessons to learn in all of boxing.

Hitting does not mean pushing. True hitting may be likened to a snap of a whip, all the energy is slowly concentrated and then suddenly released with a tremendous outpouring of power. Pushing is exactly the opposite, force being concentrated at the beginning of the blow followed by a subsequent loss of power as the arm extends. In scientific hitting the feet are always directly under the body. In pushing, the body is often off-balance as the force of the blow does not come from a pivot of the waist but from a push off the right toe.

Power in hitting comes from a quick twist of the waist, or waist pivot. This is not a swinging, swaying movement, but is a pivot over the straight left leg. As long as this straight line is maintained, as long as the hips are relaxed and free to swing, as long as the shoulders are turned through to the center line of the body before arm extension, power will result and hitting will be an art. Once the straight line of the left side of the body is broken, power is lost. The left side of the body is the anchor, the pivot point, the hinge from which power and force is generated.

So great is the power attained in this manner that an expert boxer can deliver a knockout blow without taking a single step or displaying apparent effort.

As long as the whole idea of boxing is to hit the opponent without being hit in return, then the primary purpose of hitting is to be able to hit hard and fast and to prevent the opponent from hitting back—thus scoring points and winning the match.

ANALYSIS OF THE WAIST PIVOT

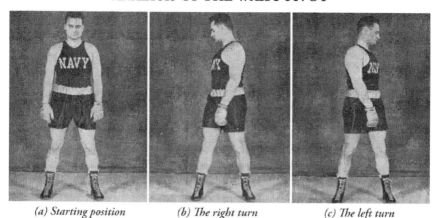

(a) Starting position   *(b) The right turn*   *(c) The left turn*

PLATE 31. THE TURN OR PIVOT

The Turn or Pivot

Stand erect, feet on a line, toes forward, one natural stance apart. Arms should hang free and easy at the sides. Imagine a rod placed directly through the head, down the spine, and into the floor. A rod so placed would allow only one movement, a turning or pivot of the body left or right. The rod would prevent swinging, swaying or bending in any direction.

With the body in the above position, turn left and right allowing the arms to swing. Be sure that the waist turns the arms. not the arms the waist. The arms will swing out freely with every turn of the body. Bring the shoulder well around on every turn with the hips swinging freely. Continue turning from left to right until this movement is firmly established. (See Plate 31a, b, c)

(a) Starting position   *(b) The right turn*   *(c) The left turn*

PLATE 32. THE CLOSE ELBOW TURN

The Close Elbow Turn

Without altering the stance, bend the arms at the elbows, open the hands and bring them to a position eight to ten inches directly in front of the eyes. The elbows are down close and in front of the body, the forearms forming a straight line from the elbow to the tip of the fingers.

Now, turn the body as in the previous exercise. Make the waist turn the body well through, with no swinging or swaying being evidenced. The turn of the body is a straight pivot. (See Plate 32a, b, c) The position of the hands does not change during this movement. Keep the chin down on the breast bone as if it were pinned there. Continue this exercise until it can be easily performed.

The Arm Extension, Palms Up

Again assuming the above position, reach out with the left arm, palm up, to a point in front of the body which represents the median or center line. The right hand, palm up, is held on the chest, directly behind the left hand, so that a straight line may be sighted between the two hands. Turn the body to the left and while turning, drive the right hand to the exact spot vacated by the left. (See Plate 33a, b) As the right hand drives out into extension, the left arm folds to the body, elbow down, palm in and at eye level. Continue turning until the arms can be driven forward like pistons.

(a) Left arm extension   *(b) Right arm extension*

PLATE 33. ARM EXTENSION, PALMS UP

Making a Proper Fist

Before attempting to hit with a closed fist, it is essential to know how to properly clench the hand to make a fist. Improper clenching of the hand, as well as the lack of knowledge of how to use the fist for hitting purposes, accounts for many broken and disfigured hands.

To make a tight fist place the fingers in the center of the palm and close the thumb over and across the phalanges of the second and third fingers so that the thumb side of the hand is perfectly flat. (See Plate 34a, b, c, d)

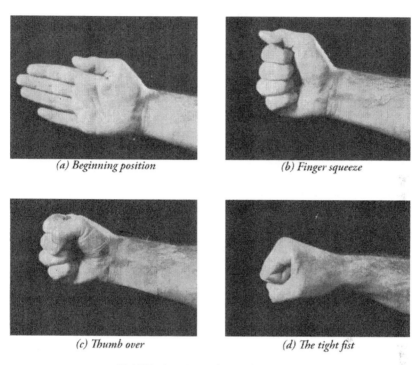

(a) Beginning position   (b) Finger squeeze

(c) Thumb over   (d) The tight fist

PLATE 34. MAKING A PROPER FIST

Driving Both Hands Through

Assume the on guard position. Perform the same hitting exercise as before but with clenched fists. In the on guard position the fist is held so that the thumb side is upward. As the body is turned to the right, and the left arm driven into extension, the wrist is turned inward, so that at the moment of impact the thumb side of the hand is in, knuckles up. This quarter turn of the wrist is a natural movement of the arm and gives a snap to the blow impossible to obtain in any other manner.

With the left arm now held out into complete extension, line the right hand up directly behind it. Quickly turn the body to the left, driving the right hand into complete extension, the left arm folding to the body, elbow down, hand up and open in position of guard, (See Plate 35a, b) Continue this exercise until it becomes automatic in execution. Remember, if the elbows are carried close, if the hands are carried high, if the plane of the fist never varies, if the body takes the elbow, if the twist of the waist furnishes the propulsion for the blow, if the principle of the rod is carefully observed, if practice is continued until skill becomes automatic, then hitting will be an art in the fullest sense.

(a) Left arm extension   (b) Right arm extension

PLATE 35. DRIVING BOTH HANDS THROUGH

COACHING HINTS

1. Hitting is done with the body, not the arms; the aims are merely the vehicles of force.

2. Body hitting means a snap blow, not a push.

3. Power in boxing is obtained through a straight turn or twist, with the shoulder and hip following through to the center line of the body.

4. The principle of the rod must be observed at all times, no swinging, no swaying, no pushing off with the right foot.

5. The left side of the body and the left leg should maintain an approximate straight line. This is the hinge around which body weight and power rotates.

6. Arm extension takes place only after the hip and shoulder are turned through to the center line of the body.

7. The plane of the fist should never vary. In other words, drive the arm straight toward a point and return through the same plane.

8. The elbows are folded to or taken by the body. Elbows never drop back past the medial line of the body.

9. In making a correct fist, the thumb side of the hand is perfectly flat.

10. The hand rotates a one-quarter turn inward as the arm is extended so that at the moment of impact, knuckles are up and the thumb side of the fist inward.

11. In teaching the hit there is a definite progression that must be followed—the principle of the turn, the close elbow turn, the arm extension, palm up, the making of a fist, and driving both hands through.

CHAPTER VII
Straight and Bent Arm Blows and Technique--The Left Lead

LEFT JAB TO THE CHIN—TECHNIQUE

The left jab is a straight left lead to the chin delivered by a quick turn of the waist without the disturbance of body weight.

It is the foundation of all boxing. Based on speed and accuracy, the left jab is used as a "feeler." While the blow stings and jars, its primary purpose is to render ineffective the opponent's attack by keeping him off balance, and to annoy him into exposing himself for solid follow blows.

The jab is the whip rather than club. It is the sign of the skilled boxer. It is both an offensive and a defensive weapon. Its perfect execution is dependent upon skill, finesse, speed and deception. The left jab is executed without disturbance of body balance, making possible further consecutive action if such is indicated. The left jab is simple in execution, being merely a quarter turn of the body to the right and the extension of the left arm.

ANALYSIS OF THE LEFT JAB

The principal movement of the left jab has already been learned in the drill on the waist pivot. In execution, the left jab is merely one-half of the complete waist pivot or turn, a quarter turn of the left shoulder to the right until the center line of the body is reached, and then the forceful extension of the left arm. (See Plate 36a, b, c, d, e, f)

(a) The original position   *(b) Quarter turn of the shoulder*   *(c) Extension left arm*

PLATE 36. THE LEFT JAB TO THE CHIN (FRONT VIEW)

(d) On guard position   *(e) Quarter turn of the*   *(f) Extension of the*
                                    shoulder   *left arm*

PLATE 36. THE LEFT JAB TO THE CHIN (SIDE VIEW)

In practicing the movement remember that as the left arm extends there is a quarter turn of the first inward, so that at the movement of complete extension the knuckles are turned up. The arm extends on a straight line slightly above shoulder height, and returns on a straight line, the plane of the first never changing, the elbow folding to the short ribs.

The initial position of the left arm is very important in the successful execution of the left jab. The left arm must be held shoulder height, to the left, so that it corresponds to the outside line of the left side of the body. The hand must always return to the same outside position. Under no circumstances should the blow start from a position inside the body line as it is easily rendered useless by the opponent who uses the stop or pin.

The right hand is held directly in front of the right shoulder, palm open toward the opponent. In the execution of the jab, as the body turns to the right, the right arm moves forward and up to a position in line with the left shoulder.

The left jab is a turn of the body and sudden arm extension, like a sudden lash of the whip. All power is concentrated away from the body, the arm then relaxing or falling back to the short ribs naturally. No effort should be exerted in bringing the left arm back to position.

In all blows but the left jab, the blow is driven through the mark or point of attack. The left jab, like a pointer, is driven to the mark, jarring and stinging, but without great power because the weight of the body is not disturbed.

The jab must be a light, easy movement, the shoulder and arm being free and relaxed. It is simple in its ordinary execution, but precise and exact in its use.

Long diligent practice is necessary in order to make the movement reflexive and so that speed, power and accuracy will result without apparent effort.

The Speed Jab

The jab as described above is the basic left lead because it derives its greatest power from the quick turn of the waist, or in other words, the body. However, if the jab is started from a position inside the body line, it becomes possible to cross it with a right.

The speed jab because of the difference in basic arm position is more difficult to "cross" with a right. The on guard or starting position is slightly different in that the left hand is held with the thumb side of the hand in, knuckles up, elbow directly down, with the hand slightly higher than in the ordinary position. The arm forms the outside line of the body.

From that position the arm is extended forcibly, without the benefit of the body pivot. The straight-on body position is maintained. Power is obtained from a forceful arm extension plus the quick advance of the body forward. The body does not bend at the waist or turn to the right. (See Plate 57 a, b)

As the arm retracts, the elbow drops to the on guard position, hand remaining high and ready.

In its proper execution, the arm extends on a straight line with shoulder, driving out with great speed and power. Because the hand is held slightly higher and closer to the shoulder, it is more deceptive than the regular jab. It depends primarily on arm action instead of an arm and trunk movement, therefore has a slightly greater speed.

(a) Starting position   (b) The arm extension
(note position of left hand)   (no shoulder turn)

PLATE 37. THE SPEED JAB

Because of the high hand position there is a tendency to raise the elbow and instead of driving straight to the mark, to slap downward. Such a jab is called a *flicker jab*.

The Flicker Jab

The flicker jab as mentioned above is a faulty version of the speed jab. It has little merit except as a diversion. It lacks power, and can easily be crossed with a right hand, therefore should not be used or imitated. Because it is a partial movement, it can be delivered quickly, but at a loss of accuracy and power.

COACHING HINTS

Basic Left Jab

1. Weight or balance should not be disturbed.

2. The power comes from the quarter turn of the left shoulder to the right and the forceful extension of the left arm.

3. The arm is driven slightly upward and returns through the same plane.

4. At the moment of impact the knuckles are up.

5. The force of the blow is away from the body. The arm merely relaxes back to the body.

6. Jab at the mark, whether eyes, nose, mouth or chin.

7. The right hand is held open and ready in position of guard.

8. The left side of the body should form a straight line throughout the maneuver.

Speed Jab

1. Left hand is held high.

2. Knuckle side of hand is up, thumb side in.

3. Blow is delivered straight from shoulder without the waist pivot.

4. Power is obtained from the forward advance as well as the arm extension.

5. Right hand is carried in the position of guard.

Flicker Jab

1. Hand is held the same as in the speed jab.

2. The elbow is raised and the hand slapped down to the target.

3. The right hand remains in the position of guard.

LEFT JAB TO THE CHIN—DEFENSE

Defense for the left jab includes all the techniques and defensive maneuvers designed to nullify attack by the left lead.

Because the left jab is the only true lead blow, it is essential that an adequate defense be developed.

Inability to defend against a left jab not only nullifies attack and counter attack, but initiates further attack from the opponent.

Defense for the left jab consists of blocking, guarding, parrying, stopping, slipping, cuffing, the quick shift, the drop shift, the rear shift, the step back, covering, folding, rolling, weaving and the snap away. Some are elementary, others are advanced. All are a part of the defense for a left jab.

Blocking

Is the first line of defense. It means taking a blow on some part of the body which is less susceptible to injury. However, considerable resistance is necessary to block a hard blow which causes contusion of the tissue, nerves, and bone. Blocking, therefore, tends to weaken rather than conserve bodily forces. A well-delivered blow, even if blocked, will disturb balance, prevent countering, and create openings for other blows.

Blocking may be used against all types of blows, either to face or body. It should be learned first and learned well. Later it should be used only when necessary.

Guarding

Is using the arms as levers to dispel the force of the opponent's blows. Such movements require subtle judgment, speed and coordination for their execution. Some contusion takes place, but not to the same degree as in blocking. Guarding is used against straight blows and often in conjunction with the counterattack.

Parrying

Is a sudden movement of the hand either from the inside or outside, deflecting the oncoming blow from its original path. It is a light, easy movement depending on timing rather than force. A blow should be parried close to the body. To parry a blow by reaching for it not only creates openings for counter blows, but enables the opponent to change the direction of his blow. Parry late rather than early.

Parrying is an extremely useful form of defense, easily learned, and easily performed. It should be used whenever possible, as openings are created which are essential to counter-fighting.

Stopping

Is the pinning of an opponent's hand or arm so that he is unable to deliver a blow. It may be used as a preventive measure when slipping or countering, or when an opponent actually intends to deliver a blow. It requires a knowledge of when an opponent is going to lead and depends on speed and skill for execution.

Slipping

Is avoiding a blow without actually moving the body out of range. It is used primarily against straight leads and counters. It calls for exact timing and judgment and to be effective must be executed so that the blow is escaped only by the smallest fraction. Performed suddenly, the slip contains an element of surprise and leaves the opponent wide open for counter blows.

Because slipping leaves both hands free to counter, it is the method preferred by the expert.

It is possible to slip either a left or a right lead. Actually, slipping is more often used on a left lead because it is safer. The outside slip, that is, dropping to a position outside of the opponent's left or right lead is safest and leaves the opponent unable to defend against a counter attack.

Slipping is a most valuable technique, the real basis of counter-fighting upon which depends the science of attack.

Cuffing

Means slapping the opponent's hands up or down, or slapping aside his leads, whether to face or body.

It tends to create openings for counters and when combined with other forms of defense can be a valuable technique.

The Quick Shift

Is the use of the side step as a means of slipping punches or moving out of range.

The Drop Shift

Is used to move forward to a position underneath an opponent's lead.

The Rear Shift

Used to move quickly to the rear thus avoiding the opponent's attack.

The Step Back

Is used to move out of the range of attack, yet retaining position for attack.

Covering

Is often referred to as the safety block. It is dropping the head in the crook of the right arm, at the same time placing the left arm over the solar plexus.

Folding

Is dropping slightly forward, hands high, so that the blow is either slipped or taken on the top of the head. It is a method of getting close enough to start the attack without taking any serious punishment.

Rolling

Means nullifying the force of a blow by moving the body with the blow. Against a straight blow, the movement is backward; against hooks, to either side; and against uppercuts, it is backward and away.

Rolling is the technique of the expert. It is almost impossible for a novice to hit an expert who is using it. It is a technique worth perfecting.

Weaving

Is an advanced defensive tactic which means moving the body in, out and around a straight lead to the head, making the opponent miss and using the opening thus created as the start of a two-fisted counter attack, Weaving is based on slipping. Thus mastery of slipping helps to create skill in weaving. It is more difficult than slipping but a very effective defense maneuver once perfected.

The Snap Away

Means rocking the body away from a straight blow so as to make the opponent miss. As the opponent's arm relaxes to the body it is possible to move in with stiff counters. It is a very effective technique against a left jab and the basis of the one-two combination blow.

PLATE 38. THE CATCH FOR THE LEFT JAB

Often referred to as the stop block

PLATE 39. THE LEVERAGE BLOCK ON A LEFT JAB

Often referred to as the inside guard

ANALYSIS OF THE METHODS OF DEFENSE

Blocking

The Catch or Stop Block—As the opponent leads a slow left jab, the lead should be caught in the palm of the open right glove and forced up and out to the right. This leaves one on the inside guard position and ready to carry the attack. (See Plate 38)

It is important that the right glove be kept open and relaxed. The blow should be caught on the lower part or butt of the hand. The movement must be kept close to the body at all times. Do not reach out to catch the opponent's blows as openings are thus created for a counter attack.

Guarding

The Leverage Block—Means using the right arm as a lever against a straight left lead. As the opponent leads a left jab, drive the right arm forward and sideways into complete extension, crossing to the inside of the opponent's jab and forcing it wide of its mark. (See Plate 39)

The elbow should be completely straightened at the moment of contact with the opponent's forearm, palm turned outward. Considerable force is required to prevent the opponent's jab from breaking through. The left arm is held in the position of guard or counter. Chin must be down.

Parrying

The Inside Parry on the Left Lead—As the opponent leads a left jab, drop slightly to the left, bringing the right hand to the inside of the oncoming jab. Turn the palm of the right hand outward, and brush the jab to the outside.

It is important to take a quick short step to the left with the left foot and to bend the body slightly inside the left lead. The left hand should be ready to stop opponent's right counter. Keep the chin down. This parry calls for a great deal of practice and coordination in order to be properly executed. (See Plate 40)

PLATE 40. THE INSIDE PARRY ON
A LEFT LEAD

PLATE 41. THE OUTSIDE PARRY ON
A LEFT LEAD

The Outside Parry on the Left Lead—Is probably the most simple defense for a left jab. The opponent's left lead is forced across the body to the left with the right hand. The movement is light and easy, force not being required.

As the opponent leads a left jab, flick the right hand across the opponent's approaching wrist, thus forcing the blow to the left and leaving the opponent's left side of the body exposed. (See Plate 41)

This movement is mainly of the wrist and hand as an arm movement would be too slow and heavy. The right hand, moving inward from the point of the elbow, flicks across swiftly, as if brushing a fly away from the nose. Speed is essential.

The right hand should strike the opponent's lead on the cuff of the glove, or on the wrist. The right elbow must remain fixed if the movement is to be performed correctly.

The Cross Parry on the Straight Left Lead—As the opponent leads a straight left, reach across with the left hand and force the oncoming lead outward, causing it to go wide of its mark, The movement is primarily one of the forearm. The elbow does not move. Hold the right hand in position to counter to the body. (See Plate 42)

PLATE 42. THE CROSS PARRY ON A STRAIGHT LEFT LEAD

Stopping

Anticipate the opponent's left lead. Reach out with right glove and place it over the opponent's left glove. In so doing, straighten the elbow and keep the body well out of range. (See Plate 43a, b, c)

In slipping, ducking and weaving, *always pin or stop the opponent's right hand when moving to the inside position.*

Slipping

To the Inside Guard Position on a Left Jab—As the opponent leads a left jab, shift the weight over the left leg, thus moving the body slightly to the left and forward, and bring the right shoulder quickly forward. In so doing, the left jab slips over the right shoulder, the right hip rotates inward, and the right knee bends slightly. The movement gains the inside position which is the preferred position for attack. The head is moved only if the slip is too close. (See Plate 44a)

To the Outride Guard Position on a Straight Left Lead—As the opponent leads a left jab, drop the weight back to a straight right leg by quickly turning the left shoulder and body to the right. The right foot remains stationary, but the left toe pivots inward. The left jab will slip harmlessly over the left shoulder.

Drop the left hand slightly, but hold it ready to drive an uppercut to the opponent's body. The right hand should be held high off the left shoulder ready to counter to the chin. (See Plate 44b)

PLATE 43. STOPPING

| *(a) Right stop on left jab* | *(b) Left stop on left jab* | *(c) Right stop on right lead* |

(a) To the inside guard position   (b) To the outside guard position

PLATE 44. SLIPPING

Cuffing

As the opponent leads a left jab, drop either the left or the right open glove down, across and over opponent's lead. This is called cuffing or knocking punches down. The movement must be sudden and can be performed with either hand. Be ready to counter to chin with the hand that is not used. (See Plate 45a, b, c, d)

If an opening to the body is desired drop either the right or left glove under the opponent's left lead and force up. This causes the lead to go high. Be ready to counter with the hand not used to cuff with. (See Plate 46a, b)

(a) Right cuff on left lead   (b) Right cuff on right lead

PLATE 45. CUFFING DOWN

The Quick Shift

As the opponent leads a left jab, shift quickly to the right thus avoiding the blow. Then either pivot into the attack or step out further yet. (See page 64 for the full explanation.)

(c) Left cuff on left lead   *(d) Left cuff on right lead*

PLATE 45. CUFFING DOWN

(a) Right cuff on left lead   *(b) Left cuff on right lead*

PLATE 46. CUFFING UP

The Drop Shift

As the opponent leads a left jab use the drop shift to attain the inside guard position, underneath the opponent's lead. (See Page 65 for the full explanation.)

The Rear Shift

As the opponent leads a left jab, step quickly to the rear. (See Page 66 for the full explanation.)

The Step Back

As the opponent leads a left jab, execute the step back technique. (See Page 66 for the full explanation.)

(a) Under a left lead *(b) Under a right lead*

PLATE 48. FOLDING

Covering

As the opponent leads a left jab, raise the right arm in half bent position forward and up under the lead, placing the head in the crook of the right arm. At the same time, cover the solar plexus with left arm. (See Plate 47)

Folding

As the opponent leads a left, drop forward from the waist, knees bending slightly. At the same time bring both arms forward, hands well up in front of face, elbows to outside line of body, forearms straight and protecting the body, hands high protecting the face. Such a movement forces the left jab up, body dropping underneath. (See Plate 48a, b)

Folding is a technique of the old school, and brings the opponent into range for the counter attack.

Rolling

On straight leads move the body backward with the blow in order to dissipate its force. On hooks move the body in the same direction as the blow. On uppercuts move backward out of range.

Weaving

To the Inside Position—On a left lead, slip to the outside position. Drop the head and upper body and move in under the extended left lead to the left. Then

(a) The outside slip *(b) Mid-position* *(c) To the inside position*

PLATE 49. WEAVING TO THE INSIDE

straighten to the on guard position. The left lead now approximates the right shoulder. Carry the hands high and close to the body. As the body moves to the inside position, place the open left glove over the opponent's right. (See Plate 49a, b, c) Later, counter with first a left, then a right and a left-handed blow as the weave is performed.

To the Outside Position—As the opponent leads a left jab, slip to the inside guard position. Move the head and body to the right and upward in a circular movement so that the opponent's left lead approximates the left shoulder. The body is now on the outside of the opponent's lead and in position of guard. Both hands are carried high and close. (See Plate 50a, b, c) As the inside slip is executed, place the left glove on the opponent's right. Later counter with both hands as slip is performed.

PLATE 51. THE SNAP AWAY

The Snap Away

As the opponent leads a left jab, shift the body weight quickly to the right leg and move back with the 0pponent's blow. As the blow falls short and opponent's left hand folds back to the body, step in with a left jab, and follow by a straight right. (See Plate 51)

COACHING HINTS

Blocking

The Catch—

1. Catch opponent's left lead in the butt of the open right hand.

2. Force the blow up and out, thus obtaining the inside position.

3. Hold the left hand ready to attack.

Guarding

The Leverage Guard—

1. Use against a straight left lead.

2. Straighten the right arm upward and outward, striking the opponent's lead from the inside and forcing it outward.

3. Lock the elbow at the moment of contact.

4. Turn the right hand outward.

5. Force must be applied.

6. Hold the left hand in a position of guard, ready to block opponent's right or to counter to face or body.

Parrying

The Inside Parry on a Straight Left Lead—

1. Drop the body slightly to the left bringing the right hand inside the left lead

2. Brush outward with the right hand, palm turned outward.

3. Hold the left hand ready to block or counter.

Outside Parry on a Straight Left Lead—

1. Brush the opponent's lead to the left with the right hand.

2. Movement is more wrist than arm. Elbow should be fixed.

3. Intercept opponent's oncoming blow on the wrist, not on the glove.

4. Lower the left hand, ready to counter to opponent's body.

The Cross Parry on a Straight Left Lead—

1. Reach over with the left hand and brush the opponent's left lead outward.

2. Perform the movement with the wrist and arm.

3. Move the elbow only as much as necessary.

4. Lower the right hand ready to counter.

Stopping

1. Reach out and place the hand over opponent's glove.

2. When slipping, ducking or weaving always pin the opponent's right hand.

Slipping

To Inside Guard Position—

1. Shift the weight over a straight left leg.

2. Turn the right shoulder forward.

3. Swing the right hip forward, with right knee bent and loose.

4. Place the left glove over opponent's right glove.

To Outside Guard Position—

1. Shift weight over a straight right leg.

2. Turn the left shoulder and hip to the right.

3. Keep the right foot stationary, left toe pointed inward.

4. Lower the left hand ready to counter to body.

5. Hold the right hand off the left shoulder in a position to guard or counter.

Cuffing

1. Knock the opponent's left lead downward by slapping with either the left or right glove. Elbows remain fixed.

2. Slap the opponent's lead upward with either the right or left glove, using the back of glove. Elbows remain fixed.

3. Movement must be sudden. Use only occasionally.

The Quick Shift	*The Drop Shift*	*The Rear Shift*	*Step Back*
See page 64.	*See page 65.*	*See page 66.*	*See page 66.*

Covering

1. Raise the right arm in a half bent position.

2. Drop head into the crook of the arm.

3. Fold left arm across solar plexus.

Folding

1. Bend the body slightly forward from the waist.

2. Raise the arms forward so that hands cover face.

3. Elbows remain down and to outside lines of body.

4. The body drops or folds under opponent's left lead.

Rolling

1. Move the body backward on straight blows.

2. Move the body to the left on left swings or hooks.

3. Move the body to the right on right swings or hooks.

4. Move body backward on uppercuts.

Weaving

To Inside Guard Position—

1. Slip to the outside guard position.

2. Drop head forward and bend trunk slightly.

3. Move the head to the left, under opponent's arm and up to position.

4. Carry both hands high and in position of guard.

5. As the body moves to the inside position, place the left glove over the opponent's right.

To the Outside Position on Left Lead—

1. Slip to the inside guard position.

2. Drop the head forward and bend the trunk slightly.

3. Then move the head to the right, under opponent's arm and up to position.

4. Carry the hands high.

The Snap Away

1. Use against a left jab.

2. Drop the weight to the right foot, moving the body back with the jab.

3. As the jab falls short, move in with a left and right to chin.

LEFT JAB TO THE CHIN—COUNTER ATTACK[*]

Counter attack means foreknowledge of specific openings which will result from an attack by the opponent. The counter attack is not a defensive action but a method of using an opponent's offense as a means of successfully completing one's own attack.

The counter attack is an advanced phase of offense. It calls for the greatest skill, the most perfect planning and the most delicate execution of all boxing techniques. It uses as tools all the main techniques of boxing, blocking, guarding, parrying slipping, weaving, ducking, sidestepping, feinting, drawing and shifting. Besides a mastery of technique, the counter attack requires exact timing, unerring judgment, and cool, calculating poise. It means careful thought, daring execution and sure control. It is the greatest art in boxing, the art of the champion.

There are numerous counters which may be used for every lead, but for each particular occasion there is one counter which should be used. Such a counter is that one most effective for the particular situation at hand. Action must be instantaneous and where there is a wide choice of action, instant action is difficult if not impossible unless the right action has been previously conditioned.

Conditioning is a process whereby a specific stimulus will cause a specific reaction. A repeated stimulus eventually creates an action pattern in the nervous system. Once this pattern is established the mere presence of the stimulus will cause a specific action. Such action is instantaneous and practically unconscious. In boxing, conditioned action should be the result of intense and concentrated practice of planned action patterns in response to certain leads. Finally, the lead itself will automatically bring the right counter.

Boxing should be done with the head, not the hands. It is true that during the time of actual boxing one does not think of how to box but rather of the weakness or strength of the opponent, of possible openings and opportunities. Boxing will never reach the state of a true art unless performance of skill is made automatic and the cortex freed to think and to associate, to make plans and to judge. The higher nerve centers always retain control but will act only when necessary.

---

[*] A general explanation is herein given in this first section on the counter attack.

In a consideration of counter blows there are three, things that must be understood.

— The lead of the opponent.
— The method of avoiding the lead.
— The counter blow itself.

The lead of the opponent is important in that it determines which side of the body is open to attack. A left lead exposes the left side of the body, while a right lead exposes almost all of the upper trunk.

In order to decide upon the method of avoiding leads, it must be decided whether the counter attack should be one or two handed. Blocking, guarding, stopping and partying all leave but one hand with which to counter. Such maneuvers as slipping, side-stepping, ducking, weaving, feinting, drawing and shifting allow a two-handed attack.

The counter blow depends upon the method used in avoiding the opponent's lead as well as the lead itself. In other words, if the opponent jabs and the blow is avoided by an inside slip, a right to the heart or a right cross is indicated.

ANALYSIS OF THE COUNTER ATTACK

THE LEFT JAB AS A COUNTER BLOW

A left jab can be used as a return jab, for parrying the opponent's left lead either to the inside or outside, and returning with a left jab.

(a) Riding with the jab   (b) The return jab

PLATE 52. THE RETURN JAB

The Return Jab

As the opponent leads a left jab, ascertain what happens after the lead is finished. Because the arm must retract back to the normal on guard position, it is possible to move in with a left jab if the timing is correct. Timing is the essence of the return jab. The rhythm of the opponent's jab must be determined, especially the withdrawal of his hand to normal position. One's own jab must then be timed exactly with the withdrawal of the opponent's arm. As the arm returns to the body, drive the left jab to opponent's chin. (See Plate 52a, b) It takes a great deal of practice and timing to make the return jab effective. Once the technique has been perfected, it becomes a very excellent counter, disturbing to the opponent and making possible further action.

The Inside Parry and Left Jab

As the opponent leads a straight left, step forward and left with the left foot, turning the left shoulder directly forward, and at the same time drive the left arm to the opponent's chin. The right arm is carried high, hand turned outward, forcing or parrying the oncoming lead outward. (See Plate 53a, b)

(a) The inside parry   (b) The left jab

PLATE 53. THE INSIDE PARRY AND LEFT JAB

COUNTER BLOWS FOR A LEFT JAB

The Outside Parry and Left Jab

As the opponent leads a left jab, parry to the outside guard position with the right hand, pinning the lead momentarily to the left shoulder. At the same time, drive the left out into extension, using the forward or drop shift to gain power. After partying the opponent's lead, the right hand is held high and ready to block or counter. (See Plate 54a. b)

The Right Cross

As the opponent leads a straight left, slip to the inside guard position by stepping forward and sideways with the left foot, shifting the body weight to the straight left leg. Keep the right hand outside of the opponent's lead. As the

(a) Complete action   *(b) Close up*

PLATE 54. THE OUTSIDE PARRY AND LEFT JAB

opponent's jab slips over the right shoulder, hook the right arm over the opponent's left lead to his chin. The position of the right arm should not vary from the half bent position. The left hand is carried high and in a position of guard. The whole action is performed as a unit. The movement of the right arm

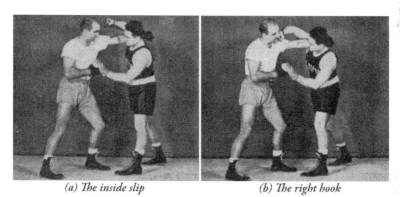

(a) The inside slip   *(b) The right hook*

PLATE 55. THE RIGHT CROSS

is up and over. (See Plate 55a, b)

The Inside Straight Right to the Chin

As the opponent leads a left jab, quickly turn the body to the left bringing the right shoulder forward to center line. From this point drive the right hand into complete extension. The opponent's lead slips to the outside of the right arm. The left hand is held in the position of guard. (See Plate 56a, b) To obtain greater power, take a short step to the left with the left foot, thus shifting the weight over a straight left leg.

The Inside Guard and Right Hook

As the opponent jabs with the left, drop directly to the left, at the same time raise the right forearm up in under the opponent's lead, forcing the lead to the

(a) Turning inside   *(b) The straight right*

PLATE 56. THE INSIDE STRAIGHT RIGHT TO THE CHIN

outside. Then raise the right elbow so that it is in a straight line with the opponent's chin, step forward and sideways with the left foot shifting the weight to the left leg, and hook a hard right hook to the opponent's chin. Carry the

PLATE 57. THE INSIDE GUARD AND RIGHT HOOK

(a) The inside guard   *(b) Raising the elbow*   *(c) Hooking to chin*

left hand in the position of guard. (See Plate 57a, b, c)

The Inside Right to the Heart

On the opponent's left lead slip to the inside position, and drive a straight right to the heart. The body should be carried low and on the same plane as the right arm, the arm protecting the head. The left hand is held high, and ready to stop the opponent's right hook. To obtain the greatest power, step forward and left, six to eight inches

**PLATE 58. THE INSIDE RIGHT
TO THE HEART**

|(a) The parry|(b) The uppercut|

PLATE 59. THE OUTSIDE PARRY AND LEFT UPPERCUT, RIGHT STEP

with the left foot, while shifting all the weight to the left leg. (See Plate 58)

The Outside Parry and Left Uppercut

On the opponent's left lead parry to the outside position with the right hand. At the same time drop the left arm perpendicular to the floor, and step across with the right foot to a position outside the opponent's left foot. As the weight shifts to the right leg, drive a hard left uppercut to the solar plexus. (See Plate 59a, b) This same movement may be repeated by stepping across with the left foot to a position outside the opponent's left foot. (See Plate 60a, b)

|(a) The parry|(b) The uppercut|

PLATE 60. THE OUTSIDE PARRY AND LEFT UPPERCUT, LEFT STEP

The Inside Guard and Left Uppercut to the Liver

As the opponent leads a straight left, drop directly to the left, and to the inside guard position. Parry the left lead outward with the right hand, pivot sharply from the waist forcing the left hand up and under the opponent's guard to the solar plexus. The weight is shifted over the left leg, which in turn becomes the

| (a) The inside guard | (b) The uppercut | (c) The pivot cut |

PLATE 61. THE INSIDE GUARD AND LEFT UPPERCUT TO THE LIVER

pivot point around which the body wheels upon completion of the blow. (See Plate 61a, b, c)

The Cross Parry and Inside Right to Chin

As the opponent leads a straight left, reach over with the open palm of the left glove and force the oncoming blow to the right. At the same time rock the weight forward to the left foot, and as soon as the parry is made drive a straight right to chin (or body). (See Plate 62a, b)

| (a) The cross parry | (b) Straight right to chin |

PLATE 62. THE CROSS PARRY AND INSIDE RIGHT TO CHIN

COACHING HINTS

The Return Jab

1. The rhythm of the opponent's left jab must be timed, especially the retraction of the left hand to the on guard position.

2. As the opponent's arm retracts to the body, step in and drive a left jab to the chin.

The Inside Parry and Left Jab

1. Shift the weight to the left leg.

2. Turn the left shoulder straight forward.

3. Drive the left hand into complete extension.

4. At the same time parry the opponent's left lead outward with the right hand

The Outside Parry and the Left Jab

1. Use the right hand to parry left lead inward.

2. Momentarily pin the left jab to the left shoulder.

3. At the same time shift the weight forward to the left leg.

4. Hold the right ready to counter.

The Right Cross

1. Step forward with the left foot without moving the right arm, allowing the opponents lead to slip over the right shoulder.

2. Hook the right arm up and over the opponents extended arm to his chin.

3. The left glove should be placed over the opponent's right in order to prevent a counter blow.

The Inside Right to the Chin

1. Shift the weight to a straight left leg.

2. Turn the right shoulder and hip through to the center line.

3. Drive a hard right to the chin inside the opponent's left lead.

4. Carry the left hand high, and ready to stop the opponent's right counter.

Inside Guard and Right Hook

1. Drop directly to the left.

2. Guard the left lead outward with the right arm.

3. Step forward and to the left shifting the weight forward.

4. At the same time raise the right elbow and hook a hard right to opponent's chin.

The Inside Right to the Heart

1. Take one step forward and sideways with the left foot, shifting the weight over the left foot.

2. Turn the hip and shoulder through to the center line allowing opponent's left lead to slip over the right shoulder.

3. Drive a hard right to opponent's heart inside his left lead.

4. Carry the left hand high and ready for the opponent's left counter.

5. Protect the head with the right arm.

The Outside Parry and Left Uppercut to the Solar Plexus

1. Parry the opponent's left lead to the outside guard position with the right hand.

2. Drop the left arm perpendicular to the floor, and step across to a position outside the opponent's left foot, with either the left or right foot.

3. Shift the weight to the front leg and then drive a hard left uppercut to the solar plexus.

4. Carry the right hand high, ready to cross to opponent's chin.

The Inside Guard and Left Uppercut to the Liver

1. Step forward and left with the left foot.

2. Parry a left lead to the outside guard position with the right hand.

3. At the same time shift the weight to the left leg and drive a left uppercut to the opponent's liver.

4. Using the left leg as a pivot, wheel the body to the right and out of range.

5. Carry the right hand high and open off the left shoulder ready for opponent's right hand counter.

The Cross Parry and Inside Right Hook to the Chin or Body

1. Reach across with the open left glove and force the opponent's oncoming left lead to the right.

2. As this is done step forward slightly with the left foot.

3. The moment the cross parry is made drive the right hand to the chin or body.

LEFT JAB TO THE BODY—TECHNIQUE

The left jab to the body is a straight left driven to the opponent's solar plexus. Power is obtained through the forward bend of the body as well as the complete and forceful extension of the left arm.

The primary use of the left jab to the body is to worry the opponent and to bring his guard down. While ordinarily not a hard blow, it will cause distress if driven directly to the solar plexus. The body must drop to the level of the target, the body being on the same plane as the arm.

ANALYSIS OF THE LEFT JAB TO THE BODY

The fundamental foot position must be correct, in order that the body will assume the proper straight forward position necessary for the execution of the left jab to the body.

Drop the trunk straight forward from the waist to a position approximately at right angles to the legs. The left leg bends slightly, the right leg more so. As the body drops, drive the left arm into forceful extension to the opponent's solar plexus. (See Plate 63a, b)

(a) Front view   *(b) Side view*
PLATE 63. THE LEFT JAB TO THE BODY

The blow is slightly upward, never downward. The right hand is carried high in front of the body ready for the opponent's left hook. Head should be held close to the extended left arm. Only the top of the head should be vulnerable to attack.

Side view

**PLATE 64. VARIATION OF
LEFT JAB TO THE BODY**

Never hold the position but return as quickly as possible to the on guard position.

A *variation* is the left jab to the body performed from a side position. The body turns directly to the right so that the left shoulder is pointed toward the opponent. The body folds directly forward as the turn is made and the left arm is driven to the opponent's solar plexus. It is a movement similar to touching the right toe with the right hand, the left arm being driven into extension as the body drops. The right hand is held forward protecting the jaw. (See Plate 64)

COACHING HINTS

1. Power is obtained through a body drop from the waist to a position where the left shoulder is directly over the left toe.

2. The greatest portion of the body drop is obtained through a bend of the right knee.

3. The left leg is kept as straight as possible.

4. The left arm is driven straight from the shoulder to the solar plexus.

5. At the moment of impact the knuckles are up.

6. The right hand is held up and open, ready to block the opponent's left hook.

7. The head is carried well forward and is protected by the extended left arm.

8. The movement must be sudden and recovery immediate.

9. On returning to the on guard position, the left hand is not dropped but is brought directly back to the left shoulder.

LEFT JAB TO THE BODY—DEFENSE

The purpose of the left jab to the body is to obtain a lowering of the hands or guard of the opponent. Therefore the defense for the left jab to the body must not only give protection, but at the same time keep the opponent from achieving his purpose.

There are several different methods of defense for the left jab to the body. One is covering the point of attack, in this case the solar plexus, with the forearm or elbow. With this type of defense, which is called blocking, it is possible to stay close enough to the opponent to deliver hard counter blows.

Another type of defense is deflecting the oncoming blow with the glove, forcing it wide of its mark. This is called parrying, or sometimes brushing.

Moving out of range of the left jab to the body is another means of defense.

ANALYSIS OF THE METHODS OF DEFENSE

The Elbow Block

As the opponent leads a left jab to the body, merely turn the body so as to take the blow on the elbow. The elbow and the body are turned as one. Ordinarily it is best to intercept the blow on the right elbow, although the blow can be taken on the left elbow. The elbow should be held tight to the body, forearm straight, hand held high and in position of guard. (See Plate 65)

The elbow block
PLATE 65. DEFENSE FOR LEFT JAB TO THE BODY

The forearm block
PLATE 66. DEFENSE FOR THE LEFT JAB TO THE BODY

The Forearm Block

As the opponent leads a left jab to the body, fold both forearms across the abdomen, right arm above the left, so that the solar plexus is completely covered. The forearms should be held close together, hugging the body. (See Plate 66) It should be noted in the use of the forearm block that the chin is exposed to the opponent's left or right counter. On a left hook, fold forward under the blow. On a straight right or hook turn the body to the right, drop the left arm along the left side of the body and raise the right hand, elbow tight to the body, to the position covering the jaw.

The Brush Away or Parry

As the opponent leads a straight left to the body, drop the open right glove down and across the opponent's wrist thus brushing the blow outward. (See Plate 67) The elbow remains in a fixed position until contact is made, then the whole arm is straightened forcibly outward to the right. Actually the movement is a circular one, dropping the right hand and forearm, first inward and then out. A cross brush with the left hand can be used on a left lead to the body. Drop the left arm downward and inward, pulling the opponent's left lead across the body to the left. Counter with a right to the body.

The brush away

PLATE 67. DEFENSE FOR THE LEFT JAB TO THE BODY

The step away

PLATE 68. DEFENSE FOR THE LEFT JAB TO THE BODY

The Step Away

Is a defensive measure whereby the point of attack is drawn out of range. As the opponent leads a left jab to the body, place the left hand to the top of his head. At the same time swing the left foot backward so that the entire weight of the body shifts to the left foot. The right foot swings free as the right hand brushes downward and inward forcing the opponent's lead outward. (See Plate 68)

COACHING HINTS

The Elbow Block

1. Intercept the opponent's left jab directly on the right elbow.

2. Don't move the elbow to meet the blow, turn the body.

3. A cross block can be used, that is, intercepting the left lead to body on the left elbow.

4.   The left hand should be held high and open ready for the opponent's counter.

The Forearm Block

1.   Use only when necessary.

2.   Fold the right arm over the left, forearms tight together.

3.   Gloves should be turned inward so that the broad side of the forearms are rotated outward.

4.   Chin is exposed so be ready to fold under blows so directed.

The Brush Away

1.   The movement is downward and inward with the right hand, forcing the opponent's left lead to the body outward.

2.   The right elbow remains fixed until contact is made with the opponent's oncoming left lead, then the whole arm straightened forcibly outward.

3.   Always use a right brush for a left lead to the body. A cross brush with the left hand can be used.

4.   The left hand is held high in position of guard, ready for the opponent's counter.

The Step Away

1.   Drive the open palm of the left hand forcibly to the opponent's head.

2.   Drop the left foot back to the right, shifting the weight to the left foot.

3.   As the right leg swings free, brush outward with the right hand forcing opponent's left jab to the body wide.

LEFT JAB TO THE BODY—COUNTER ATTACK

The left jab to the body is not an effective counter blow because of its limited power. When used as a counter its effectiveness results because of the tendency of the opponent to lower the guard, thus creating openings for other and more potent counters. On the other hand, the left jab to the body can be effectively countered with uppercuts.

ANALYSIS OF THE COUNTER ATTACK
THE LEFT JAB TO THE BODY AS A COUNTER BLOW

The Outside Slip and Left Jab to the Body

On the opponent's left lead, shift the weight forward, bending the body slightly forward and to the right, allowing the left lead to slip over the left shoulder At the same time drive a straight left to opponent's short ribs. (See Plate 69)

PLATE 69. THE OUTSIDE SLIP AND LEFT   PLATE 70. THE INSIDE SLIP AND LEFT
         JAB TO BODY   JAB TO BODY

The Inside Slip and Left Jab to the Body

On the opponent's left lead, shift the weight over a straight left leg allowing the opponent's jab to slip over the right shoulder. At the same time drive a left jab to opponent's solar plexus. (See Plate 70)

COUNTER BLOWS FOR A LEFT JAB TO THE BODY

The following counter blows for a left jab to the body are fully covered in other sections of the book:

The Inside Parry and Left Uppercut to Body

Turn to Page 126 for a full description.

Cross Parry and Right Uppercut to Body

Turn to Page 176 for a full description.

COACHING HINTS

THE LEFT JAB TO THE BODY AS A COUNTER BLOW

The Outside Slip and Left Jab to the Body

1. Slip to the outside position by dropping forward and to the right.

2. As the body drops forward drive a left jab to opponent's midsection.

3. The use of the drop shift will add power to the counter.

The Inside Slip and Left Jab to the Body

1. Slip to the inside guard position.

2. As the body drops forward, drive a left jab to the solar plexus.

3. Power is obtained through the use of the drop shift. Carry the right hand high ready to block or counter.

LEFT JAB TO THE BODY—COMBINATIONS

The term combinations as herein used denotes a series of blows delivered in a natural sequence. The objective is to maneuver the opponent into such a position or create such an opening that the final blow of the series will find a vulnerable spot, resulting in a knockout or near knockout blow.

The difference between an expert and a novice boxer, is that the expert makes use of each opportunity to score, and follows up each opening with a series of blows, while the novice delivers only single blows. Blows should be delivered in a well-planned series, each blow resulting in other openings until finally the desired setup is obtained. Some blows might be termed "follow" blows in that they always come after or follow certain leads. For instance the straight right is a follow blow for the left jab and a left hook is a follow blow for a straight right. It seems natural to punch straight, then hook, as it does to punch first to the head and then to the body. Follow or combination blows have rhythm and "feel" as their basic element. Every boxer should make use of natural sequences. Sequence hitting or the use of combination blows require a great deal of practice in order that correct performance will result. Any combination of blows may be used, as long as a final opening results. Each boxer should develop combinations effective for himself. However, there are combinations of proven value which should be learned.

At this particular stage of development, the number of effective combinations is naturally limited. One very fundamental combination should receive a great deal of practice at this time. It is the left lead to head and body, or to body and head.

ANALYSIS OF THE COMBINATIONS

The Double Left Jab to the Chin

From the on guard position jab to the chin. Before complete recovery is obtained, jab again. The double left jab must have speed of execution in order to be effective.

The Left Jab to the Chin Followed by the Left Jab to the Body

Lead a left jab to the chin. Then drop forward from the waist, weight carried well forward, and drive a left jab to the solar plexus. The right hand should be carried high and open ready for opponent's left hook. (See Plate 71a, b, c)

The Left Jab to the Body Followed by the Left Jab to the Chin

This is the reverse of the above combination. It is one of the most effective combinations in boxing. Drop the body forward and jab to the body. From that position, straighten the body, step in and deliver a quick jab to the chin.

The Double Left Jab to the Body

Drop forward with a left jab to the body. Keep the body low and weight carried well forward. Then drive the left hand to the solar plexus a second time.

(a) Left jab to chin   (b) Mid-position   (c) Left jab to body
PLATE 71. THE LEFT JAB TO THE CHIN AND LEFT JAB TO BODY

COACHING HINTS

The Double Jab to the Chin

1.   If the first jab makes contact, follow with a second jab.

2.   Do not retract hand too far.

3. Step with the first jab. Use arm and body power to gain force for the second jab.

4. Carry the right hand high in a position of guard.

The Left Jab to the Chin Followed by the Left Jab to the Body

1. Is an effective feint as well as a combination blow.

2. The first blow should be light with emphasis on speed.

3. The jab to the body should be low with the intention of making the opponent drop his guard.

The Left Jab to the Body Followed by the Left Jab to the Chin

1. It is an effective feint as well as a combination blow.

2. The left jab to the body carries very little power but has speed.

3. The opponent's guard must be brought down.

4. The left jab to the chin should be a clean hard blow.

The Double Left Jab to the Body

1. Is a combination that depends upon deception and speed.

2. The first blow is to the body. While the second blow is also to the body, the opponent must be made to feel that it is going to be delivered to the chin.

LEFT HOOK TO THE CHIN—TECHNIQUE

The left hook is the most difficult blow in boxing to properly learn. It has tremendous power and can be used either as a counter or as a finishing blow. It can be used to create openings for straight blows.

The left hook is a short blow rarely traveling over eight inches. It obtains power through a shift of the body weight at the moment of contact. It should never be led, but used only when actual openings are present. It is best used as a follow blow for a left jab when starting the attack, and as a short arm jolt when in close or when coming out from the attack. It has a very real use against an opponent who overreaches with either the right or left. The so-called body hooks are in reality uppercuts of poorly executed straight blows.

ANALYSIS OF THE LEFT HOOK TO THE CHIN

The left hook uses the principle of the hinge. The right side of the body becomes the pivot point around which force is propelled. It calls for more perfect execution than any other blow, therefore requiring greater coordination. Because of these factors it is a very difficult blow to execute properly.

(a) Starting position   *(b) Foot pivot*

PLATE 72. THE LEFT HOOK TO THE CHIN

The left hook is composed of three movements, the first of which is the foot pivot. From the regular stance turn on the toes of both feet to the right until the body position is exactly reversed, that is the right foot is flat on the deck and the left toe off the deck, left knee bent. The whole body must turn as a unit so that at the final execution of the pivot the left side of the body faces directly toward the opponent. (See Plate 72a, b)

The second part of the movement is the body turn, a modification of the foot pivot. Hold the left hand high off the left shoulder. Turn the body to the right and away from the left arm. The left hand remains stationary, not moving, but the elbow raises so that the forearm is practically on the line with the hand. This is called turning away from the hand. (See Plate 73a, b)

On the third movement, the left shoulder and hip turn through to the center line, the left hand remaining stationary until the turn of the body starts the arm forward. The arm is then whipped laterally across the body with all the force possible, to the right shoulder. The arm remains in a right angle, or bent arm position throughout the blow. At the moment of contact, the thumb side of the hand is up, knuckles out. The right hand folds in close to the left shoulder in a position of guard. At the completion of the blow the weight is directly over the right leg, the left side of the body is turned toward the opponent, the left arm

(a) Starting position   *(b) Turning away from*   *(c) Follow through*
                            the head

PLATE 73. THE LEFT HOOK TO THE CHIN

has been pulled across the body in a bent arm position, The left hand approximates the position of the right shoulder. The right arm is held inside the left arm and near the left shoulder. (See Plate 73c)

The hand position is sometimes held so that the knuckles are up, thumb side of the hand turned inward toward the body.

COACHING HINTS

1. Turn the left hip and shoulder through to the center line of the body and away from the left arm and hand, which retains its original position.

2. The left elbow raises slightly.

3. The weight shifts back to a straight right leg.

4. The body turns to the right, the left hand is whipped in an arc to the right shoulder.

5. Drive through the target, not at it. The left hand does not telegraph the blow in any manner.

6. At the movement of impact, knuckles are pointing outward, palm inward, thumb side of the hand up.

7. The right hand is carried off the left shoulder, open and in position of guard.

LEFT HOOK TO THE CHIN—DEFENSE

There are three methods of defense for the left hook to the chin. One is blocking or taking the hook on some part of the body less susceptible than the chin. The second is dropping underneath the hook, or making the opponent miss by ducking. The third is merely stepping out of range of the hook.

The forearm block does not disturb body position so counter blows can be used. Ducking allows a two fisted attack to be initiated, while stepping away is purely a defensive movement.

ANALYSIS OF THE METHODS OF DEFENSE

Forearm Block

As the opponent leads a short left hook, raise the right arm as if to salute. Hand should be high and close, knuckles turned outward. The forearm must be straight, in a firm and fixed position, elbow down. The force of the blow is taken on the wrist, forearm and elbow. A slight turn to the left helps to dissipate the force of the blow. (See Plate 74)

Forearm block   *Ducking*
PLATE 74. DEFENSE FOR A LEFT HOOK   **PLATE 75. DEFENSE FOR A LEFT HOOK**

Ducking

As the opponent leads a left hook drop underneath the blow by bending at the knees and waist, thus evading the blow. (See Plate 75.) It is practically a straight drop, the body maintaining more or less of an upright position. Hands are held high and in position of guard.

The Step Back

For an analysis of this technique, turn to Page 65.

Circling to the Left

One of the most effective means of defense is to nullify the opponent's strong blow. In this case it would be the left hook. Therefore, the proper procedure would be to circle to the left, using the left foot as a pivot point about which to wheel the body to the right. Circling constantly to the left will render the opponent's left hook ineffective. Carry the right hand high in a position of guard.

COACHING HINTS

The Forearm Block

1. This movement is similar to a salute.

2. The arm must be held close and tight to the body, forearm straight, elbow down, chin well-guarded.

Ducking

1. Bend the trunk forward from the waist and dip both knees forward, causing the body to drop underneath the hook.

2. Carry the hands high, chin well down.

The Step Back

Coaching hints for this technique are listed on Page 65.

Circling to the Left

1. Step twelve to fifteen inches to the left with the left foot.

2. Use the left foot as a pivot point and wheel the body to the right.

3. The right hand should be held high in position block.

4. Left toe should be kept pointed toward opponent.

LEFT HOOK TO THE CHIN—COUNTER ATTACK

The left hook is primarily a counter blow. It is a short jolting blow delivered while in close. It is used as a counter against the left jab and is a most effective counter for the straight right. It calls for exact timing and precision of movement.

Although an effective counter blow, and used both as a lead and a follow blow, the left hook can easily be countered. Either the left jab or the straight right are effective counter blows against the left hook. A left hook is never used with impunity and one should be conscious of the counters that can be used against it.

ANALYSIS OF THE COUNTER ATTACK
THE LEFT HOOK AS A COUNTER BLOW

The Inside Guard and Left Hook to the Chin

As the opponent leads a left jab, step to the left with the left foot. At the same time move the right arm, palm outward, inside of the opponent's oncoming blow, forcing it wide. As the movement is executed, pivot sharply over the left foot and drive a short left hook to the chin. (See Plate 76a, b)

(a) The inside guard   (b) Left hook to the chin

PLATE 76. THE INSIDE GUARD AND LEFT HOOK TO THE CHIN

The Inside Hook on a Straight Right Lead

As the opponent leads a straight right to the chin, shift the weight quickly to the right foot and drive a short hook to the chin, inside of the oncoming blow. Speed and timing are absolute requisites of the counter. (See Plate 77a, b)

(a) Starting position   (b) The inside hook

PLATE 77. THE INSIDE HOOK ON A STRAIGHT RIGHT LEAD

The Cross Parry and Left Hook to the Chin on a Straight Right Lead

Parry the opponent's straight right lead across to the left, using the right glove. This forces the opponent's blow to the outside line of the body and slightly downward. Drive a hard left hook inside to the opponent's chin. As the movement of the cross parry is made, the body pivots to the left, left hand swinging wide over opponent's right. As the left hook is delivered the body pivots sharply to the right, the right hand guarding against the opponent's left. The whole movement is like the swing of the pendulum across to the left and the return swing to the right. (See Plate 78a, b)

(a) The cross parry   (b) The left hook

PLATE 78. THE CROSS PARRY AND LEFT HOOK TO THE CHIN
ON A STRAIGHT RIGHT LEAD

COUNTER BLOWS FOR A LEFT HOOK TO THE CHIN

The Left Jab

As the opponent leads a left hook, step forward and to the left and drive a straight left to the chin. The movement must be performed quickly. The right hand should be held high ready for opponent's left hook. Because the left hook is a short inside blow, the jab will land before the hook, throwing the opponent off balance. (See Plate 79)

The Straight Right to the Chin

While the left hook is a natural counter against a straight right, the straight inside right is a natural counter against a left hook.

To counter with a straight right on a left hook, step to the left and forward with left foot, shifting the weight well forward. Turn the right shoulder and hip through to the center line and drive a hard right to the opponents chin inside the left hook. (See Plate 80)

PLATE 79. THE LEFT JAB AS A COUNTER FOR THE LEFT HOOK TO THE CHIN

PLATE 80. THE STRAIGHT RIGHT AS A COUNTER FOR THE LEFT HOOK TO THE CHIN

The Straight Right to the Body

For a full description see the Straight Right to the Body, Page 163.

The Return Left Hook to the Chin

It is an old axiom, fight fire with fire. It applies in certain cases to boxing. If an opponent has a good left hook, be ready to block the hook. Catch the blow on the right forearm, step forward and to the left, body wheeling to the right, and drive a left hook to the opponent's chin. The whole action is one movement. (See Plate 81a, b)

(a) The block

(b) The return hook

PLATE 81. THE RETURN LEFT HOOK TO THE CHIN

Forearm Block and Left Uppercut to the Body

For full description see the Left Uppercut, Page 124.

The Duck with a Left Hook to Body

As the opponent leads a left hook to the chin, duck underneath. the blow allowing it to pass harmlessly over the head. At the same time step forward and to right with right foot, and hook the left glove to the opponent's solar plexus. Thumb side of the hand should be up. (See Plate 82a, b).

(a) The duck   (b) The left hook

PLATE 82. THE DUCK WITH A LEFT HOOK TO THE BODY

COACHING HINTS

THE LEFT HOOK AS A COUNTER BLOW

The Inside Guard and Left Hook to Chin

1. Step forward and to the left.

2. Parry the opponent's lead outward.

3. Wheel the body to right and hook a hard left to the chin.

The Inside Hook on a Straight Right Lead

1. Step to right and forward with the right foot.

2. Drive a short hook inside the lead.

The Cross Parry and Left Hook to the Chin on a Straight Right Lead

1. While cross parrying with the right hand turn the body to the left.

2. Allow the left hand to rotate with body to the left.

3. Force opponent's right lead outward and slightly downward with the right glove. This is absolutely essential to the proper execution of the counter.

4. Hook the left to opponent's chin, body now pivoting to the right.

5. The right hand is ready to block the opponent's left.

COUNTER BLOWS FOR THE LEFT HOOK TO THE CHIN

The Left Jab

1. Execution is practically the same as the regular jab.

2. The right hand should be carried in position of a forearm block, ready to block opponent's hook.

3. Jab as the opponent starts to hook.

4. Is a very safe counter against a left hook.

The Return Hook to Chin

1. Hold the left arm in position of a forearm block.

2. On opponent's lead, wheel the body to the right while blocking with the right forearm.

3. Hook the left hard to the opponent's chin.

The Duck and Left Hook to Body

1. Duck under opponent's left hook.

2. Step to the right with right foot and drive a hook to the solar plexus.

LEFT HOOK TO THE CHIN—COMBINATIONS

The more blows that are used the greater the number of possible combinations. With the left jab to face and body already learned, effective combinations now become possible through the addition of the left hook to the chin. One of the most effective movements in boxing is the jab-hook combination. Ninety percent of all boxing is done with this combination and every boxer should be familiar with it.

ANALYSIS OF COMBINATIONS

The Jab, Step and Hook

The jab, step and hook is one of the most fundamental movements in boxing. It should be broken down into its component parts in order to aid the learning process.

The Extended Arm Hook—From the on guard position extend the left arm to the jab position. Now turn the body to the right, shifting weight to the right foot. Do not move the left arm. Once the pivot is completed pull the left arm in a wide arc to the right shoulder. Arm retains a half-bent position throughout the movement. (See Plate 83a, b, c, cl)

PLATE 83. THE EXTENDED ARM HOOK

|) Starting position | (b) The turn | (c) The hook | (d) The follow through |

The Jab-Hook—Instead of starting with the arm extended as in the above drill, jab first, then pivot the body, and as the weight shifts to the right foot, hook the left arm in a wide arc to the right shoulder. (See Plate 84a, b, c)

| *(a) The jab* | *(b) The hook* | *(c) The follow through* |

PLATE 84. THE JAB-HOOK

Jab-Step-Hook—This is a combination of the above three drills. Execute a left jab. As the arm retracts, step forward one step with the left foot and from that position, turn the left shoulder and hip to the right shifting the weight to the right foot, and hook the left arm in an arc to the right shoulder. (See Plate 85a, b, c)

(a) The jab   *(b) Arm fold and step*   *(c) The hook*

PLATE 85. THE JAB-STEP-HOOK

In actual use a double step is necessary. Step with the first jab, then take another step as the left arm retracts to the on guard position. From that position turn body to the right, shifting weight to the right foot, and hook the left arm in an arc to the right shoulder. (See Plate 86a, b, c) When boxing the whole movement is shortened, in that the hip and shoulder are already turned to the center line, and weight has been shifted to the right foot before stepping in.

(a) The step and jab   *(b) The step and arm fold*   *(c) The hook*

PLATE 86. THE STEP AND JAB-STEP AND HOOK

The Left Jab to the Body and Left Hook to the Chin

Jab to the solar plexus, dropping the body well forward. From that position, step forward and to the right with the right foot and as the body reassumes the upright position, hook the left to opponent's chin. (See Plate 87b, c, d)

The Left Jab to the Chin, the Left Jab to the Body and the Left Hook to the Chin

Jab a left to the opponent's chin. Drop quickly and drive a straight left to the body. Move the right foot forward and to the right, and as the body reassumes the upright position, hook a left to the chin. The primary function of the left jab to the body is to make the opponent drop his guard, so that the left hook following will find a clean opening. (See Plate 87a, b, c, d)

PLATE 87. THE LEFT JAB TO CHIN, LEFT JAB TO BODY, LEFT HOOK TO CHIN

| *) Jab to chin | (b) Jab to body | (c) Mid-position | (d) Left hook to chin |

COACHING HINTS

The Jab-Step and Hook

1. Step in with a left jab to the chin.
2. As the left arm retracts, step forward one step with the left foot.
3. Turn the left shoulder and hip through to the center line.
4. Weight drops back to the right foot.
5. The left arm is hooked in an arc to the right shoulder.
6. Movement must be executed smoothly and with speed.

The Left Jab to the Body and a Left Hook to the Chin

1. Jab to the body.
2. Shift weight to the right foot.
3. Straighten body and hook a left to the chin.

The Left Jab to the Chin, the Left Jab to the Body and a Left Hook to the Chin

1. Step in with a left jab to the chin.

2. Follow with a left jab to the body, body dropping low.

3. Step to the right with the right foot, straighten the body and hook to the chin.

LEFT UPPERCUT TO THE BODY*—TECHNIQUE

The left uppercut to the body is strictly a counter blow. Its most effective delivery is to the liver, often referred to as the left hook to the liver. Such a blow slows the opponent and makes him more vulnerable to attack.

The left uppercut to the body is dangerous in execution because of the necessity of dropping the left hand. An opening for the opponent's right is thus created.

(a) *The drop*   (b) *The pivot*   (c) *The uppercut*

PLATE 88. THE LEFT UPPERCUT TO THE BODY

ANALYSIS OF THE LEFT UPPERCUT TO THE BODY

Bend sideward, to the left and slightly forward, until the left elbow is touching the left leg a few inches below the hip line. The left arm is carried in a half bent position, forearm parallel to the floor, palm up. The right elbow remains close to the body, forearm covering the right side of the body and face. Turn the left shoulder and hip to the right, carrying the left arm to the center line of the body. Then straighten the body and whip the left arm upwards to the solar plexus. (See Plate 88a, b, c)

---

* The uppercut is a body blow. Seldom, if ever is it used to the chin.

COACHING HINTS

1. Bend the body sideward and slightly forward.

2. The left arm should be in a half bent position, forearm parallel to the deck.

3. Pivot the body to the center line.

4. Straighten the body and whip a left uppercut to the opponent's solar plexus.

LEFT UPPERCUT TO THE BODY—DEFENSE

The most effective defense against uppercuts to the body is merely stepping back a few inches out of range. However, an uppercut can easily be parried or blocked.

ANALYSIS OF THE METHODS OF DEFENSE

The Brush

On a left uppercut to the body, drop the right glove downward and inward across the opponent's forearm, forcing the blow outward.

A cross brush, that is, dropping the left hand downward and inward across the opponent's forearm forcing the blow to the left, can be used on occasion. However, it leaves the chin somewhat unprotected against a right hand blow. (See Plate 89)

The brush
**PLATE 89. THE DEFENSE FOR THE
LEFT UPPERCUT TO THE BODY**

The forearm block
**PLATE 90. THE DEFENSE FOR THE
LEFT UPPERCUT TO THE BODY**

The Forearm Block

On a left uppercut to the body, drop the right forearm forcibly downward across the opponent's wrist. The hand is inward, forearm straight, elbow to the outside. (See Plate 90)

The Step Back

Is a standard technique for moving out of range. See page 65 for a full description of the technique.

COACHING HINTS

The Brush

1.   Drop the right glove downward and inward across the opponent's wrist.

2.   Force outward to the right.

The Forearm Block

1.   Drop the right forearm forcibly downward across the opponent's wrist.

The Stepaway

See page 107.

LEFT UPPERCUT TO THE BODY—COUNTER ATTACK

The left uppercut is an effective counter for a left jab to the chin providing it is used with skill, speed and deceptiveness, and providing the opponent is not too good a right hand puncher. On a straight right lead, the left uppercut can be used effectively with the inside slip or the cross parry.

The safest use of the left uppercut as a counter is after partying to the outside guard position on a left jab. Such a counter is absolutely safe.

The left uppercut to the body leaves the chin exposed for numerous counters, such as the left jab, the left hook, the straight right. Its use must be sudden and unexpected, and as a follow, not a lead blow.

ANALYSIS OF THE COUNTER ATTACK

THE LEFT UPPERCUT AS A COUNTER BLOW

The Outside Parry and Left Uppercut to the Solar Plexus on a Left Lead—Right and Left Steps

As the opponent jabs, parry to the outside guard position with the right hand. At the same time drop the left arm perpendicular to the floor and step across with the right foot to a position outside the opponent's left foot. As the weight shifts to the right leg, whip the left uppercut to the solar plexus. (See Plate 59a, b, Page 99)

Exactly the same technique can be repeated by stepping across with the left foot to a position outside the opponent's left foot. This is a more precise movement than stepping across with the right foot and therefore can be used against a faster left jab. While it has more speed, it loses the power obtained through stepping across with the right foot. (See Plate 60a, b, Page 99)

The Inside Guard and Left Uppercut to Liver

As the opponent leads a straight left, drop directly to the left, and to the inside guard position. Parry the left outward with the right hand, pivot sharply from the waist, and drive a hard left up and under the opponent's guard to the liver. The weight is shifted over the left leg which becomes a pivot around which the body wheels as the blow is completed. (See Plate 61a, b, c, Page 100)

The Cross Parry and Left Uppercut to the Liver, on a Straight Right Lead

As the opponent leads a straight right to the chin, cross parry with the right hand, forcing the oncoming blow to the outside position. As the cross parry is made, the left hand drops perpendicular to the body from where it is whipped to the opponent's liver. (See Plate 91a, b) Force is gained by pivoting to the right as the left arm is whipped upward.

(a) The cross parry   (b) The left uppercut
PLATE 91. THE CROSS PARRY AND LEFT UPPERCUT TO THE LIVER, ON A STRAIGHT RIGHT LEAD

COUNTER BLOWS FOR THE LEFT UPPERCUT TO THE BODY

The Left Jab to the Chin

On a left uppercut to the body, step forward with a left jab to chin, blocking the opponent's uppercut with the palm of the open right glove. The left jab will force the opponent off balance, rendering his uppercut impotent.

Straight Right to the Chin

As the opponent starts a left uppercut to the body, step in with hard right to his chin. Use a cross brush to block opponent's uppercut if necessary.

Right Hook to Chin

As the opponent starts a left uppercut to the body, step in with hard right hook to the chin. Block opponent's uppercut with a cross brush.

Return Left Uppercut

As the opponent starts a left uppercut to the body, block with the open right glove, and step in with a return left uppercut.

COACHING HINTS

THE LEFT UPPERCUT AS A COUNTER

The Outside Parry and Left Uppercut to the Solar Plexus on a Left Lead

1. Parry to the outside guard position on the opponent's left lead. Parry with the right hand.

2. As parry is executed drop the left arm perpendicular to the floor, and step across to a position outside the opponent's left foot with either the left or the right foot.

3. As the weight shifts forward whip the left uppercut to the solar plexus.

4. Carry the right hand high, ready to cross to the chin.

The Inside Guard and Left Uppercut to the Liver

1. Drop left and slightly forward.

2. Guard to the inside position with the right hand.

3. Shift the weight to the left leg and drive a left uppercut to the liver.

4. Wheel the body to the right and out of range.

5. Carry the right hand off the left shoulder in position of block for the opponent's right counter.

The Cross Parry and Left Uppercut to the Liver on a Straight Right Lead

1. Execute a cross parry with the right glove on the opponent's right lead.

2. Drop the right hand perpendicular to the body.

3. Turn the body to the right and drive a hard left uppercut to the opponent's liver.

COUNTER BLOWS FOR THE LEFT UPPERCUT TO THE BODY

The Left Jab to the Chin

1. The left jab must be executed with speed.

2. The jab should force opponent off balance before the uppercut can be fully executed.

3. Use the right hand to block with.

The Straight Right to the Chin

1. Should force opponent off balance before the uppercut can be consummated.

2. Step forward with the blow.

3. Block with the left hand.

The Right Hook to Chin

1. Step with the hook, shifting weight to left foot.

2. Perform block with the left hand.

The Return Left Uppercut

1. Block opponent's left uppercut.

2. Step in with a left uppercut to the solar plexus.

LEFT UPPERCUT TO THE BODY—COMBINATIONS

The ability to whip the left hand to head or body, in a jab-hook-uppercut combination, is the mark of the effective workman in boxing. Left arm combinations should be drilled on regularly, so that as soon as contact is made with the left jab, a left hook or uppercut follows naturally to the head or body. Because ninety percent of all hitting is done with the left hand it is important to be proficient in the use of all left hand blows, either singly or in combination.

While the left jab to either face or body together with the left hook to the chin is a very fundamental combination, the most effective left hand sequences combine the left jab, left hook and the left uppercut.

ANALYSIS OF THE COMBINATIONS

The Left Jab to the Chin and the Left Uppercut to the Body

This is a very effective combination. jab first to the chin, drop the arm and body directly to the left, pivot the left shoulder forward, and drive a left uppercut to the solar plexus. (See Plate 92a, b, c) The right hand should be held high in a position of guard.

(a) Jab to chin   (b) Mid-position   (c) Left uppercut to body

PLATE 92. THE LEFT JAB TO CHIN AND LEFT UPPERCUT TO THE BODY

The Left Uppercut to the Body and the Left Jab to the Chin

This is not a smooth combination as some because a straight blow is seldom used as a follow blow for an uppercut. However, at times, it can be used very effectively.

Bend the body to the left, pivot the body to the right from the waist and drive a hard left uppercut to the solar plexus. Suddenly straighten up, and drive a straight left to the chin. The tight hand and arm covers the head and body. (See Plate 92b, c)

(a) The left hook   (b) Mid-position   (c) The left uppercut

PLATE 93. THE LEFT HOOK TO THE CHIN AND LEFT UPPERCUT TO THE BODY

The Left Hook to the Chin and the Left Uppercut to the Body

A smooth combination that develops terrific power on the hook to the chin. Whip a hard left uppercut to the solar plexus. Rock the weight back to the right leg, and drive a short left hook to the chin. Carry the right hand high and in position of guard. (See Plate 93a, b, c)

The Jab, Hook and Uppercut

A very potent triple combination. Step in with a jab-hook to the chin. Then turn the body to the left, drop the left hand and whip an uppercut to the solar plexus. The right hand should be carried high in position of guard. (See Plate 94a, b, c, d)

PLATE 94. THE JAB, HOOK AND UPPERCUT

(a) The jab	(b) The hook	(c) Mid-position	(d) The uppercut

The Jab, Uppercut and Hook

Jab to the chin. Follow immediately with a left uppercut to the body. Then turn the body sharply to the right, shifting weight over a straight right leg, and hook a hard left to the chin. Right hand must be carried high in position of guard, ready to block either a left or right hand counter. (See Plate 95a, b, c, d)

(a) The jab	(b) The uppercut	(c) Mid-position	(d) The hook

PLATE 95. THE JAB, UPPERCUT AND HOOK

COACHING HINTS

The Left Jab to the Chin and Left Uppercut to the Body

1. Jab hard to the chin.
2. Bend the shoulder and body to the left.
3. Drop the left hand, then whip it to the solar plexus.
4. Carry the right hand high in position of guard.

The Left Uppercut to the Body and the Left Jab to Chin

1. Dip the left shoulder and drive a hard uppercut to the body.
2. Straighten suddenly and jab to the chin with the left hand.

The Left Hook to the Chin and the Left Uppercut to the Body

1. Hook the left hand hard to the chin.
2. Pivot body to the left.
3. Drop the left arm and whip it upward to the solar plexus.
4. Carry right hand high in position of guard.

The Left Uppercut to the Body and the Left Hook to the Chin

1. Step in with left uppercut to the body.
2. Shift weight to the right leg.
3. Hook hard with the left to the chin.

The Jab, Hook and Uppercut

1. Execute the jab-hook combination.
2. Drop the left shoulder and drive a hard left uppercut to the solar plexus.
3. Carry the right hand high in position of guard.

The Jab-Uppercut and Hook

1. Execute the jab-uppercut combination.
2. Shift the weight to the right leg.
3. Hook hard with the left to the chin.
4. Carry right hand high in position of guard.

CHAPTER VIII
Straight and Bent Arm Blows and Technique—The Right Lead

STRAIGHT RIGHT TO THE CHIN—TECHNIQUE

The straight right is a power blow. It is the 16 inch gun in action. Such power should be used sparingly and only when openings are created. It is delivered with a twist of the waist, and the forceful extension of the right arm. At the moment of impact the weight shifts forward over a straight left leg, which gives the power necessary for use as a finishing blow.

The secret of power in the straight right is using the left side of the body as a hinge, and allowing the right side of the body to swing free. It is the same idea as slamming a door shut.

The right is essentially a counter blow. It should never be led because in so doing the whole body turns to the left, exposing and uncovering many vital openings to the opponent. Therefore—do not lead with the right.

ANALYSIS OF THE STRAIGHT RIGHT

The straight right is a very easy blow to execute properly. In principle, for any power or force blow, the body structure must be so aligned as to form one straight body side or line. This enables the bone structure to support the weight of the body, freeing the musculature for purpose of pivoting or turning the other side of the body forward. Thus terrific power is created.

The straight right is executed by shifting the weight of the body directly over the straight left leg. The left side of the body now forms a straight line. Now turn the right hip and shoulder through to the center line of body and drive the right hand into forceful extension. The arm drives out at shoulder height. At the moment of impact the knuckles of the hand are turned up. The arm then *relaxes* back to the on guard position. (See Plate 96a, b, c) Propulsion for the blow comes from the twist of the waist, the shifting of the weight forward and forceful arm extension. As the right arm drives into extension, the left arm is held close to the left side, hand high, forearm straight, elbow down. The movement in its final execution is relaxed and easy, the arm driving out with such force that it pulls on both the shoulder and the elbow joint. It is like the snap of a whip. The right hand should he *driven through the target, not at the target.*

(a) On guard position   *(b) Right shoulder and hip*   *(c) Extension of right arm*
                          to center line

PLATE 96. THE STRAIGHT RIGHT TO CHIN

COACHING HINTS

1. Body weight must be shifted directly over the straight left leg.

2. Hip and shoulder must turn through to the center line.

3. The right arm is then driven into complete extension.

4. At the moment of impact the knuckles are up and the thumb side of the hand turned inward.

5. The plane of the fist does not vary. The blow is delivered on a straight line, and returns on a straight line.

6. All force is away from the body. The arm relaxes back to position.

7. The left arm folds to the body in position of guard.

8. The right hand is driven through the target, not at one.

STRAIGHT RIGHT TO THE CHIN—DEFENSE

A good defense against right hand blows is practically an essential. Such a defense should be developed early and be as complete as possible.

ANALYSIS OF THE METHODS OF DEFENSE

The Stop

As the opponent leads a straight right, catch the blow in the open left glove, raise slightly and force the lead inward and to the right. (See Plate 97)

The stop
PLATE 97. DEFENSE FOR A
STRAIGHT RIGHT

The leverage block
PLATE 98. DEFENSE FOR A
STRAIGHT RIGHT

The Leverage Block

As the opponent leads a straight right, drive the left hand for the tip of the opponent's right shoulder, then forcing to the left. This causes the arm to cross inside of the opponent's lead, deflecting it to the outside. The left arm must be completely straightened, elbow locked at the moment of contact. The palm of the left hand should be turned outward. The arm is raised slightly as it is extended and should be driven out forcibly. This block is best performed by stepping inward as it is executed. Carry the right hand high, in position of guard. (See Plate 98)

The Inside Parry

As the opponent leads a straight right, shift slightly to the right, at the same time turn palm of left hand outward and parry or push the oncoming lead to the left. Carry the right hand high in position of guard. (See Plate 99)

The Outside Parry

As the opponent leads a straight right, brush the oncoming lead to the right with the left hand. As the parry is performed, drop the right hand ready to

The inside parry
PLATE 99. DEFENSE FOR A
STRAIGHT RIGHT

The outside parry
PLATE 100. DEFENSE FOR A
STRAIGHT RIGHT

counter to the body. This movement is more effective, if as the opponent leads a straight right, a short step is taken to the left and forward with the left foot (See Plate 100)

The Cross Parry

As the opponent leads a straight right, brush the oncoming lead to the left with the right hand, forcing it to the outside. Keep the elbow low. Make it as much a wrist and forearm movement as possible. Drop the left hand slightly. If the opponent counters with a left hook, drop the head forward into the crook of the right arm, folding under the blow. (See Plate 101)

The cross parry
**PLATE 101. DEFENSE FOR A
STRAIGHT RIGHT**

The shoulder block
**PLATE 102. DEFENSE FOR A
STRAIGHT RIGHT**

The Shoulder Block

As the opponent leads a straight right to the chin, turn the body to the right so as to intercept the oncoming blow on the deltoid, or shoulder muscle of the left shoulder. At the same time, tip the left shoulder upward, and shift the body weight back to the left leg. The left arm drops to a position covering the left side of the body. The right hand is carried open and directly of the left shoulder. (See Plate 102)

Slipping to the Inside Guard Position

As the opponent leads a straight right, drop the weight back to the right leg by quickly turning the left shoulder and body to the right. The right foot remains stationary but the left foot pivots inward. This movement allows the right lead to slip over the left shoulder and obtains the inside guard position. (See Plate 103)

Slipping to inside guard

**PLATE 103. DEFENSE FOR A
STRAIGHT RIGHT**

Slipping to outside guard

**PLATE 104. DEFENSE FOR A
STRAIGHT RIGHT**

Slipping to the Outside Guard Position

As the opponent leads a straight right, shift the weight left and forward over the left leg, right shoulder swinging forward. The blow slips over the right shoulder. A short step forward and left with the left foot facilitates the movement. Hands should be carried high in position of guard. (See Plate 104)

The Step Back

This is a fundamental movement used for moving out of range of all blows. For a full description turn to Page 65.

Circling Away from the Right Hand

The proper strategy for beginners is to circle away from the opponent's strongest blow. In case of a straight right, it is best to circle to the right or away from opponent's right. The movement is executed by moving one step to the right with the right foot, following with the left leg quickly to position.

The left hand should be carried high, ready to block the opponent's attempted right leads. The right hand should be carried high, and in position to guard, ready to block any left hand leads or counters.

Circling into a Right Hand

The force of any blow can be nullified before it is started. Speed and power do not result until after force has been exerted. Applying this to boxing, and especially to the principle of defense, it indicates that a sound defense for a right hand is to move directly into or toward it. In this manner it is simple to control or stop a right lead altogether.

By crowding a right hand, that is, circling or moving directly into it, the left hand high and in position of guard, it is almost impossible to properly execute a straight right so that power will result. It becomes necessary to anticipate the blow so that the crowding movement toward the opponent's right is started before blow can be executed. A continuous circling or crowding of right handed blows will smother attempted leads so that they can be controlled by stopping with the open left glove.

COACHING HINTS

The Stop

1. Carry the left hand high, palm open.

2. Catch the opponent's right lead in the open palm of the left glove.

3. Force upward and to the right.

4. The right hand should be carried in position of guard.

The Leverage Block

1. Start the left as if to jab, but instead, drive hard for the tip of the opponent's right shoulder, crossing underneath the oncoming right lead.

2. Palm should be turned outward.

3. The left arm must be straight, elbow locked at the moment of contact.

4. The right hand should be carried high in position of guard.

The Inside Parry

1. Step to the right.

2. Brush the opponent's right lead to the left with the left glove.

3. Glove should be turned outward.

4. Right hand should be carried high in position of guard.

The Outside Parry

1. Step to the left and forward, as the opponent leads a straight right.

2. Brush inward with the left glove, forcing the lead to the right.

3. Drop the right hand to counter to the body.

The Cross Parry

1. Brush across the body to the left with the right hand forcing the opponent's right lead to the left and downward.

2. Movement should be light and fast without too much arm movement.

3. Left hand should be held high ready to counter to chin.

The Shoulder Block

1. Turn the body to the right so as to catch the blow high on the left shoulder.

2. Tilt the left shoulder upward by dropping the body weight back over the straight right leg.

3. The left arm drops to a position covering the left side of the body.

4. The right hand is carried high and open, directly off the left shoulder.

Slipping to the Inside Guard Position

1. Shift the weight to the right leg but keep well forward.

2. Turn the left shoulder through to the center line.

3. Hold the right foot stationary with the left toe turned inward.

4. Hold the left hand ready to counter.

5. Drop the right glove over opponent's left glove.

Slipping to the Outside Guard Position

1. Take a short step forward and sideways with the left foot.

2. Shift the weight to the left leg.

3. The right shoulder, hip and leg should swing forward and to the left.

4. Lower the right hand ready to counter to the body.

5. Carry the left hand high in position of guard.

The Step Back

1. Move back one step as the opponent leads a straight right.

2. The on guard position must not be disturbed.

Circling Away from the Right Hand

1. Step to the right to avoid opponent's right lead.

2. Carry both hands high, in position of guard.

Circling into a Right Hand

1. The idea is to smother the opponent's right hand.

2. By stepping to the left and keeping close to the opponent's right, the power of the blow is nullified.

3. Use a left stop on opponent's right hand before blow is started.

STRAIGHT RIGHT TO THE CHIN—COUNTER ATTACK

The straight right is a natural counter for a left lead and as such is a potent weapon. It should never be used as a lead blow.

A straight right, used either as a lead or follow blow, is open to counter blows.

ANALYSIS OF THE COUNTER ATTACK
THE STRAIGHT RIGHT AS A COUNTER BLOW

The Inside Straight Right to the Chin

This is really slipping to the inside guard position before delivering a straight right to the chin. As the opponent leads a left jab, quickly turn the body to the left, bringing the right shoulder forward to the center line. From this point drive the right hand into complete extension. The opponent's left lead slips to the outside of the right counter. A short step to the left, shifting the weight over a straight left leg, can be used to obtain more power. (See Plate 56a, b, Page 98)

The Inside Guard and Straight Right to the Chin

As the opponent leads a left jab, step to the left and forward with the left foot, and at the same time bring the right hand to the inside of the oncoming jab forcing it to the outside. Once the guard has been made and the right hip and shoulder turned through to the center line, a short straight right is delivered to the chin.

The Cross Parry and Straight Right to the Chin

As the opponent leads a left jab, brush to the right with the open left glove forcing the oncoming blow outward. At the same time step forward and drive a hard straight right to the chin. (See Plate 62a, b, Page 100)

The Outside Slip and Straight Right to the Chin

As the opponent leads a left jab to the chin, move to the outside position, the blow slipping over the left shoulder, weight transferring to the right leg. Straighten the body, shift the weight to the left leg, and drive a straight right to the chin. (See Plate 105a, b)

(a) Starting position   (b) The straight right
PLATE 105. THE OUTSIDE STOP AND STRAIGHT RIGHT TO CHIN

The Outside Parry and Straight Right to the Chin on a Right Lead

As the opponent leads a straight right to the chin, step left and forward, weight shifting to the left foot. Parry with the left glove, forcing and momentarily pinning the right lead to the right shoulder. At the same time, counter with a hard right to the chin, on the outside of the opponent's right lead. (See Plate 106)

PLATE 106. THE OUTSIDE PARRY AND STRAIGHT RIGHT TO THE CHIN ON A RIGHT LEAD

This is an effective counter, if instead of driving the right to the chin, a right uppercut to the body is used.

The Inside Parry and Straight Right to Chin on a Right Lead It

As the opponent leads a straight right to the chin, parry the blow outward with the left hand, and at the same time drive a straight right to the chin. Step slightly forward as the parry is executed so that weight rocks to the left as the counter is delivered. (See Plate 107a, b)

(a) The inside parry   (b) The straight right to chin
PLATE 107. THE INSIDE PARRY AND STRAIGHT RIGHT TO CHIN

The counter can well be a straight right or a right uppercut to the solar plexus instead of the chin.

COUNTER BLOWS FOR A STRAIGHT RIGHT TO THE CHIN

The Left Jab

As the opponent leads a straight right to the chin step to the right and drive a straight left to the chin. The right glove should be held high and in position of guard. (See Plate 108)

The left jab
**PLATE 108. COUNTERS FOR A
STRAIGHT RIGHT TO THE CHIN**

PLATE 109. THE INSIDE LEFT HOOK

The Inside Left Hook

As the opponent leads or delivers a straight right to the chin, step to the right shifting the weight over the straight right leg, and hook a short left inside the lead to the chin. (See Plate 109)

The Straight Right to Body

As the opponent leads or delivers a straight right to the chin, step left, dropping the body under the lead, and drive a straight right to the body. Turn to Page 163 for further analysis of the straight right to the body.

The Inside Parry and Right Uppercut to the Solar Plexus

As opponent leads or delivers a straight right to the chin, parry to the inside position with left hand, and at same time drop the right shoulder and drive a right uppercut to the solar plexus.

The Outside Parry and Right Uppercut to the Body

As the opponent leads or delivers a straight right to the chin, step forward and left with the left foot, brushing inward with the left hand, forcing the opponent's blow to the right. At the same time drop the right shoulder and drive a right uppercut to the solar plexus. See Page 171 for further analysis of the right uppercut.

The Outside Parry and Right Hook to the Chin

As the opponent leads or delivers a straight right to the chin, step forward and left with the left foot, brushing inward with the left hand, forcing the opponent's blow downward and to the right. At the same time raise the right elbow and hook a hard right to the opponent's chin. See Page 151 for further analysis of the right hook.

The Cross Parry and Left Uppercut to the Body

As the opponent leads or delivers a straight right to the chin, reach across the body with the right hand and parry the lead outward to the left, at the same time drop the left glove and drive a hard left uppercut to the body.

The Cross Parry and Left Hook to the Chin

As the opponent leads a straight right to the chin, reach across with the right glove and force opponent's lead outward and to the left. As the cross parry is performed, hook a short left inside to opponent's chin. If possible, step to the right with the right foot adding greater power to the hook. (See Plate 78a, b, Page 116)

COACHING HINTS
THE STRAIGHT RIGHT AS A COUNTER BLOW

The Inside Right to the Chin

1. Shift the weight to a straight left leg.
2. Turn the right shoulder and hip to center line.
3. Drive the right arm directly under opponent's left lead to chin.
4. Carry left hand high and ready to stop opponent's right counter.

The Inside Guard and Straight Right to Chin

1. Step left with left foot.
2. Move the right glove, palm up, inside of opponent's jab.
3. Guard momentarily, then drive straight right to chin as the weight shifts to the left leg.

The Cross Parry and Straight Right to Chin

1. Force the opponent's left lead to the right with the left glove.

2. Step forward and left, at the same time drive a straight right to the chin.

3. The left hand, after executing the parry, is in a position of block ready for opponent's right.

The Outside Slip and Straight Right to the Chin

1. Slip to the outside guard position.

2. Shift the weight to the left foot, straighten body, and drive a straight right to the chin.

The Outside Parry and Straight Right to the Chin on a Right Lead

1. Step forward and left with left foot.

2. Slip the blow over the right shoulder.

3. Drive a straight right to chin to the outside of the opponent's right lead.

The Inside Parry and Straight Right to the Chin on a Right Lead

1. Parry to the inside guard position with the left glove.

2. Drive a straight right to the chin.

3. Step forward with left foot to obtain more power.

COUNTER BLOWS FOR A STRAIGHT RIGHT TO THE CHIN

The Left Jab

1. Step to the right.

2. Deliver a fast jab to the chin.

3. Carry the right hand high and in position of guard.

The Inside Left Hook

1. Step to the right shifting weight to the right leg.

2. Hook a short right to the opponent's chin inside the right lead.

3. Carry the right hand high and in position of guard.

The Straight Right to the Body

1. Step left and drive a straight right to the solar plexus,

2. Opponent's right lead slips over the right shoulder:

3. Carry the left hand high and in position of guard.

The Inside Parry and Right Uppercut to Solar Plexus

1. Parry the opponent's right lead outward with left glove.

2. Drive a right uppercut to the solar plexus.

The Outside Parry and Right Uppercut to Body

1. Parry the right lead to the right with the left glove.

2. Step forward and to the left with the left foot.

3. Drive a hard right uppercut to the body.

The Outside Parry and Right Hook to Chin

1. Parry the right lead to the right and downward with the left glove.

2. Step forward and to the left with the left foot.

3. Hook a hard right to the chin.

The Cross Parry and Left Uppercut to Body

1. Brush opponent's right lead to the left with right glove.

2. Drop the left arm and glove.

3. Drive a left uppercut to opponent's solar plexus.

The Cross Parry and Left Hook to Chin

1. Brush opponent's right lead to the left and slightly downward with the right glove.

2. Step to the right with the right foot.

3. Drive a short inside hook to the chin.

4. The right hand assumes the position of block after the parry.

STRAIGHT RIGHT TO THE CHIN—COMBINATIONS

Until this time all combination blows have been with the left hand. The ability to use left hand combinations before right arm combinations have been learned is the greatest single factor in the development of boxing skill.

Too often the ability to hit with the right hand spoils the development of the left. Yet, the left is the lead blow with which over eighty percent of the boxing is done. Only after the left has been fully developed should work on the right be started, notwithstanding the fact that it may be the "Sunday School punch."

Right hand power is best utilized as a finishing blow. With the addition of the right, more effective combinations become possible.

ANALYSIS OF THE COMBINATIONS

The One-Two to the Chin

This is one of the oldest and most favorite of all the combinations—the left jab combined with the straight right to the chin. In the one-two, the arm and feet work as one. As the left jab is led, a step with the left foot is taken. As the right foot moves up to position, the right hand is driven into extension. Without the feet working in unison with the arms, the one-two is of little consequence. Jab high in order to obscure vision. Follow immediately with a straight right to the chin. The rhythm is o-n-e---two! This is the basic movement of all triple blows. (See Plate 110a, b)

(a) The left jab   (b) The straight right
PLATE 110. THE ONE-TWO TO THE CHIN

The Jab-Cross and Hook and Jab-Cross and Uppercut

This is a triple blow designed to obtain a clean opening or a finishing blow. Three blows are driven in sequence to the chin. When the opponent feels there is nothing to fear, and that his defense is adequate, change the last blow of the sequence to the body.

Jab the left hand high for the eyes. Follow with a straight right to the chin. Step to the right and hook a hard left to the chin as the weight shifts to the right leg. The rhythm is one-two---three! (See Plate 111a, b, c) Now change so that

(a) The jab   *(b) The cross*   *(c) The hook*

PLATE 111. THE JAB-CROSS AND HOOK

the last blow of the combination will be an uppercut. After the one-two to the chin, drop the left hand and whip a hard uppercut to the body. (See Plate 112a, b, c)

(a) The jab   *(b) The cross*   *(c) The uppercut*

PLATE 112. THE JAB-CROSS AND UPPERCUT

The Jab-Hook and Cross-and-Jab-Hook and Uppercut

This is a triple blow to the chin. When the opponent feels his defense is adequate, switch so that the last blow of the combination is to the body.

Jab the left hand to the chin, shift the weight to the right leg and follow with a hard left hook to the chin. Rock the weight forward to the left leg and drive a straight right to the chin. (See Plate 113a, b, c) Now switch so that the last blow of the combination will be an uppercut to the body. (See Plate 114a, b, c)

(a) The jab   (b) The hook   (c) The cross

PLATE 113. THE JAB-HOOK AND CROSS

(a) The jab   (b) The hook   (c) The uppercut

PLATE 114. THE JAB-HOOK AND UPPERCUT

The Straight High-Low

Fling the left hand forward and upward in front of the opponent's face. Drop suddenly by bending the right knee and twist the body to the left. As the right shoulder and hip turn through to the center line, drive the right arm for the opponent's midsection. (See Plate 115a, b)

(a) The left jab to chin   (b) The straight right to body

PLATE 115. THE STRAIGHT HIGH-LOW

| *(a) The left hook* | *(b) Mid-position* | *(c) The left uppercut* | *(d) The straight right* |

PLATE 116. THE HIGH-LOW AND CROSS

The High-Low and Cross

After jabbing several times, step in with a left hook to the chin. Whip a left uppercut to the body and as the opponent drops his hands to block, drive a straight right to the chin. The rhythm is one-----one-two! (See Plate 116a, b, c, d)

The Low-High and Uppercut

Step in with a wide hook to the body. Hesitate so that the opponent will anticipate the hook to the chin. Then hook to the chin, but follow immediately with a right uppercut to the solar plexus. The rhythm is the same, one -------- one, two! (See Plate 117a, b, c)

| *(a) The left uppercut* | *(b) The left hook* | *(c) The right uppercut* |

PLATE 117. THE LOW-HIGH AND UPPERCUT

COACHING HINTS

The One-Two to the Chin

1. Jab with the left hand for opponent's eyes, and step forward with the left foot.

2. Follow by moving the right foot immediately to position, at the same time driving the right to the chin.

3. The rhythm is o-n-e---two!

The Jab-Cross and Hook and the Jab-Cross and Uppercut

1. Drive a one-two to the chin.

2. Step to the right with the right foot.

3. Follow with a hard left hook to the chin.

4. Instead of hooking to the chin, drive a hard right uppercut to the solar plexus.

The Jab-Hook and Cross and the Jab-Hook and Uppercut

1. Execute a jab-hook to the chin, weight shifting to the right leg on the left hook.

2. Shift the weight forward over a straight left leg and drive a hard, straight right to the chin.

3. Fold the left arm close to the body in a position of guard.

4. Instead of crossing the last blow to the chin, whip a right uppercut to the solar plexus.

The Straight High-Low

1. Fling the left arm forward and upward.

2. Drop the body forward and drive a right to the heart.

3. Hold the left arm and hand ready to block the opponent's right.

The High-Low Cross

1. Remember that if the first blow is high the last blow is also high.

2. Lead a wide hook to the chin. Hesitate, then drive a left uppercut to the body.

3.   Follow with a straight right to the chin,

4.   The rhythm is one---two, three!

The Low-High and Uppercut

1.   Lead a wide, left hook to the body.

2.   Hesitate, then hook a left to the chin.

3.   Follow immediately with a right uppercut to the solar plexus

4.   The rhythm is the same, one---two, three!

RIGHT HOOK TO THE CHIN—TECHNIQUE

The right hook is seldom called by its correct name, yet ninety percent of the right hand blows are right hooks. The right hook is a hard power blow to the chin, often referred to improperly as a "cross." It is primarily a counter blow, but can be; used when coming out of or going into a clinch. A right "cross" is a right hook crossed over the opponent's left jab. The blow itself is a right hook, the term "cross" referring to its use as a counter.

Force is obtained because the principle of the hinge is in operation, the left side of the body being hinged, the right side of the body pivoting to the left.

The right hook is a difficult blow to deliver unless used as a counter. It is a natural follow blow for all other curved arm blows, is effective during close exchanges, and is a valuable aid to infighting.

ANALYSIS OF THE RIGHT HOOK TO THE CHIN

Shift the weight over the straight left leg, turn the right shoulder and hip through to the center line, raise the right elbow in a half-bent position, and whip it in an arc toward the left shoulder. (See Plate 118a, b, c)

There is a tendency to straighten the arm and not to follow through with the arm in a bent position. This dissipates power, prevents follow through and makes it impossible to take advantage of the body shift in weight.

(a) On guard position   *(b) elbow raised, left turn*   *(c) The right hook*

PLATE 118. THE RIGHT HOOK TO THE CHIN

COACHING HINTS

1. Shift the weight over a straight left leg.

2. Turn the right hip and shoulder through to the center line.

3. Raise the right elbow, and with the arm in a half-bent position, whip it in an arc toward the right shoulder.

4. At the moment of impact, knuckles should be turned outward, thumb side of the hand up.

5. Wrist must be kept straight.

6. The left arm is held in position of guard.

RIGHT HOOK TO THE CHIN—DEFENSE

The right hook being a power blow requires a strong defense. It can be either blocked or ducked or one can move out of range, or move with the blow.

A high left shoulder and left hand, chin down, is the best defense for a right hook.

The right hook is a comparatively slow blow, allowing time for the defense to adjust. Actually one should not be hit often with the right hook, except in an exchange of blows.

ANALYSIS OF THE METHODS OF DEFENSE

The Stop

The stop is a defensive technique which stops the hook before it can start, hence its name. As the opponent delivers a right hook, step straight forward, driving the butt of the left hand to the opponent's right shoulder, inside of the right hook. The movement also can be executed by placing the open left hand around the opponent's right biceps. (See Plate 119a, b)

In both movements the arm must be straightened and locked at the moment of contact. If performed properly, it jars the opponent, spinning him off balance and into a right hand counter.

(a) *The shoulder stop*   (b) *The biceps stop*

PLATE 119. DEFENSE FOR THE RIGHT HOOK TO CHIN

The Duck

As the opponent leads a right hook, dip both knees and bend the body from the waist, dropping the body underneath the blow. Hands should be carried high and in position of guard. Body should maintain a fairly upright position. (See Plate 120)

The duck   *The forearm block*

PLATE 120. DEFENSE FOR THE RIGHT   **PLATE 121. DEFENSE FOR THE RIGHT**
HOOK TO CHIN   **HOOK TO CHIN**

The Forearm Block

As the opponent hooks a right to the chin, raise the left elbow, left arm and forearm in a firm and fixed position, fist clinched, and take blow on the wrist and forearm. Turn slightly to the right as the movement is executed. Carry the right hand high and in position of guard. (See Plate 121)

Circling to the Right

As the opponent hooks a right to the chin, execute a right step, left hand held high, right hand held ready to block.

The Step Back

As the opponent hooks a right to the chin, step back with the right foot, and follow immediately back to position with left foot. Hands should be held high, the on guard position should be maintained throughout.

COACHING HINTS

The Stop

1. As the opponent raises his elbow to deliver a right hook, drive the open left glove to his right biceps or shoulder.

2. Straighten the arm completely, elbow locked.

3. Carry the right hand high and ready to block or counter.

The Duck

1. Dip both knees and drop straight down.

2. Carry the hands high.

The Forearm Block

1. Raise the left hand as if to salute.

2. The arm must be in a firm and fixed position.

3. Carry the elbow tight to the body, glove shut.

Circling to the Right

1. Execute the right step as the opponent hooks.

2. Carry the left hand high, right hand in front of the chin.

The Step Back

1. Move the body directly backward—feet under the body.

2. Carry the hands high in position of guard.

3. Be ready to step in to attack.

RIGHT HOOK TO THE CHIN—COUNTER ATTACK

A right hook is a natural counter for the left jab. It can be used with a parry, a cross parry, or by slipping to inside or outside guard position.

It is the one counter for a left lead that practically every boxer is familiar with. It is powerful blow carrying a knock-out punch.

The right hook can easily be countered because it is a comparatively slow blow.

ANALYSIS OF THE COUNTER ATTACK

THE RIGHT HOOK AS A COUNTER BLOW

The Right Cross

As the opponent leads a straight left, slip to the inside guard position by stepping forward and sideways with the left foot, weight shifting over the straight left leg. Keep the right hand to the outside of the opponent's guard. As the jab slips over the right shoulder, the right arm, now in a half-bent position, is hooked over the opponent's lead and to the chin. The left hand is carried high and in a position of guard. The whole action must be performed as a unit. The hook is first over and then down. (See Plate 55a, b, Page 97.)

(a) Variation   (b) Variation
PLATE 122. THE RIGHT CROSS

Actually, the above description is the only correct performance of the right cross. However there are several variations that should be noted.

As the opponent leads a left jab, raise the right elbow and drive a right to the outside of head, and to his jaw. The blow is slipped by rocking the body slightly to the left without altering the position of the right arm. The arm, however, instead of remaining in a bent position is straightened at the finish of the counter. It is more of a straight cross, not carrying as much power, but requiring a greater ability to slip blows. (See Plate 122a, b)

Another so-called right cross is to slip the lead over the left shoulder by bending the body slightly to the right, then hooking a right to the chin. (See Plate 123a, b) Actually the right hook does not cross the left lead, therefore technically speaking, it is not a right cross.

(a) Variation   (b) Variation
PLATE 123. THE RIGHT CROSS

The Inside Guard and Right Hook

As the opponent jabs with the left, lean slightly to the left, raise the right forearm inside opponent's left and block the lead to the right. Tip the right elbow upward so that the forearm is in line with opponent's chin, step sideways and forward with the left foot, shifting the weight to the left leg, and drop a short right hook to opponent's chin. Carry the left hand in position of guard. (See Plate 57a, b, c, Page 98)

The Cross Parry and Right Hook

As the opponent leads a straight left, brush across the body with the open left glove forcing the lead.' outward and to the left, hooking a hard right to the opponent's chin. (See Plate 124a, b)

(a) The inside guard   (b) The right hook
PLATE 124. THE INSIDE GUARD AND RIGHT HOOK

COUNTER BLOWS FOR A RIGHT HOOK TO THE CHIN

The Left Jab

The left jab as a counter depends on its speed to establish contact before the opponent can complete his right hook. As the opponent starts his right hook, step in smartly with a left jab. Carry the right hand off left shoulder ready to block opponent's right hook.

The Left Uppercut to the Body

As the opponent delivers a right hook to the chin, step forward with the right foot and counter with a hard left uppercut to solar plexus. Carry the right hand off the left shoulder blocking the opponent's hook.

The Straight Right to the Body

As the opponent delivers a right hook to the chin, drop forward to the left countering with a straight right to the body. The hook passes harmlessly over the head. This is a hard blow which will do much to slow up the opponent. Carry the left hand off the right shoulder ready to block.

The Left Jab to the Body

As the opponent leads a right hook to the chin, drop forward with a straight left to the solar plexus. Hold the right hand high ready to counter.

The Return Right Hook

As the opponent leads a right hook, step in and execute the stop or forearm block with the left, at the same time countering with a hard right hook to the chin.

COACHING HINTS

THE RIGHT HOOK AS A COUNTER BLOW

The Right Cross

1. Step forward and left with the left foot without moving the right arm.

2. The weight shifts forward, allowing the opponent's lead to slip over the right shoulder.

3. Hook the right arm up and over the opponent's lead to the chin.

4. The left hand should be placed over the opponent's right hand in order to prevent a counter blow.

The Inside Guard and Right Hook to Chin

1. Lean slightly to the left.

2. Parry the left lead outward with the right hand.

3. Step forward and to the left with the left leg, shifting the weight forward.

4. At same time raise the right elbow, hooking to the opponent's chin.

The Cross Parry and Right Hook to Chin

1. Cross parry opponent's left lead.

2. Shift the weight forward and hook a hard right to the chin, inside the opponent's left lead.

3. After partying, the left hand guards against the opponent's right.

COUNTER BLOWS FOR A RIGHT HOOK TO THE CHIN

The Left Jab

1. Step in and jab fast.

2. Carry the right hand off the left shoulder in order to block opponent's right hook.

The Left Uppercut to the Body

1. Shift the weight forward to the right foot and drive a left uppercut to the liver.

2. The blow is inside the right hook.

3. The right hand is held off the left shoulder, ready to block opponent's hook.

The Straight Right to the Body

1. Step left and forward, driving a hard right to the opponent's liver.

2. The opponent's right hook slips harmlessly over the head.

3. Carry the left hand off the right shoulder.

The Left Jab to the Body

1. Drop forward under the opponent's right hook.

2. Carry the right hand high in position of block.

The Return Right Hook

1.   Block the opponent's right hook with a forearm block.

2.   Step in and hook a hard right to the chin.

RIGHT HOOK TO THE CHIN—COMBINATIONS

The right hook forms an effective combination with any of the left handed blows. Combinations, using the right hook as the finishing blow, should receive a great deal of emphasis. All the combinations listed below have speed and power, and for that reason are very dangerous.

ANALYSIS OF THE COMBINATIONS

The Left Hook—Right Hook

Hook a hard left to the opponent's chin, shifting body weight over a straight right leg. Right hand should be held high and in position of guard. Rock the weight to the straight left leg and hook a hard right to the chin. The left hand is held in a position of guard. (See Plate 125a, b, c, d)

PLATE 125. THE LEFT HOOK, RIGHT HOOK

| *(a) On guard position* | *(b) The left hook* | *(c) Beginning of right hook* | *(d) The right hook* |

The Left Jab—Left Hook--Right Hook

Jab to the opponent's chin. Shift the weight to the right foot and hook the left to the chin. Right hand is held open in position of guard. Follow, by driving a hard right hook to the chin, weight shifting over the left leg. The left arm is held close to the body, in position of guard. (See Plate 126a, b, c)

(a) The left jab   *(b) The left hook*   *(c) The right hook*
PLATE 126. THE LEFT JAB, LEFT HOOK, RIGHT HOOK

The Left Jab to the Body—Right Hook to Chin

Step in with a left jab to the body. Right hand is held high and open. After the jab is executed, straighten the body and drive a hard right hook to chin. The left hand folds to body assuming a position of guard. (See Plate 127a, b)

(a) Jab to body   *(b) Right hook to chin*
PLATE 127. THE LEFT JAB TO THE BODY.
RIGHT HOOK TO CHIN

The Left Uppercut to the Body—Right Hook to Chin

This is a natural sequence and a most dangerous one. Drive a hard left uppercut to the solar plexus, right hand held high and open in front of chin. As the uppercut makes contact, turn the body sharply from the waist to the left and drive a hard right hook to the chin. The left hand is held high and open, guarding the chin. (See Plate 128a, b, c, d, e) On the left uppercut, weight shifts to right leg; and on the right hook, weight shifts to the left leg.

(a) Beginning position *(b) Beginning the left uppercut* *(c) The left uppercut*

(d) Start of right hook *(e) The right hook*

PLATE 128. THE LEFT UPPERCUT TO THE BODY, THE RIGHT HOOK TO THE CHIN

The Left Hook to Chin, the Left Uppercut to the Body and the Right Hook to the Chin

A hook-uppercut sequence. Drive a left hook to the chin, drop the left hand and drive a hard left uppercut to the body. As uppercut is executed the right hand is held high and to the right of the chin. From this position, lift the elbow and hook a hard right to the chin. (See Plate 129a, b, c, d) Weight remains forward over the left foot. After the uppercut to the body, the left hand folds to a position of guard.

(a) The left hook   *(b) Beginning left uppercut*   *(c) The left uppercut*   *(d) The right hook*

PLATE 129. THE LEFT HOOK TO CHIN, THE LEFT UPPERCUT TO BODY, RIGHT HOOK TO CHIN

The Left Uppercut to the Body, the Right Hook to the Chin and the Left Hook to the Chin

This combination makes use of the left uppercut-right hook sequence. Drive a hard left uppercut to the body. Turn the body to the left and hook a hard right to the chin. Then rock the weight which has been forward over the left leg, back to the right foot, and hook a hard left hook to the chin. (See Plate 130a, b, c) The hand always assumes a position of guard after the execution of the blows.

(a) The left uppercut   *(b) The right hook*   *(c) The left hook*

PLATE 130. THE LEFT UPPERCUT TO BODY, RIGHT HOOK TO
CHIN, LEFT HOOK TO CHIN

COACHING HINTS

The Left Hook, Right Hook

1. Shift the weight to the right leg on the left hook.

2. Rock the weight to left leg on the right hook.

3. Always carry the opposite hand in position of guard.

4.   Are effective blows in close.

5.   Should never be used as a lead combination.

The Left Jab, Left Hook, Right Hook

1.   Is an effective lead combination.

2.   Use the jab-hook to the Chin; carry the right hand high.

3.   Shift the weight back to the left foot and hook a hard right to the chin.

The Left Jab to the Body and the Right Hook to the Chin i I

1.   An effective lead combination.

2.   Feint several times to the body before actually jabbing.

3.   As the jab is performed, step in.

4.   Straighten body and hook a hard right to the chin.

The Left Uppercut to the Body and the Right Hook to the Chin

1.   Is a natural combination carrying a lot of power.

2.   Drop under the left lead with a left uppercut to the body, right hand high and open.

3.   Hook a hard right to the chin, left hand being held in position of block.

The Left Hook to the Chin, Left Uppercut to Body and Right Hook to the Chin

1.   Use a left hook, left uppercut sequence on first two blows.

2.   Then shift weight to the left foot.

3.   Hook a hard right to the chin. Left hand is held in the position of guard.

The Left Uppercut to Body, Right Hook to Chin and a Left Hook to the Chin

1.   Hook a hard right to the chin after driving a left uppercut to the body.

2.   Shift the weight to the right leg and hook a left to the chin. The left hand assumes the position of guard.

STRAIGHT RIGHT TO THE BODY—TECHNIQUE

The straight right to the body is a power blow, used either as a counter or a lead blow after a preliminary feint with the left hand. As in the left jab to the body, the body follows the blow, although added force is obtained through the use of a body pivot.

ANALYSIS OF THE STRAIGHT RIGHT TO THE BODY

Drop the body forward from the waist to a position almost at right angles to the legs. Turn to the left so that the right hip is carried to the center line of the body, and the right shoulder approximates a position directly above that of the left toe. From this position drive the right arm into a forceful extension. The left elbow is down, hand high, guarding against the opponent's right hand. The head is carried close to the right arm. (See Plate 131a, b, c) In teaching the straight right to the body, start with the body bent forward, right shoulder directly over the left toe, the right arm hanging downward. From this position have cadets raise their right arms forward until it forms a straight line to the opponent's solar plexus. Hold the left hand high and open off of the left shoulder.

(a) Shoulder-toe position   *(b) The straight right to body*   *(c) Side view*
PLATE 131. THE STRAIGHT RIGHT TO THE BODY

COACHING HINTS

The Straight Right to the Body

1. Power is obtained through a turn of the body to the left and a drop of the body forward over the left foot.

2. The body drop is obtained primarily through the bend of the right knee. The left leg is held as straight as possible.

3. As the right shoulder approximates a position over the left toe, the right arm is driven into forceful extension.

4. The body follows the arm at all times.

5. The right arm is driven on a straight line from the shoulder to the solar plexus.

6. At the moment of impact knuckles are up, thumb side of the fist turned inward.

7. The on guard position should be recovered immediately, the arm following the body.

8. The left arm is held in a position of guard, waiting and ready for a right hand counter.

STRAIGHT RIGHT TO THE BODY—DEFENSE

The defense for the straight right to the body is for all purposes exactly the same as that which is used for the straight left to the body.

ANALYSIS OF THE METHODS OF DEFENSE

The Elbow Block

As the opponent leads a straight right to the body, turn so that the blow is taken on the left elbow. The elbow must be tight to the body, forearm straight, hand high and in front of the chin. The elbow should not be moved without turning the body. (See Plate 132)

The elbow block
PLATE 132. DEFENSE FOR STRAIGHT RIGHT TO BODY

The forearm block
PLATE 133. DEFENSE FOR STRAIGHT RIGHT TO BODY

It is possible to block a straight right to the body by taking the blow on the right elbow. The left hand should be carried high, in position of guard.

The Forearm Block

As the opponent leads a straight right to the body, fold the forearms across the midsection, left arm under the right, completely covering the solar plexus.

(See Plate 133) The forearm block is dangerous in that the chin is exposed to a counter blow.

The Brush Away

As the opponent leads a straight right to the body, drop the open left glove downward and inward across the opponent's wrist, thus brushing the blow to the left. The elbow remains in a fixed position until contact is made when the arm is moved outward from the body. (See Plate 134a) It is possible to cross brush with the right hand, forcing the opponent's right lead to the right. (See Plate 134b) The left hand should be carried high and in position of guard.

(a) The brush away   (b) The cross brush
PLATE 134. DEFENSE FOR STRAIGHT RIGHT TO BODY

The Step Away

It is purely a defensive movement. As the opponent leads a straight right to the body, drive the left arm forcibly to the top of his head. At the same time slide the left foot back to the right foot, the weight shifting entirely to the left foot, and allowing the right foot to swing free. The right hand cross brushes the opponent's right to the body, forcing it outward and to the right.

COACHING HINTS

The Elbow Block

1.   Turn the body and intercept the right lead on the left elbow.

2.   A cross block can be used, that is, blocking the blow with the right elbow.

3.   Be ready to counter with a right uppercut.

The Forearm Block

1.   Fold the forearms across the body, hugging the body tight.

2. Fold the left arm under the right.

3. Be ready to drop under any counter blow directed to the chin.

The Brush Away

1. Brush down and inward with the left hand, forcing the opponent's right lead to the left.

2. The elbow remains fixed until contact is made, when the arm is straightened.

3. A cross brush with the right hand can be performed.

The Step Away

1. Place the left hand directly on top of the opponent's head.

2. Drop the left foot back to the right, shifting body weight to the left foot.

3. The right leg swings free.

4. The right hand cross brushes the opponent's right lead forcing it to the right.

STRAIGHT RIGHT TO THE BODY—COUNTER ATTACK

All effective counters are combinations of blows to the head and body. In other words, an up-down or down-up sequence.

The straight right to the body is an effective counter because it is a power blow. It is a very safe counter for left jab to the chin. Its effectiveness is increased when it is combined with the right hook or right cross to the chin. Reversibly, a straight right to the body can be easily countered because it is difficult to maintain body position on such a blow. The uppercuts are the most effective counters for the straight right to the body.

ANALYSIS OF THE COUNTER ATTACK

THE STRAIGHT RIGHT TO THE BODY AS A COUNTER BLOW

The Inside Right to the Heart

As the opponent leads a left jab to the chin, slip to the inside guard position and drive a straight right to the heart. The body is low and on the same plane as the right arm, arm protecting the head. The left hand is held high, ready to stop the opponent's right hook. (See Plate 58, Page 98) To obtain the greatest power, step forward and left, six to eight inches with the left foot, shifting all the weight over the left leg.

The Outside Slip and Straight Right to the Heart on a Straight Right Lead to the Chin

On the opponent's right lead to the chin, step forward and to the left, slipping to the outside guard position. At the same time drive a hard straight right to the heart. The body is low, the right arm protecting the head. The left hand is held high and in position of guard. (See Plate 135)

PLATE 135. THE OUTSIDE SLIP AND STRAIGHT RIGHT TO THE HEART ON A STRAIGHT RIGHT LEAD

COUNTER BLOWS FOR THE STRAIGHT RIGHT TO THE BODY

The Left Jab

The left jab is one of the very best counters for the straight right to the body. As opponent starts his right, step in with a left jab to the chin. Carry the right hand low, ready to block the opponent's right.

The Left Uppercut

As the opponent leads a straight right to the body, step forward and to the right with the right foot, dropping the left hand and driving a left uppercut inside the lead and to chin or body. The right hand should be held high ready to cross parry the opponent's straight right.

The Right Uppercut

As the opponent leads a straight right to the body, brush downward with the left glove, forcing the opponent's blow to the left. At the same time drive a hard right uppercut to the opponent's body or chin.

The Left Hook to the Chin

As the opponent leads a straight right to the body, step right with right foot, weight shifting to the right leg, and hook a hard left to the chin.

COACHING HINTS

THE STRAIGHT RIGHT TO THE BODY AS A COUNTER BLOW

The Inside Right to the Heart

1.   Step forward and to the left with the left foot.

2. Shift the weight to the left leg, body dropping forward, allowing the opponent's lead to slip over the right shoulder.

3. Drive the right hand inside of the opponent's left lead and to the heart.

4. Carry the left hand high and ready for the opponent's left counter.

5. Protect the head with the right arm.

The Outside Slip and Straight Right to the Body on a Straight Right Lead

1. Step forward and left with the left foot, dropping the weight forward over left leg.

2. Carry the left hand high and open, ready to cross parry the opponent's right lead.

3. As the opponent's lead slips over the right shoulder, drive a straight right hand to the heart.

COUNTERS FOR THE STRAIGHT RIGHT TO THE BODY

The Left Jab

1. Jab hard as the opponent starts a straight right to the body.

2. The right hand should be in the position to block the lead.

The Left Uppercut

1. On opponent's lead, step to the right with right foot, and drive left uppercut to the chin or body.

2. Carry the right hand high and in position of guard.

The Right Uppercut

1. Brush the opponent's right to the body to the left with the left glove.

2. At the same time, drive a right uppercut to the chin or body.

The Left Hook to the Chin

1. Shift the body weight to the right leg.

2. Hook the left to the chin.

3. Be ready to block the opponent's right lead to the body with the right hand.

STRAIGHT RIGHT TO THE BODY—COMBINATIONS

By adding the straight right to the body, new and more effective combinations become possible. The straight right to the body can be combined with the left jab to the chin, the left hook to the chin, and the left jab to the body.

ANALYSIS OF THE COMBINATIONS

The Left Jab to the Chin and the Straight Right to the Body

Step in with a jab to the chin. Drop suddenly and drive a straight right to the solar plexus. The jab should be high, the drop sudden, in order to make the combination work. (See Plate 114a, b, c, Page 148)

The Left Hook to the Chin and the Straight Right to the Body

Hook a short left to the chin shifting the weight to the right leg. Then shift the weight to the left foot, driving a straight right to opponent's solar plexus. This combination depends upon the first blow being high followed by a sudden drop (See Plate 136a, b, c, d)

PLATE 136. THE LEFT HOOK TO THE CHIN AND THE STRAIGHT RIGHT TO THE BODY
| *(a) On guard position* | *(b) Left hook to the chin* | *(c) Mid-position* | *(d) Straight right to body* |

The One-Two to the Body

Step in and drive a left jab to the body. Pendulum the body to the left and as the right shoulder swings forward, drive a hard right to the body. (See Plate 137a, b, c)

(a) The left jab to body   *(b) Mid-position*   *(c) Straight right to body*

PLATE 137. THE ONE-TWO TO THE BODY

COACHING HINTS

The Left Jab to the Chin and the Right to the Body

1. The jab must be high and drop must be sudden.

2. The right to the body is a powerful blow.

The Left Hook to the Chin and the Right to the Body

1. Drive a high left hook to the chin, shifting the weight over a straight right leg.

2. Shift the body weight forward over the left foot and drive a straight right to the body.

3. The movement must be sudden, especially the drop with the right, if the counter is to be effective.

The One-Two to the Body

1. Use as a threat to the body.

2. Step in with a left jab to the body.

3. Swing the body to the left, driving a straight right to the body.

RIGHT UPPERCUT TO THE BODY—TECHNIQUE

The right uppercut to the body is a power blow. While its principal use is that of a counter, it is effective during infighting, and when coming into or going out of a clinch.

It is a short blow, best used to the body. Occasionally, it can be used to the chin.

While the technique of the right uppercut is easily learned, it requires considerable experience before it can be used in action. It is the "stock in trade" of the tall boxer against the shorter opponent.

ANALYSIS OF THE RIGHT UPPERCUT TO THE BODY

Drop directly to the right and slightly forward so that the right elbow is touching the right leg below the hip. The right arm is in a half bent position, parallel to the floor, palm up. Rotate the body to the left, turning the right hip and shoulder through the center line. Then suddenly straighten the body and whip a right hand uppercut to the solar plexus. The left arm covers the left side of the body and face throughout. (See Plate 138a, b, c)

(a) Side drop   (b) The turn to center line   (c) The uppercut

PLATE 138. THE RIGHT UPPERCUT TO THE BODY

The Right Uppercut Combined with Foot Movement

The correct usage of the right uppercut means the ability to step forward, backward, to the left or to the right, and still be in a position to execute the blow.

Step forward with the left foot and as the right foot is brought to position, drop the right hand and whip it upward to the solar plexus. Left hand remains in the on guard position, carried high and off the left shoulder. (See Plate 139a, b, c)

In moving to the rear, as the weight shifts to the left foot, drop the right hand and as left foot is brought to position, shift the weight forward to the left foot and drive a hard uppercut to the body. The left hand remains high and in position of guard.

(a) Starting position　　　　*(b) The left step*　　　　*(c) The uppercut*

PLATE 139. THE RIGHT UPPERCUT, COMBINED WITH THE ADVANCE

On the left step and right uppercut, step to the left with the left foot shifting the weight to the left leg. As the right foot moves to position, drive a hard right uppercut to the solar plexus. Left hand remains high and in position of guard.

On the right step and right uppercut, as the right step is taken, drop the right hand. As the left foot moves to position, shift the weight forward to the left foot and whip right uppercut to the solar plexus.

COACHING HINTS

Right Uppercut

1. Drop the body directly sideways to the right.

2. The arm should be in half bent position, parallel to the floor, palm up.

3. Pivot the body to the center line.

4. Straighten the body and drive the right uppercut to the solar plexus.

Right Uppercut with the Advance

1. Step forward with the left foot.

2. As right foot moves to position, execute the right uppercut.

3. Carry hands high in position of guard.

The Right Uppercut with Retreat

1. Step back with the right foot, dropping the right hand as the left foot follows to position.

2. Shift the weight forward, driving the right uppercut to the solar plexus.

3. Carry the left hand high in position of guard.

The Right Uppercut with Left Step

1. Step left with the left foot, shifting the weight forward.

2. As the right foot moves to position, drive a hard right uppercut to the body.

3. Carry the left hand high, in position of guard.

The Right Uppercut with Right Step

1. Step to the right with the right foot, and as the left foot moves to position, rock the weight to the left foot and drive a hard right to the solar plexus.

2. Carry the left hand high, in position of guard.

RIGHT UPPERCUT TO THE BODY—DEFENSE

Because the right uppercut is a short inside blow, it can be easily defended against by merely moving out of range. The right uppercut can be blocked either by the use of the brush away or the forearm blow.

The defense for the right uppercut to the body is exactly the same as the defense for the left uppercut to the body.

ANALYSIS OF THE METHODS OF DEFENSE

Brush Away

On a right uppercut to the body, drop the left glove, palm open, forward and inward, crossing the opponent's lead from inside and forcing it outward, and to the left. (See Plate 140)

The brush away
**PLATE 140. THE DEFENSE FOR THE
RIGHT UPPERCUT TO THE BODY**

The forearm block
**PLATE 141. THE DEFENSE FOR THE
RIGHT UPPERCUT TO THE BODY**

The Forearm Block

On a right uppercut to the body, drop the left forearm forcibly downward, striking the oncoming blow from the inside and forcing it outward. Power should be used. The left forearm is actually placed in the crook of the opponent's right arm. Carry the right hand high in position of guard. (See Plate 141)

The Step Back

On a right uppercut to the body, drop the left forearm forcibly downward, move the body out of range, ready for either attack or defense. The body must be maintained in an upright position. (See Plate 142a, b)

(a) Starting position   *(b) The step back*
PLATE 142. THE DEFENSE FOR THE RIGHT UPPERCUT TO THE BODY

COACHING HINTS

The Brush

1. Drop the left glove downward and inward, crossing the oncoming blow from the inside forcing it outward to the left.

2. The elbow should remain fixed until contact is made.

3. The palm of the left hand should be open.

4. The right hand should be carried high in position of guard.

Forearm Block

1. Bend slightly forward, dropping the left forearm forcibly across the opponent's right arm.

2. If possible, the left forearm should be placed in the crook of the opponent's right arm.

3. Carry the right hand high and open in position of guard.

RIGHT UPPERCUT TO THE BODY—COUNTER ATTACK

With the addition of the right uppercut the possibilities of the counter attack are complete. It is now possible to counter with either hand to the head or body, using straight blows, hooks and uppercuts.

The right uppercut is a most powerful counter when properly used. It is easily countered, however, and does not lend itself to promiscuous use. . .

The natural counter blow for the right uppercut to the body is the left handed blow, either the left jab to the chin or left hook to the chin.

ANALYSIS OF THE COUNTER ATTACK

THE RIGHT UPPERCUT TO THE BODY AS A COUNTER BLOW

The Inside Slip and Right Uppercut to the Body on a Left Lead

As the opponent leads a left jab to the chin, step forward and to the left with the left foot. Slip the blow over the right shoulder, drop the right hand and drive a hard right uppercut to the solar plexus. (See Plate 143)

The left hand should be carried high and in position of guard, open and ready for the opponent's right hand counter.

PLATE 143. THE INSIDE SLIP AND RIGHT UPPERCUT TO THE BODY, LEFT LEAD

The Cross Parry and Right Uppercut to the Body on a Left Lead

As the opponent leads a left jab to the chin, reach over with the left hand and force the opponent's lead to the right. At the same time step forward with the left foot, drop the right hand and drive a hard right uppercut to the body. (See Plate 144a, b)

PLATE 145. THE OUTSIDE SLIP AND RIGHT UPPERCUT TO THE BODY, RIGHT LEAD

PLATE 146. THE INSIDE PARRY AND RIGHT UPPERCUT TO BODY, RIGHT LEAD

After the cross parry has been executed with the left hand, move the left hand quickly to position ready to stop opponent's right counter blow.

The Outside Slip and Right Uppercut to the Body on a Straight Right Lead

As the opponent leads a. straight right to the chin, step left and forward with the left foot, weight shifting to the left foot. At the same time, drop the right hand and drive a hard right uppercut to the solar plexus. Carry the left hand high and open off the left shoulder. (See Plate 145)

The Inside Parry and Right Uppercut to the Body on a Straight Right Lead

As the opponent leads a straight right to the chin, move the left hand upward and to the inside of the lead, forcing it to the left. At the same time, step forward with the right foot and drive a hard right uppercut to the body. (See Plate 146)

After executing the parry, the left hand crosses over to the right shoulder, open and ready for opponent's left hand counter.

THE COUNTER BLOWS FOR THE RIGHT UPPERCUT TO THE BODY

The Left Jab

As the opponent leads a right uppercut to the body, step directly forward and jab a hard left to the chin. The right hand should be held ready to block the opponent's right uppercut to body.

The Left Hook to the Chin

As the opponent drops his glove to execute a right uppercut to the body, shift the weight to the right foot and hook a hard left to the chin.

The right hand should be ready to block the opponent's left uppercut.

The Return Right Uppercut

(a) The cross parry   (b) The right uppercut
PLATE 144. THE CROSS PARRY AND RIGHT UPPERCUT TO BODY, LEFT LEAD

As the opponent leads a right uppercut to the body, brush outward with the left hand forcing the opponent's lead wide. At the same time, step forward with the left foot rocking the weight forward, and drive a right uppercut to the solar plexus.

COACHING HINTS

THE RIGHT UPPERCUT TO THE BODY AS A COUNTER BLOW

The Inside Slip and Right Uppercut to the Body

1. Slip the left lead over the right shoulder.

2. Step forward and to the left with the left foot.

3. Drop the right glove and drive a right uppercut to the opponent's solar plexus.

4. Carry the left hand high, in position of guard.

The Cross Parry and Right Uppercut to the Body

1. Cross parry the opponent's left lead with the left glove.

2. Step to the left and forward with the left foot, driving a hard right uppercut to the body.

3. After executing the parry, the left hand should be ready to stop a right hand counter.

The Outside Slip and Right Uppercut to Body on a Straight Right Lead

1. Step forward and to the left with the left foot.

2. Slip the opponent's right lead over the right shoulder.

3. Drop the right hand and drive a right uppercut to the body.

4. Carry the left glove in a position of guard.

The Inside Parry and Right Uppercut to the Body on a Straight Right Lead

1. Parry the opponent's right lead outward with left glove.

2. Step to the left and forward with the left foot.

3. Drop the right hand and drive a hard uppercut to the solar plexus.

4. After executing the parry, the left hand assumes a position off the right shoulder, ready to guard the opponent's counter.

THE COUNTERS FOR THE RIGHT UPPERCUT TO THE BODY

The Left Jab

1. The left jab is faster and has more reach than the opponent's right uppercut.

2. Step in fast with a left jab.

3. Be ready to block the opponent's right uppercut with the right hand.

The Left Hook to the Chin

1. As the opponent drops his right glove to uppercut, step to the right and hook a hard left to the chin.

2. Carry the right hand off of the right shoulder, ready to block the left counter.

The Return Right Uppercut

1. Block the opponent's right uppercut with the left brush away.

2. At the same time, step left and forward with left foot.

3. Drop the right hand and drive an uppercut to the solar plexus.

4. The left hand, after executing the brush, moves to a position of guard oif the left shoulder.

RIGHT UPPERCUT TO THE BODY—COMBINATIONS

An expert boxer, after making contact with his lead blow, will follow with a series of blows herein described as combinations. The idea of the combination blow is to confuse the defense so that the final follow blow will find a clean opening resulting in a possible knockout. All good combinations, or series, start as fundamental blows. If contact is made, other blows follow in sequence to head and body.

Combination blows take advantage of the fact that the best defense can only block a small proportion of the blows led. Blows delivered in combination are the acme of boxing offense.

With the addition of the right uppercut, any of the eight fundamental blows can be used in any sequence or combination. The left hand blows are, the left jab and left hook to the chin, the left jab and left uppercut to the body. The right hand blows are the straight right and right hook to the chin and the straight right and right uppercut to the body.

ANALYSIS OF THE COMBINATIONS

The Left Jab and Right Uppercut to the Body

Step in with a left jab to the chin. As the weight shifts to the left foot, follow with a right uppercut to the body, the right foot moving to position. The left hand folds to the body in a position of guard after the execution of the left jab. (See Plate 147a, b, c)

(a) *The left jab*   (b) *The step*   (c) *The uppercut*

PLATE 147. THE LEFT JAB, RIGHT UPPERCUT TO THE BODY

The Right Hook and Right Uppercut to the Chin

One of the most important combinations in boxing is the use of the same hand to chin or body. Such a drill should be highly perfected.

(a) *The right hook*   (b) *Mid-position*   (c) *The right uppercut*

PLATE 148. THE RIGHT HOOK, AND RIGHT UPPERCUT TO CHIN

Shift the weight over the straight left leg and hook a right to the chin. Step forward with the left foot, drop the right hand, and drive a right uppercut to the body. (See Plate 148a, b, c)

The Right Uppercut and Right Hook to Chin

This is the exact opposite of the above combination, but is distinct, and should not be confused with it.

Step forward with the left foot and drive a hard right uppercut to the body. Then shift the weight to the straight left leg, lift the right elbow and hook a hard right to the chin. (See Plate 149a, b, c, d)

PLATE 149. THE RIGHT UPPERCUT AND RIGHT HOOK TO CHIN

| (a) Beginning uppercut | (b) The right uppercut | (c) Beginning right hook | (d) The right hook |

The Left Hook and Right Uppercut

This is one of the most dangerous combinations in boxing. It has an advantage of combining two power blows, one to the chin and the other to the body.

The right uppercut is a natural follow blow for the left hook.

Shift the weight to the right leg, and hook a hard left to the chin. Step forward, rocking the weight to the left leg, and move in with a hard right uppercut to the body. While hooking with the left, the right hand is held high in position of guard. After executing the hook, the left hand assumes a position of guard. (See Plate 150a, b, c)

(a) The left hook   *(b) Mid-position*   *(c) Right uppercut*

PLATE 150. THE LEFT HOOK AND RIGHT UPPERCUT

The Left and Right Uppercuts

This drill is used for infighting, or coming into and going out of clinches. Rock the weight to the right leg. Drop the left hand and drive a hard uppercut to the solar plexus. Follow by shifting the weight to the left leg, dropping the right hand, and driving an uppercut to the solar plexus.

The right hand is held high and open, in position of guard off the left shoulder, while executing the left uppercut. The left hand is high and open, off the right shoulder in a position of guard, while executing the right uppercut. (See Plate 151a, b, c, d)

PLATE 151. THE LEFT AND RIGHT UPPERCUTS

(a) Beginning left uppercut   *(b) The left uppercut*   *(c) Beginning right uppercuty*   *(d) Right uppercut*

(a) The left hook   *(b) Beginning right hook*   *(c) Right hook*   *(d) Beginning left uppercut*

(e) Left uppercut   *(f) Beginning right uppercut*   *(g) Right uppercut*

PLATE 152. THE LEFT HOOK, RIGHT HOOK, LEFT UPPERCUT, RIGHT UPPERCUT

The Left Hook, Right Hook, Left Uppercut, Right Uppercut

This is one of the most essential drill combinations that can be learned. It teaches the use of hooks and uppercuts as natural follow blows. Shift the weight to the right foot and hook a left to the chin. Follow immediately with a right hook to chin, weight shifting to the left foot. Then drop the left hand and whip a left uppercut to the solar plexus, weight remaining forward over the left leg. Follow by dropping the right hand and whipping a hard uppercut to solar plexus. (See Plate 152a, b, c, d, e, f, g)

The hand not used for striking is held in the position of guard. On the left hook, the right hand is held off the left shoulder, inside of the left arm. On the right hook, the left hand is held high and in front of the chin. After the left hand drops to execute the left uppercut, the right hand shifts to position off the left shoulder. After executing the left uppercut, the left hand assumes a position off the right shoulder as the right uppercut is executed.

(a) Starting left uppercut   *(b) The left uppercut*   *(c) Starting left hook*   *(d) Left hook*

(e) Starting right uppercut   *(f) Right uppercut*   *(g) Starting right hook*   *(h) Right hook*

PLATE 153. THE LEFT UPPERCUT, LEFT HOOK, RIGHT UPPERCUT, RIGHT HOOK

The Left Uppercut, Left Hook, Right Uppercut, Right Hook

An uppercut, hook sequence. Drive a hard left uppercut to the solar plexus, weight shifting to the right leg. Turn the left hip through to the center line and hook the left to the chin. Then drop the right arm and drive a hard right uppercut to solar plexus, weight shifting to left leg. Raise the right elbow and hook the right hand to the chin, weight remaining forward. (See Plate 153a, b, c, cl, e, f, g, h)

(a) Position   *(b) Left hook*   *(c) Beginning left uppercut*   *(d) Left uppercut*

(e) Beginning right hook   *(f) Right hook*   *(g) Beginning right uppercut*   *(h) Right uppercut*

PLATE 154. THE LEFT HOOK, LEFT UPPERCUT, RIGHT HOOK, RIGHT UPPERCUT

The Left Hook, Left Uppercut, Right Hook, Right Uppercut

This too, is a combination that is important for teaching the hooks and uppercuts as natural follow blows for each other. In this combination the hook-uppercut sequence is used. Drive a hard left hook to the chin, weight shifting to the right foot, then as weight rocks back to left foot, drop the left hand and whip an uppercut to the solar plexus. During this action the right hand is in the position of guard, high and in front of chin. Immediately after the execution of left uppercut, weight being over the left leg, a right hook is indicated and driven hard to the chin.

The left hand is in a position of guard. Immediately rock the weight back to right foot, dropping the right hand, and driving a hard uppercut to solar plexus as weight shifts back to the left foot. Left hand is held high and in position of guard. (See Plate 154a, b, c, d, e f, g, h)

(a) Beginning position   (b) Left hook   (c) Beginning right uppercut   (d) Right uppercut

(e) Beginning left uppercut   (f) Left uppercut   (g) Beginning right hook   (h) Right hook

PLATE 155. THE LEFT HOOK, RIGHT UPPERCUT, LEFT UPPERCUT, RIGHT HOOK

Left Hook—Right Uppercut, Left Uppercut—Right Hook

In this combination two power blows are used together in a body-chin sequence. The shift is from left to right and right to left. Alternate blows are used in sequence to chin and body. Hook a hard left to the chin, weight shifting to the right foot, right hand being held high and open in position of guard in front of chin.

Drop the right hand and step forward with the left foot, weight rocking forward, and drive a hard right uppercut to the solar plexus. The left hand is held high and in position of guard.

Now drop the left hand, right hand being held off left shoulder in a position of guard, and without shifting weight, whip the left hand to the solar plexus. With the weight still over the left leg, raise the right elbow and hook hard to the chin, left hand being held open and in position of guard. (See Plate 155a, b, c, d, e, f, g, h)

The Inside Triple

As the opponent leads a left jab, slip to the inside guard position with a right to the heart. Then weave under the opponent's extended left arm and as the weight of the body shifts to the right leg hook the left hand to the solar plexus. From this outside position, cross the right to the opponent's chin. (See Plate 156a, b, c)

(a) Straight right to body   *(b) Left hook to body*   *(c) Right cross to chin*

PLATE 156. THE INSIDE TRIPLE

The Outside Triple

The inside triple and outside triple, were made famous by Jack Dempsey. As Jack would say, "hit them in the stomach and hit them on the chin."

The first two blows of this combination are designed to bring down the guard and to create openings for the final or finishing blow.

On the outside triple, as the opponent leads a left jab, slip to the outside guard position and swing a wide left hook to the midsection. The right hand should be open and carried off the left shoulder. Step inward and to the left with the left foot, the body moving under the opponent's left lead, and hook a right hand to the body. The left hand drops over the opponent's right, in the position of stop.

Now straighten the body and whip the left uppercut to opp0nent's chin. The right arm is carried off the left shoulder open and in position of guard. (See Plate 157a, b, c)

PLATE 157. THE OUTSIDE TRIPLE

(a) Left hook to body   *(b) Right hook to body*   *(c) Left uppercut to chin*

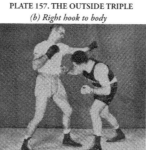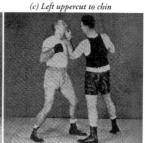

COACHING HINTS

The Left Jab, Right Uppercut

1. Step in with a left jab.

2. Follow with a hard right uppercut to the opponent's solar plexus.

3. Be sure to shift the weight over the straight left leg.

4. The left jab should be high and to the eyes. The left uppercut should follow quickly after the jab.

5. The left hand should assume a position off the left shoulder, ready and open for opponent's counters.

The Right Hook, Right Uppercut

1. To be used only when in close, or in an exchange of blows.

2. It is never a lead combination.

3. Jab with the left, then step in with a hard right hook to the chin and follow with a right uppercut to the body.

The Right Uppercut, Right Hook

1. This is the same combination as described above.

2. After riding in on a left jab, drive a right uppercut to the body and whip a right hook to the chin.

The Left Hook, Right Uppercut

1. This is a powerful combination.

2. It should be used coming into a clinch, while infighting, or when stepping out of a clinch.

3. Once contact has been made with left hook, drop the right shoulder and whip a right uppercut to the body.

The Left and Right Uppercuts

1. Use only while in close, in an exchange of blows, or while infighting.

2. Step with the left foot and drive a left uppercut to the body.

3. As the left uppercut is delivered, move the right foot on a line parallel with the left.

4. Bend the knees slightly and drive out with a right then a left uppercut to the body in rapid succession.

The Left Hook—Right Hook, Left Uppercut—Right Uppercut

1. In this combination the uppercut always follows the hook, whether you start with the left or the right hook.

2. The follow blow is the left or right uppercut.

3. Use only while infighting, coming in or going out of a clinch.

The Left Uppercut—Left Hook, Right Uppercut—Right Hook

1. In this combination the hook always follows the uppercut, whether it be a left or right uppercut.

2. It is used only while infighting, coming in or going out of a clinch.

The Left Hook—Right Uppercut, Left Uppercut—Right Hook

1. In this sequence the uppercut follows the hook in the first series, but the hook follows the uppercut in the second part of the series.

2. It is used while infighting, or coming in or going out of a clinch.

The Inside Triple

1. Is a combination-counter, in which the first blow is a right to the body, inside the opponent's left lead.

2. As the weight shifts to the right leg, a left hook to opponent's body is delivered.

3. Weight then shifts back to left foot, body straightens and a right hook is driven to the opponent's chin.

4. Keep the body low until the final movement.

5. Weight is first shifted to the left leg, then to the right leg, and then back again to the left leg.

The Outside Triple

1. A combination-counter used on a left lead.

2. Slip to the outside guard position and swing a wide left to the opponent's midsection.

3. Move the left foot sideways and forward as the body moves to the inside guard position.

4. Hook the right to opponent's ribs and at the same time use the stop on the opponent's right with the left hand.

5. Then straighten the body and drive a hard left uppercut to the opponent's chin.

6. Body must be kept low until the final blow.

7. Weight is shifted first to the right foot and then to the left.

CHAPTER IX
Feinting and Drawing, Clinching and Infighting

FEINTING

Feinting is Characteristic of the expert boxer. It requires using the eyes, the hands, the body and the legs in a single effort to deceive the opponent. Such movements are decoys, and if the opponent attempts to adjust his defense, advantage is then taken of the openings created. Feinting is also used to ascertain what the opponent's reactions will be to each movement.

Feinting creates only momentary openings. To be able to take advantage of the openings created means instant reflexive action, or a foreknowledge of what openings will be created by specific feints. Such familiarity presupposes the practice of many feints against all kinds of opponents so that a general reaction tendency can be determined.

In boxing, as in football, an opening should be "set up." Once an opening is created by a certain feint, that opening should not be used until a clean sure blow will result.

A good boxer knows what openings will result before he feints, and makes use of this knowledge and initiates his follow-up action almost before the opening results. Whenever two boxers of equal speed, strength and skill are matched, the one who is the master of the feint will be the winner.

The essential elements in feinting are rapidity, change, deception, and precision, followed by clean crisp blows. Feints used too often in the same manner will enable the opponent to "time" them for a counter attack, thus defeating their very purpose.

Feinting is the art of using the body in feigning attack at one point, and then attacking another. It involves the use of footwork, the knees, hands, eyes, arms, and trunk. Feints against the unskilled are not as necessary as against the skilled. Combinations of feints should be practiced until they are natural movements.

ANALYSIS OF FEINTING

It is best to practice feinting before a full length mirror. Each method should be tried, the deception of each being noted.

BODY FEINTS

The Arm Swing

Assume the on guard position. Advance slowly, allowing the left arm to swing free. If the arm is held loose and relaxed, on each forward movement of the left foot, the left arm will swing slightly to the rear and then forward. This action is produced entirely by the movement of the body, but gives the impression that the left hand is being extended. This is a fundamental feint that should be mastered by every boxer.

The Knee Faint

While advancing slowly, quickly bend the left knee. This gives the impression that the arms are moving as well as the legs. In reality, the arms are entirely relaxed and ready.

The Body Drop

Make a quick forward bend of the upper body, at the same time bending the left knee and moving the left hand slightly forward.

The Side Bend

While advancing slowly, drop the body to the right and forward creating the impression that a right hand lead is about to be executed.

ARM FEINTS

These feints are more specific than those described as body feints, and can be used to obtain a specific result.

The Up-Down Feint

Means feinting a left to the chin, and then to the body, or feinting a blow to the body or the chin with the right hand, without follow-up action. Such feints are used to ascertain how the opponent reacts, and to establish plans as to the further use of the feint.

The Draw-Back Feint

This is a right hand feint using the same principle as in frightening an animal. This is done by drawing the arm back as if to strike, rather than in a striking movement itself. To execute, drop the weight back to the right foot, and draw the right hand back, as if to deliver a hard right hand blow.

The Shift Feint

This too, is a right hand feint to the chin, using the striking motion to "fake out" the opponent. Shift the weight forward over the left foot, raising the right elbow slightly. Turn the right hip to the center line as if to strike with the right hand. A hard hook to the chin can be delivered off this feint.

SPECIFIC ARM FEINTS

— Feint a left jab to the chin and then drive a straight left to the solar plexus.

— Feint a left jab to the solar plexus and then step in with a left jab to the chin.

— Feint a left jab to the chin, shift the weight to the right foot, and feint a right to the chin. Then step forward with a left jab to the chin.

— Feint a straight right to the jaw, and hook the left to the body.

— Feint a jab to the chin and deliver a hard right uppercut to the body.

— Step forward with the left foot, as in the quick advance, and jab without hitting the opponent. From this close position, pull the left arm back to position, and jab to the chin.

COACHING HINTS

1. Always "build-up" an opening before making use of it.

2. Feints must be precise of action, rapid and decisive.

3. Each feint will bring a characteristic reaction, which should be known before the feint is made. This means practice.

4. Never use the same feint more than twice in a row. Change is all important.

5. Use the whole body, eyes, hands, the bend of the waist, and a bend of the knees to fake action desired.

6. Arm feints are specific, leading to certain openings or reactions of the opponent.

DRAWING

Drawing is closely allied to feinting. Whereas in feinting an opening is created, in drawing, some part of the body is left unprotected in order that the opponent will lead a specific blow against which a counter attack can be executed. Feinting then, is but one phase of drawing which uses also the methods of strategy, which is the method of crowding and forcing. Advancing while apparently open to attack, drawing the attack and at the same time executing a successful counterattack, is a phase of boxing that few ever develop. Many boxers refuse to lead. Then to be able to draw or force a lead becomes very important.

ANALYSIS OF DRAWING

By Exposing the Body to Attack

In drawing a left lead to the chin, carry the right hand low, thus exposing the chin. On the lead, step in or out, countering with either hand. To draw a left lead to the body raise the right elbow. Be ready to drop a right hand blow to the opponent's chin, or to step inside of the lead with a straight right.

To draw a right hand lead to the head, carry the left hand low. Be ready to slip to the inside or outside guard position, thus leaving either hand free to counter. To draw a right hand lead to the body, carry the left elbow high. Be ready to brush or cross parry the opponent's right lead.

By Forcing

Advance slowly and continuously to the attack, thus forcing or bringing forth a left lead. Be ready to slip to the inside or outside guard position, countering either to body or chin. To force a specific lead, advance slowly forward at the same time exposing a particular part of the body which will draw the lead desired. For instance, if the right hand lead to the body is desired, advance slowly forward while carrying right arm high and clear of the body.

By Feinting

Experience alone will tell which feint to use in order to draw a specific blow. Only practice will give knowledge of what blow each feint will draw.

COACHING HINTS

1. A blow may be drawn by exposing the body, by forcing or by feinting.

2. After drawing, the counter attack is indicated.

3. Drawing is a necessary art against an opponent who will not lead.

4. Its success is dependent on speed, timing and judgment.

CLINCHING

Clinching means holding the opponent's arms in such a manner that he is unable to strike a blow. It is used as a means of protection after missing a blow, and when hurt or fatigued. There are many methods of clinching, but only one which is absolutely safe and sure. All types should be practiced.

In clinching it is important to keep the body as close to the opponent as possible. Do not allow the opponent to move away. Stay close until the referee orders a break. If possible, keep the left shoulder against the opponent's chest, and the left leg close to his body. This reduces the possibility of punishment. Only when coming into, or going out of a clinch, is a boxer liable to get "hurt."

ANALYSIS OF CLINCHING

(a) The start

(b) Arm slide

(c) The clinch

(d) Showing position of left hand

PLATE 158. THE SAFETY CLINCH

The Safety Clinch

It is important in clinching to grasp the hands or arms but not the body. The only sure way to find the arms or hands is to start directly at the shoulders and slide the hands down the arms. To do this both hands must start from the inside position. As the opponent leads a left, move both hands forward in A movement similar to that of the breast-stroke in swimming. From the opponent's shoulder move the left hand down and around his right biceps, and at the same time move the right hand down to his left elbow, forcing his left glove up and under the right armpit. Grasp the opponent's left elbow with the right hand. (See Plate 158a, b, c, d)

After the arm is locked under the armpit, turn the body to the right, and drop the weight on the opponent's right arm. As the opponent tries to free himself, spin him off balance by using his left arm as a lever.

PLATE 159. BICEPS CLINCH

Biceps Clinch

In this method place the open hands around both of the opponent's biceps. As the opponent tries to punch, throw the body weight against the biceps, forcing him off balance, and rendering his effort impotent. (See Plate 159)

Arm Encirclement

If no other method is effective throw both arms around the opponent and hold tight. Keep the body close and the arms locked tightly. (See Plate 160)

PLATE 160. ARM ENCIRCLEMENT

PLATE 161. THE DOUBLE LOCK

The Double Lock

The double lock means forcing both the opponent's gloves up in under the armpits, and locking the hands in front of the body. (See Plate 161)

Spinning Out of a Clinch

Generally speaking, in moving out of a clinch, hold the hands high and well extended until the opponent is out of range. (See Plate 162a, b) It is always a good plan to force the opponent off balance by spinning either to the right or left.

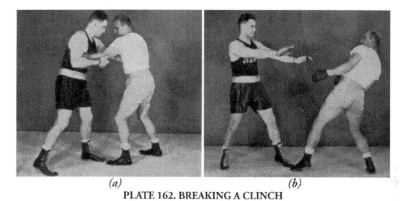

(a)   (b)
PLATE 162. BREAKING A CLINCH

Place the left hand behind the opponent's left elbow, and the right hand in back of his left shoulder Push to the left with the left hand, pull with the right, spinning the opponent off balance. (See Plate 163a, b, c)

(a) The clinch   (b) Right arm push   (c) Left arm follow through
PLATE 163. SPINNING OUT OF A CLINCH—THE LEFT

To spin the opponent to the right, place the left hand in back of the opponent's right elbow and the right hand on opponent's left shoulder. Pull forward with the left hand, and push with the right hand, thus spinning opponent to his left. (See Plate 164a, b, c)

| (a) The clinch | (b) Left arm push | (c) Right arm push |

PLATE 164. SPINNING OUT OF A CLINCH—TO THE RIGHT

COACHING HINTS

1. From the inside guard position, run the hands down the opponent's arms.

2. Place the open left glove around opponent's right biceps.

3. Tuck the opponent's left glove up in under the right armpit, and hold it tight to the side.

4. Shift all the weight to the opponent's left arm.

5. Break the clinch only at the referee's order.

INFIGHTING

Infighting is the art of boxing at close range. It takes skill to get in close and skill to stay there.

To obtain the inside position, it is necessary to slip, weave, duck, draw, or feint. Once the inside position is obtained, drive both hands to the opponent's midsection, occasionally switching to the chin.

ANALYSIS OF INFIGHTING

Infighting Technique

Draw a left lead and slip to the inside guard position, hands carried high. Place the forehead on the opponent's breastbone and push forward. This will force the opponent off balance. At the same time, drive short left and right uppercuts to the midsection. (See Plate 165a, b)

| (a) | (b) |

PLATE 165. INFIGHTING TECHNIQUE

Shifting with the Opponent

From the inside position, it is possible to shift with the opponent. As the opponent leads a left to the body, drive a right uppercut inside his blow to the body. As the opponent shifts to deliver a right, drive a left uppercut inside, and to the body. Continue pommeling the body until the opponent drops his guard. Then shift the attack to his head. (See Plate 166a, b)

(a)   (b)

PLATE 166. SHIFTING WITH THE OPPONENT

Switching the Attack

After driving hard blows to the body, straighten the body and drive a straight right arm blow to the opponent's right shoulder, spinning him to the right and into a left hook. (See Plate 167a, b, c) Again straighten the body, drive a straight left arm to the opponent's left shoulder, spinning him into a right hook. (See Plate 168a, b, c)

(a) Block blows   *(b) Cross over with right*   *(c) Left hook*

PLATE 167. SWITCHING THE ATTACK

(a) Block blows   (b) Cross over with left   (c) Right hook

PLATE 168. SWITCHING THE ATTACK

A Defense Against the Infighter

If the opponent obtains the inside position and starts to infight, place the open palm of both hands against his shoulders and push slightly forward. Slide the right hand to the side of the opponent's left shoulder, forcing him to the right, while pushing forward with the left hand. This will spin the opponent off balance.

COACHING HINTS

1. The inside position must be obtained through slipping, weaving, ducking and drawing.

2. Place the forehead on the opponent's breastbone.

3. Force forward with the head, pushing the opponent off balance.

4. Keep driving both hands to the opponent's midsection.

5. Maintain the inside position at all times.

6. Shift with the opponent.

7. If the opponent drops his arms, switch the attack to the head.

CHAPTER X
Ring Science

Ring craft is the ability to meet and successfully solve problems as they arise in the ring. Ring generalship is a general plan of battle thought out in advance of the bout, which attempts to nullify the opponent's strength and take advantage of his weakness.

Ring craft means the faculty to successfully adapt one's self to the opponent's style. It means the ability to out-smart and out-think the opponent in the ring. Ring craft depends upon knowledge, skill and physical condition to guarantee good performance. Real ring craft is based upon experience. While a boxer may be naturally wary and cautious, and show a tendency toward good ring craft from the very beginning, the expert is one who is wise in the ways of the ring, who has experienced the situations that are most likely to occur and knows best how to meet them.

In general, ring craft means ascertaining as soon as possible, the opponent's weakness or strength, his favorite mode of attack and his general manner of defense. It means learning the opponent's moves, his timing and his whole style of boxing. It means forcing the opponent to fight out of style, t tire him out and to frustrate his attack.

Ring generalship means a general knowledge of boxing styles and the most successful way of meeting each style. A plan of battle may be mapped out before a bout. If this is done, it necessitates knowing exactly what style of boxing the opponent uses. It is probably best to map out the exact plan of battle after boxing a round or so. The plan will then fit the style the opponent is using at that moment.

ANALYSIS OF RING CRAFT

There is no special technique of ring craft. Experience seems to be the only teacher, although in general there are certain techniques which have proven useful. These techniques are hereby presented as ring strategems.

Ring Strategems

1. Use your head, fight with your head, not your hands. Out-think the other man and you can out-hit him.

2. Be in condition—nothing will make up for good physical condition.

3. Relax! If you are tense, your reaction time is slow. Don't try too hard.

4. Know the fundamentals—there will be many chances to use them.

5. Appear confident at all times. If hurt or tired, don't show it.

6. Never forget that the opponent is as tired or is hurt as badly as you are.

7. The left hand is the safest lead. Use it.

8. Keep moving. To stand in one spot means you make a good target. However, do not jump around or make unnecessary movements.

9. Carry the hands high at all times.

10. Keep the chin tucked to the breast-bone.

11. Punch the moment the opponent is in range. Don't wait, otherwise you will be punched. Don't hold your blows.

12. If a blow is missed or you are off balance, clinch and wait for the referee to break.

13. Puzzle the opponent by a variety of maneuvers. Never do the same thing twice in succession.

14. Once the inside guard position is gained, stay close and keep punching.

15. Never underestimate an opponent. Remember, they are all tough.

16. Keep the feet under the body at all times. When off balance the body is open to attack.

17. Hit hard when you hit! Mean business. Snap a blow, don't push.

18. Punch only when there is an opening. Don't punch just to be doing something.

19. Punch through an object, not at one.

20. Step in to hit. It is impossible to hit hard while moving backward.

21. Do exactly what your opponent doesn't want you to do.

22. Never stop trying. Remember, it only takes one.

23. The safest place in boxing is in close, head waist high, hands high.

24. There are two times when you are most likely to get "hurt," while coming in to attack, or coming from attack.

25. Whenever the opponent gets set to hit, move.

26. Note carefully the reaction of your opponent just preceding his leads.

27. Make a mental note of any peculiarities.

28. The natural counter for a left jab is a right cross, therefore act accordingly.

29. Realize that ordinarily a straight punch will "beat" a hook.

30. The two handed attack to be effective must start from the inside guard position.

31. The outside guard position is the safest place from which to start an attack.

32. Right hand leads and short hooks are counter blows. Unless you want to get hit, do not lead them.

ANALYSIS OF RING GENERALSHIP

Because generalship is primarily concerned with a plan of action against different styles of boxing, some of the styles will be herein considered.

How to Box a Tall Opponent

This situation is often encountered. A tall opponent has more to protect, making it difficult for him to guard against all opening. Often he is slower and *therefore there are more openings.* However, to offset these disadvantages, the tall man has the longer reach and probably more power due to better leverage.

In general, the best plan is to keep moving in and out attempting to draw a left lead. On the lead, slip in fast, countering hard and often. Once the inside guard position is gained, place the forehead on the opponent's chest and force him backward and off balance. At the same time lift short arm jolts to the solar plexus.

A method of deception that can be used is to gradually edge the left foot nearer the opponent without altering the position of the body itself. If the stance is spread, it will be easier to reach the opponent when stepping in.

How to Box a Croucher

Any opponent who continually crouches is a difficult man to hit effectively. He fights from a "shell," well covered up.

Some crouchers bend directly forward, In this case, use speed, stepping in and out with short inside uppercuts. Never stay in close.

If the opponent crouches to either the left or the right side, jab to the front shoulder and try to force or spin him off balance. If this is done, follow up and stay close, taking advantage of each opening.

How to Box a Rusher

The rusher is chronic to the sport of boxing. He is the unskilled worker who must force himself to close range in order to score.

The sidestep was made for the rusher. As the opponent rushes, step smartly forward with the left foot and drive the left hand to the chin. Follow with a straight right. Once in close, clinch, resting the weight on the opponent, Wait until the referee calls for a break. As the opponent rushes again, repeat.

Straight blows will score before swings and hooks. Keep the blows high, chin down. If a hit is scored, follow up, if missed, clinch

How to Box a Jabber

Some boxers use only one blow, the left jab. To rope with this style, keep the body low. The inside position must be obtained by slipping, weaving or sidestepping, Punch while going in, use a right to the heart or a left hook to the body. Once in close, pin the forehead on the opponent's chest and stay right there. Drive both hands to the opponent's body.

The ability to fold under a left jab is an effective way of moving in close. As the opponent leads, drop the head into the crook of the right arm, This forces the jab over the top of the head. Carry the left hand low, ready to counter.

How to Box a "South-Paw" (The Left Handed Boxer)

Special technique is required to box a "southpaw." There are three principles that should be followed: (1) Make the southpaw lead first. (2) Circle to the left, away from the southpaw's left hand. (5) Use the right hand as the major weapon of offense. As a general rule this will bring good results. It should be varied as circumstances indicate.

---

* Many coaches and seconds maintain that the proper method of boxing a southpaw is to carry the attack. From a personal knowledge gained through handling "southpaws" it has been found that they prefer the attack to be carried to them. If forced to lead they are not only wide open, but off balance as well.

Circling left against a "southpaw" nullifies his best hand, his left. A "southpaw" usually has a terrific power in his left hand, which he invariably hooks. By circling away from the left hook, not only is power nullified, but a better position is obtained from which to deliver a right counter. However a right hook may be encountered. If possible, "feint out" the right hook. Usually on a feint, the "southpaw" will draw back his right arm ready to cross. If he does, step in with a straight left arm, hand open, to the opponent's right biceps or shoulder. This will spin him off balance and into a right counter.

The Slugger

Some men are endowed with the ability to hit hard with either hand. These men seldom take the trouble to learn how to box or to hit straight. They depend mainly on powerful hooks. They are always dangerous opponents.

Heavy hitters must "get set" in order to deliver their blows, therefore, the best defense is to keep moving. Inability to "get set" will lessen the hitter's power and make him less dangerous. Moving around does not mean jumping around but means moving efficiently and easily to prevent the opponent from getting ready to hit.

Each time the opponent sets himself to hit, move. Such a plan will render his attack ineffective.

A good piece of strategy is to suddenly stop moving and step in quickly catching him unprepared and off balance. This must be done Suddenly, moving in and then out before the opponent can "set" himself to hit. Do not attempt to "slug" with him.

A boxer who stands still is a "catcher." Move constantly, in and out, not vigorously, but easily.

The Counter Fighter

The counter fighter is a dangerous opponent. He turns the force of his opponent's blows back against the opponent. A counter fighter is dependent upon the lead of his opponent. Therefore, to thwart his attack do not lead, and especially, do not lead the blows expected. If possible, force the counter fighter to lead by feinting or drawing. If this is not successful, do what he expects, only be ready to counter the counter blow.

An aggressive attack with speed and power is an effective method in some cases. Such a procedure keeps a counter fighter off balance and thus ineffective.

COACHING HINTS

How to Box the Tall Opponent

1. Keep moving.

2. Draw a left lead.

3. Slip to the inside guard position.

4. Commence infighting.

How to Box a Croucher

1. Sidestep and counter.

2. Step in with a one-two to the chin.

3. If a hit is scored, follow up. If the blows are missed, clinch.

Haw to Box a Jabber

1. Keep low.

2. Slip to the inside or outside guard position.

3. Counter to the body.

4. Try to time a right cross.

5. Force continually.

How to Box a "Southpaw"

1. Don't lead, make the "southpaw" come to you.

2. Circle left away from the opponent's left hook.

3. Use the right hand to the head or body, straight or hooked.

How to Box the Slugger

1. Keep moving. Don't let the opponent get set.

2. Make the attack sudden.

3. Move out immediately, don't slug.

The Counter Fighter

1. Force a lead if possible.

2. If the opponent won't lead, carry the attack but be ready to counter his counter.

3. Constant aggressive action will keep the counter fighter off balance.

TEAM STRATEGY AND HANDLING

The successful coach is one who not only can get his team in good physical condition and teach them how to fight, but is one who can make them want to fight. Other things being equal, the ability to instill a will to win is the most important single factor of team handling. A group of superior technicians will be defeated by a group of boys who really want to win. This also holds true for the superior conditioned boys. Condition alone will not make a fighter.

General team handling resolves itself to the teaching, conditioning and inspiring of a mental set that is satisfied only with winning. It is concerned with getting the boys physiologically and psychologically ready to fight.

Team strategy on the other hand, is concerned with how to get the most out of a team once it is prepared to fight.

TEAM HANDLING

There is no place in boxing for the easy leader. The easy leader will fail to inculcate into the cadet those qualities and traits essential to a fighting man. The coach must be absolutely fair and impartial, treating all alike with no favoritism being shown.

Selecting a Squad

The tournament method of selecting a varsity squad is the fairest way of determining team personnel. Thirty-two cadets is considered a well-balanced squad, four to each weight. Once the squad has been picked, it is important to become well acquainted with each cadet. Find out his background, his interests, his ambitions, his habits, Take a personal interest. Help him achieve those things that he want; to do.

Analyze his boxing style, his background in boxing, his weaknesses and his strength. Map out a personal program of development so that a balanced technique will result. Talk to the cadet concerning this plan. Have him set certain objectives of accomplishment and encourage him to constantly try and work toward their successful completion. If a cadet can be motivated so that his one objective is to make himself it better boxer, he will become a better boxer.

Indoctrination

The squad selected should receive definite training in the building of specific attitudes. Talk to them about working up to their full capacity; that they can't be hurt unless they will be; that they are never tired. Such a precept must be followed during actual drills and coaching periods. Talk to them about what is required; then force them to practice such requirements.

Training Rules

Determine what training rules you want followed. Have them mimeographed and given out to each cadet. Go over each rule with the squad, explaining their purpose and what is expected as regards training. Be very strict in the application of the rules. Discipline immediately, any cadet who breaks the rules. Place him on the fourth team, select somebody else to fight in his place. If the case demands it, drop the cadet from the squad, but first tell him the reason for such action.

Workouts

Have a certain definite time and plan for each workout, Drive the cadets at top speed. Work them hard. Stop them while they are still fresh. Vary the type of work in order to keep their interest.

Appearance of the Team

All team members should be issued certain prescribed items of gear. No item of special gear should be issued to any of the team members. Training clothes should be easily laundered. They should be issued weekly. Hair should be worn short so it will not bother vision and so that it can be easily dried after showering.

Winning teams are a part of established tradition. The trick is to start the tradition, which in many cases means a winning team. A winning team forms a background of example which helps to perpetuate the idea of winning.

TEAM STRATEGY

"Keying up" a Team

There are some who advocate "keying up" a team for a match. This is done by talking to the team, appealing to them, giving them the so-called "pep talk."

Others believe that if a team isn't ready by the time of the match, then there is little that can be said which will aid in the winning oi the match. Ordinarily speaking, it is best to give each man definite instructions, and then hope that he will perform the way he should. The bout itself will "key up" the cadet except for some extraordinary circumstance, when something special must be done. In that case, the so-called "pep talk" might help.

Beginning with a Win

Some coaches lay great stress on winning the first match. One win, supposedly, spurs on the rest of the team to greater performance. Therefore, the strategy is to always have the 112, or the 120-pound division the strongest. Naturally, it does not follow that a beginning win means continued wins--or that the talent will be in the above mentioned weights.

Pre-Contest Strategy

Rest and relaxation before a bout is in order for all participants. It is probably best to leave the cadet by himself, because if he is not mentally set or if he is nervous, there is little that can be done to relieve him. Each cadet must fight his own battle, both before going into the ring and while in the ring. If he can't win the first battle; he probably won't win the second.

Arrive at the place of the bouts in plenty of time and be well provided with all necessary equipment. Have plenty of time to wrap each cadet's hands individually, unless they are expert and desire to wrap their own.

Once the cadets are dressed and ready for competition, have them rest until they are ready to go on.

Handling the Bout

The coach should see that an expert second is on hand to administer first aid in case it is necessary; he should have already instructed the cadet to act in the ring; how to loosen up; how to come out of a corner; what to do when returning to the corner; how to sit on a stool; how to relax himself between rounds; and lastly, how to listen.

Some advocate having the contestant sit toward the corner facing the coach or second so that he can be talked to while first aid or the freshening-up process is being administered.

The job of the second is to refresh and rest the contestant, that of the coach to give advice. During the last fifteen seconds of the rest period, plain simple advice emphasizing and repeating one idea, should be given. Never tell a cadet that he is ahead. If he asks, he is either behind or just about even. Always help the cadet off the stool, and move the stool in place as soon as the round is over,

The cadet should be coached to watch the corner, and if possible be near the corner when the bell rings.

After the bout is completed, and before the decision, the cadet should be cleaned up, and his robe put on. He then should await quietly the decision. Whether the decision is favorable to him or not, he must be sure to congratulate his opponent.

Directly after the bout, if possible, the contestant should take a good hot shower or whirlpool bath for ten minutes or more, allowing the hot water to loosen and relax his body. A body massage, soothing and relaxing, can be given. No food should be eaten within an hour after the fight, and then only a light lunch.

Glossary

Alertness Drill—A special drill designed to keep the attention of the class at all times. Should be mixed in with the regular drills.

Blocking—Taking a blow on some part of the body less susceptible to injury.

Blocking Drill—A method of teaching proper defense for specific blows.

Brush-away—A defense against straight blows to the body.

Butting—Using the head to strike the opponent while at close quarters.

Button—Refers to the point of the chin.

Cauliflower Ear—Often referred to as a "tin ear." Is the result of a blow on the ear causing a blood tumor, which if not given proper attention will cause connective tissue to form, obliterating all regular ear marking, leaving a crinkled mass known as a cauliflower ear.

Catch—A fundamental block for the left jab.

Circling Left—Moving sideward and to the left.

Circling Right—Moving sideward and to the right.

Clinching—Holding the opponent in such a manner that he is unable to strike a blow.

Combination Blows—A series of blows delivered in a natural sequence.

Controlled Boxing—Limiting the offense to certain specified blows.

Counter Attack—Using the opponent's lead as a means of successfully completing the attack.

Countering—Allowing the opponent to lead and then through some defense technique nullify the lead, taking advantage of the opening created to land solid blows to head or body.

Covering—Folding the arms in such a manner as to give almost complete protection.

Cuffing—Slapping the opponent's hands, or lead blows, up, down or aside.

Cross Parry—Forcing the opponents lead to the outside using the same hand as the opponent's lead.

Defensive Boxing—A boxing drill developed to teach defensive technique under actual boxing conditions. In this drill one student is on defense only.

Dementia Pugilistica—A condition often referred to as "punch drunk." Caused by many severe beatings about the head.

Drawing—Leaving some part of the body unprotected in order that the opponent will lead a certain blow.

Drop Away—A defense against a looping overhand right.

Drop Shift—The method of quickly dropping to the inside or outside guard position.

Drying Out—Abstinence from liquids for a period of twenty-four hours before a bout.

Ducking—Dropping under hooks and swings to the head.

Elbow Block—A defense against straight blows to the body.

Feinting—The art of using the body in feigning attack at one point, and then attacking at another.

Flicker Jab—A faulty version of the speed jab.

Folding—Is dropping forward under the opponent's blows.

Footwork—The ability to move the body easily and efficiently so that balance is not disturbed.

Forced Retreat—A sudden movement backward without loss of balance.

Forearm Block—Defense against straight blows to the body.

Goldbricking—Trying to get out of activity by pretending sickness, injury or the like.

Guarding—Is using the arms as levers to dispel the force of the opponent's blows.

Handwraps—Special bandages for the express purpose of protecting bones in the hand and wrist.

Head Protector or Helmet—A head harness developed to give protection to the eyes and ears. The new Navy helmet protects the nose and jaw as well.

Hitting—The art of obtaining maximum power in blows with a minimum of effort.

Hitting Drill—A drill in which one individual holds his glove as a target for the other to practice his blows.

Hooks—Bent arm blows to the chin.

Infighting—An exchange of blows while at close quarters.

Instructional Program—That phase of the athletic program given over to the teaching of basic skills.

Jab—See left jab.

Leading—Delivering the initial blow.

Left Jab—A quarter turn of the left shoulder inward followed by the complete extension of the left arm.

Left Jab to the Body—A straight left lead to the body, used to lower the opponent's guard.

Left Hook—A short bent arm blow to the chin.

Lesson Plan—The organization of material for teaching.

Leverage Guard—Using the arms as levers to deflect opponent's blow.

Long Hooks—Are really wide uppercuts to the body.

Mass Instruction—Instructing large groups at one time.

Mouthpiece—A rubber teeth grip designed to prevent chipping of the teeth.

On Guard Position—That position which is most favorable to the mechanical execution of the skills and technique of boxing.

One-Two—A combination of a left jab followed by a straight right to the chin.

Parrying—A sudden movement of the hand inward or outward deflecting the opponent's blow from its original path.

Physiological Conditioning—The preparation of the body for intense neural and muscular action.

Protection Cup—A piece of equipment designed to protect the scrotum against injury.

Psychological Conditioning—Creating a mental set which will permit all-out effort in order to win.

Quick Advance—A sudden movement forward without loss of balance.

Quick Shift—The shifting of weight and changing of the feet without disturbing balance; sometimes referred to as the side step.

Rabbit Punch—Striking with the edge of the hand to the back of the neck.

Rear Shift—A defensive maneuver designed to carry the body quickly out of range.

Right Cross—A right hook crossed over the opponent's left lead.

Right Hook—A short bent arm blow to the chin with the right hand.

Right to the Body—An inside counter to the body on a left lead.

Ring Craft—Successfully adapting one's self to the opponent's style.

Ring Generalship—A general knowledge of the methods used to cope with the different styles of boxing.

Rockaway—Swaying the body just out of range of the opponent's blows and "riding" in with straight counters.

Rolling—Nullifying the force of a blow by moving the body in the same direction as the blow.

Shadow Boxing—Practicing the various blows and movements of boxing.

Shoulder Block—Turning the left shoulder to intercept the opponent's right lead.

Shoulder Catch—Catching the opponent's right hook in the open right glove which is held directly off the left shoulder.

Sidestepping—Shifting the weight and changing the foot positions without disturbing balance.

Slipping—Is avoiding a blow without actually moving the body out of range.

Slow Advance—Moving slowly forward without disturbance of balance.

Slow Retreat—Moving slowly backward without disturbance of balance.

Solar Plexus—The second longest nerve center in the body controlling the sympathetic nervous system. It is situated above the middle line of the upper border of the pancreas just opposite the margin of the diaphragm.

Speed Jab—A variation of the basic jab.

Sports Program—The same as an intra-mural or competitive sports program.

Staleness—Lack of pep, listlessness. No interest or enthusiasm due to overwork and neural fatigue.

Step Away—A defense against straight blows to the body.

Slap Back—A defensive maneuver used to quickly move the whole body out of range without disturbing the on guard position.

Stopping—Is the pinning of an opponent's hand or arm so that he is unable to deliver a blow.

Straight Right Lead—Is the powerful extension of the right arm from the center line of the body to the point of attack.

Technique Drill—Practice on the proper technique of a skill or a part of a skill.

Telegraphing Blow—Giving away the intent of the following action.

Timing—Delivery of blows or execution of defense at the right time so as to assure successful action.

Training Bag—A large, heavy bag, filled with resilient material, used to develop power in hitting.

Uppercuts—Bent arm blows to the body.

Weaving—Moving the body in, out and around opponent's straight lead.

Spartan Sport Service, Michigan State College, Fred Stabley

SYRACUSE HEAVYWEIGHT TAKES NATIONAL COLLEGIATE

Marty Crandell, left, plants a left to the head of Don Schaeffer of San Jose State, after slipping Schaefer's left jab during the final round for the national collegiate heavyweight title. Note competitive headgear worn by Crandell.

APPENDIXES

The Naval Aviation Boxing Program

Last-Minute Reminders and Hints on Safety

Prior to beginning mass boxing instruction, the physical training officer should check the equipment as follows, re-checking periodically for safety:

A. Specialized Gear

1. See that the ring meets specifications—well-padded with covering of canvas; flooring of ring extended at least 30 inches beyond the lower ropes; ropes wrapped to prevent burns.

2. Gloves should be conscientiously inspected for tears and rips; those badly scuffed should be discarded or used for body bag work only. Metal tips at end of lace should be removed. Gloves should be kept off floor and cleaned according to a rigid schedule in order to prevent eye infections and cuts. '

3. The head protector or helmet should be worn at all times when boxing. (Note—The National Collegiate Boxing Association has just added Section 4 under Rule 5 which reads: "As a protection against eye cuts, ear and head injuries, a light competitive head guard must be worn by each participant in dual meets in tournament competition. Such head guards must provide for a layer of sponge rubber 1/2 inch in thickness covering the ears, eye ridges, temples and back of head.")

B. Personal Gear

1. Mouthpieces should be used at all times when boxing. (Note—Rule 5, Section 3 of the National Collegiate Boxing Code reads: "Rubber guards for the teeth must be used." A note under this section reads: "It is recommended that each individual be provided with a moulded guard that will fit his teeth.")

2. See that handwraps are being worn properly. (A daily spot-check is advised if boxers are wrapping own hands.)

3. Protective cups should be worn by each contestant when boxing.

In addition to the wearing of head protectors, other safety measures employed by colleges have proven themselves through the years, so it is suggested that these too be put to use. They are:

1. A contestant knocked down *must* take a full count of nine before being allowed to resume. This is to prevent over-anxious boxers from resuming action before they have fully recovered from a blow.

2. A bout is automatically stopped should one of the contestants be cut. Should this cut occur during the *first* round, the bout, when stopped, shall be declared "no contest." Should this cut occur during the *second* or *third* round, the bout, when stopped, shall be awarded to the contestant who is ahead on points.

For prompt treatment of injuries, it is recommended that a physician or a trainer be on hand whenever there is boxing competition, either of the practice or meet variety. The attendance of a medical representative will help greatly in developing confidence in the boxers.

APPENDIX I

The Drills for the Teaching of Mass Boxing

Mass boxing has made necessary certain adjustments in the teaching techniques and methods employed when instructing a small group or class, or in coaching a varsity team. Essentially, however, the two travel a similar path. Only the magnitude of mass boxing makes certain Changes necessary.

It calls for greater organization of time, space, equipment and facilities. It calls for greater organization of material. Techniques must be simply explained, commands must be exact and specific in order to bring forth correct action. Power and form for both offensive and defensive skills must be developed without loss of time or efficiency. Such is the need for drills in mass teaching.

The drills herein listed are those which have been tried and tested. They incorporate the best known methods of teaching boxing, making use of the technique drill, the hitting drill, the blocking drill and both defensive and controlled boxing.

All drills are included which are necessary to the various stages of the Naval Aviation Boxing program. In combination they form the basic teaching unit of the thirty lesson plans listed in the appendix.

The drills can be used singly or re-combined to form various types of courses to fit the need of the group. The simple rudiments of boxing can be taught using only the beginning drills. There are drills of an advanced nature which will motivate and encourage the experienced boxer if it is so desired.

Athletic officers with Operational Flight Training, at foreign bases or with the fleet, have ample source material on boxing to meet their specific needs and as the occasion demands.

The drills have been designed so as to bring most quickly the desired results. The inexperienced instructor will find them invaluable; the experienced teacher a source of great aid in handling large groups with greatest efficiency.

DRILL 1—THE ON GUARD POSITION

Technique Drill

1. Explain and demonstrate the following elements of the on guard position:

— Foot position.
— Trunk control.
— The position of elbows.
— The position of hands.
— The position of head.

2. Have the class practice the on guard position.

— Command—*On Guard, Hep!*

3. Have the group hold the on guard position. Correct those who need help. Call attention to common errors.

4. The command to return to position is—*Steady, Front!*

DRILL 2—THE SLOW ADVANCE AND THE SLOW RETREAT; THE QUICK ADVANCE AND THE QUICK RETREAT

Technique Drill

1. Explain and demonstrate:

— Slow advance.
— Slow retreat.
— Quick advance.
— Quick retreat.

2. Have the class practice the slow advance.
   Command—*Advance, Hep!* Shorten to *Hep!*

3. Have the class practice the slow retreat.
   Command—*Retreat, Hep!* Shorten to *Hep!*

4. Have the class practice the slow advance and slow retreat.
   Command—*Advance, Hep! Retreat, Hep!* Now give this type of command—*Advance six steps, Retreat six, Ready, Hep!*

5. Have the class practice the quick advance.
   Command—*Retreat, Hep!* or *Hep!*
6. Have the class practice the quick retreat.
   Command—*Retreat, Hep!* or *Ready, Hep!*

7. Have the class practice the quick advance and the quick retreat.
   Command—*Advance, Hep! Retreat, Hep!*

8. Have the class practice the slow advance interspersed with the quick advance. Have class move forward using the slow advance. On command all practice the quick advance.
   Command—*Ready, Hep!*

9. Practice the above drill interspersing the quick retreat with the slow retreat.

10. Have the class practice the slow advance interspersed with the quick retreat.
    Command—*Retreat, Hep!* or shorten to *Hep!*

11. Have the class practice the slow retreat interspersed with the quick advance.
    Command—*Advance, Hep!* or shorten to *Hep!*

DRILL 3—THE LEFT STEP, THE RIGHT STEP, THE STEP BACK. THE STEP IN-STEP OUT

Technique Drill

1. Explain and demonstrate:
   — The left step.
   — The right step.
   — The step back.
   — The step in-step out.
2. Have the class practice the left step.
   Command—Left step, Ready, Hep! Shorten to Ready, Hep! then to Hep!

3. Have the class practice the right step.
   Command—Right step, Ready, Hep! Shorten as above.

4. Have the class practice both the right and left steps.
   Command—Right step, Hep! Left step, Hep!

5. Have the class practice the advance, retreat, left and right step. Mix in every possible combination and sequence.
   Command—Advance, Hep! Retreat, Hep! Right step, Hep! Left step, Hep! etc.
   Now practice advancing four steps, retreating four steps, left step four steps, right step four.
   Command—Ready, Hep!

6. Have class practice the step back.
   Command—Step back, Ready, Hep! Shorten to Ready, Hep! finally to Hep!

7. Have the class practice the step in-step out.
   Command—Ready, One, Two! On One, step in; on Two, step out; or Ready, In: Ready, Out!

8. As above, but on command of Two, move to the right or left instead of to the rear.

DRILL 4—THE QUICK SHIFT, THE DROP SHIFT, THE REAR SHIFT

Technique Drill

1. Explain and demonstrate the:
    — Quick shift.
    — Drop shift.
    — Rear shift.
    —

2. Have the class practice the quick shift.
   Command—Quick shift, Ready, Hep! Shorten to—Ready, Hep.

3. Have the class use the slow advance, practicing the quick shift on command.
   Command—Ready, Hep! or Hep!

4. Have the class use the slow retreat, practicing the quick shift on command.
   Command—Ready, Hep! or Hep!

5. Have the class practice the drop shift.
   Command—Drop shift, Ready, Hep! Shorten to—Ready, Hep!

6. Have the class use the slow advance, practicing the drop shift on command.
   Command—Ready, Shift! or Ready, Hep!

7. Have the class practice the rear shift.
   Command—Ready, shift, Ready, Hep! Shorten to—Ready, Hep!

8. Have the class use the slow advance, practicing the rear shift on cornmand.
   Command—Ready, Shift! or Ready, Hep!

9. Have the class use the slow retreat, practicing the rear shift on'command.
   Command—Ready, Shift! or Ready, Hep!

Hitting Drill

1. Inboard men—On command, lead a slow left jab.
   Outboard men—Practice the quick shift.
   Command—Ready, Strike! or Ready, Shift!

2. Inboard men—On command, lead a slow left jab.
   Outboard men—Practice the drop shift.
   Command--Ready, Strike! or Ready, Hep!

3. Inboard men—On command, lead a slow left jab.
Outboard men—Practice the rear shift.
Command—Ready, Step! or Ready, Strike!

DRILL 5—THE WAIST PIVOT

Technique Drill

1. Explain and demonstrate the waist pivot:
    — The turn or pivot.
    — The close elbow turn.
    — The arm extension, palms up.
    — Making a proper fist.
    — Bring both hands through.
    —

2. Have the class practice the turn or pivot, one turn on each command. Once the idea has been developed, allow free practice.
Command—Ready, Turn, Turn, Turn, etc. or 1—2—3—4.

3. Have the class practice the close elbow turn. Allow free practice on the close elbow turn.
Command—Ready, turn! or 1--2—3—4, as above.

4. Have the class practice the arm extension, palm up. Start with left arm extended, right hand lined up directly behind.
Command—Ready, Strike! Shorten to—Strike!

5. Have the class practice making a fist. Have them hold the fists in front of body in order that you may check form. Watch for "loose" thumbs.

6. Have the class practice driving both hands through. Start with left arm in extended position. Give commands with force to keep action moving.
Command—Ready, Strike! Shorten to—Strike!

7. Have the class practice driving both hands through, always bringing the thumb back to the nose.
Command—Ready, Strike! Shorten to—Strike!

8. Have the class practice as above, but watching only the returning hand. The hand should always be brought back to a position directly in front of the face.
Command—Ready, Strike! Shorten to—Strike!

9. Have the class practice driving both hands through for two minutes. Form must be maintained. Work for speed.
Command—Ready, Begin!

DRILL 6—THE LEFT JAB TO THE CHIN

Technique Drill

1. Explain and demonstrate the left jab to the chin.
   — The extension of the left arm.
   — The quarter-turn of the body.
   — The quarter-turn and left arm extension.
   —

2. Have the class practice the left jab.
Command—Left jab, Ready, Strike! Shorten to—Strike!

3. Have the class practice the step-jab. As the jab is delivered with the left hand, step forward with the left foot, foot and hand landing together, right foot remaining in place. As the hand folds to the body, the left foot returns to the proper position.
Command—Ready, Strike!

4. Have the class practice the double jab, two jabs in succession.
Command—Double jab, Ready, Strike!

5. Have class practice the slow advance and left jab. As the left jab is landed, step forward with left foot, moving right foot immediately to position. The left hand and left foot work in unison. As the left arm retracts to the body, the right foot moves to position.
Command—Advance, Ready, Strike! Shorten to—Ready, Strike! Then to just—Strike!

6. Have the class practice the left jab and quick advance. Action is the same as described above.
Command—As above.

7. Have the class practice the left jab and slow retreat. Step back with the right foot, and as the weight shifts to the right foot, jab the left arm into extension. The left arm folds to the body as the left foot moves to position.
Command—Retreat, Ready, Strike! Shorten to—Ready, Strike!

8. Have the class practice the left jab and quick retreat. Action is the same as described above.
Command—Retreat, Ready, Strike!

9. Have the class practice the left jab combined with the left step. As the left step is taken, jab with the left hand. As the arm folds to the body move the right foot to position.
Command—-Left step, Ready, Strike!

10. Have the class practice the left jab combined with the right step. As the right step is taken jab the left arm into extension as the weight is shifted to the right leg. As the left arm folds to the body, move the left foot to position.

Command—Right step, Ready, Strike!

Hitting Drill

1. Inboard men—Hold the right glove, palm open and toward partner, directly in front of the right shoulder.

Outboard men—On command, drive a left jab to the target.

Command—Ready, Strike! Shorten to—Strike!

2. Inboard men—Hold right glove as described above.

Outboard men—On command, drive a double left jab to target.

Command—Ready, Strike!

3. Inboard men—Hold both hands, palm open and toward partner, directly off the left and right shoulders respectively.

Outboard men—On command, jab first to partner's right glove, then to his left glove. One blow on each command.

Command—Ready, Strike! (Jab to partner's right glove). Ready, Strike! (Jab to partner's left glove). Later, on command, deliver two jabs consecutively, first to the partner's right glove, then to his left.

Command—Ready, Strike! (Two jabs in succession).

DRILL 7—THE STOP BLOCK FOR THE LEFT JAB TO THE CHIN—THE INSIDE OR LEVERAGE GUARD FOR THE JAR TO THE CHIN

Blocking Drill

1. Inboard men—On command, lead a slow left jab to the chin.
Outboard men—Practice the stop block for the left jab.
Command—On Guard, Hep! Left jab, Ready, Strike! Shorten to—Ready, Strike!

2. Both men—On command. practice the return jab and stop.
Command—Start each student with his arm extended, his glove hand placed in the open palm of his partner's left glove. On the command of Ready! both men retract their left to the on guard position. Then on the command of Strike! drive a left jab to the partner's open right glove. Then on the command of Ready! both men retract their left arms ready to jab again on the command of Strike!

3. Inboard men—On command, lead a slow left jab.
Outboard men—Practice the inside guard.
Command—On guard, Hep! Left jab, Ready, Strike! Shorten to—Ready, Strike!

4. Inboard men—On command, lead a slow left jab to the chin.
Outboard men—Practice the stop block or the inside guard.
Command—Ready, Strike! Shorten to—Strike!

5. Inboard men—On command, lead a slow left jab.
Outboard men—-Practice either the stop block or the inside guard.
Command—Ready, Strike! Shorten to—Strike!

Defensive Boxing

1. Inboard men-—Use only the left jab to the chin.
Outboard men—On defense only. Use of stop block should be stressed.

2. Inboard men—Use only the left jab to the chin.
Outboard men—On defense only. Use of the inside guard should be stressed.

Controlled Boxing

1. Inboard men—Use only the left jab to chin and the stop block.
Outboard men—Use only the left jab to chin, and the inside guard.

2. Both men—Use the left jab to chin and the stop block and the inside guard.

DRILL 8—PARRYING TO THE INSIDE GUARD POSITION ON A LEFT JAB—PARRYING TO THE OUTSIDE GUARD POSITION ON A LEFT JAB—THE CROSS PARRY ON A LEFT JAB—STOPPING ON A LEFT JAB

Blocking Drill

1. Inboard men—On command, lead a slow left jab to the chin.
Outboard men—Practice partying to the inside guard position.
Command—Ready, In! or Ready, Strike!

2. Inboard men—On command, lead a slow left jab to chin.
Outboard men—Practice parrying to the outside guard position.
Command—Ready, Out! or Ready, Strike!

3. Inboard men—On command, lead a slow left jab to chin.
Outboard men—Practice the cross parry.
Command—Ready, Strike!

4. Inboard men—On command, lead a slow left jab to chin.
Outboard men—Practice either the inside or the outside parry—depending or command given.
Command—Ready, In! Ready, Out!

5. Inboard men—On command, lead a slow left jab to chin.
Outboard men—Practice either the inside parry or the cross parry.
Command—Ready, Strike!

6. Inboard men—On command, lead a slow left jab to chin.
Outboard men—Practice inside parry, the outside parry or cross parry.
Command—Ready, Strike!

7. Inboard men—On command, lead a slow left jab to chin.
Outboard men—Practice stopping with both right and left gloves.
Command—Ready, Strike!

Defensive Boxing

1. Inboard men—Use only the left jab to the chin.
Outboard men—On defense, practicing the inside parry.

2. Inboard men—Use only the left jab to the chin.
Outboard men—On defense, practicing the outside parry.

3. Inboard men—Use only the left jab to the chin.

Outboard men—On defense, practicing the cross parry.

4. Inboard men—Use only the left jab to the chin.
Outboard men—On defense, practicing stopping on opponent's lead.

Controlled Boxing

1. Both men—Use only left jab to chin, and any defensive movements known.

DRILL 9—SLIPPING TO THE INSIDE GUARD POSITION ON A LEFT JAB—SLIPPING TO THE OUTSIDE GUARD POSITION ON A LEFT JAB— CUFFING ON A LEFT JAB

Technique Drill

1. Explain and demonstrate:
Slipping to the inside guard position.
Slipping to the outside guard position.
Cuffing up.
Cuffing down.

2. Have the class practice slipping to the inside guard position.
Inboard men—Hold left arm in extended jab position.
Outboard men—Slip to the inside guard position.
Command—Ready, Hep! or Ready, In!

3. Have the class practice slipping to the outside guard position.
Inboard men—Hold left arm in extended jab position.
Outboard men—Slip to outside guard position.
Command—Ready, Hep! or Ready, In!

4. Have class practice slipping to either the inside or outside guard position.
Inboard men—Hold left arm in extended jab position.
Outboard men—Slip either to the inside guard position or to the outside guard position as indicated by command.
Command—-Ready, In! Ready, Out!

5. Inboard men—As above.
Outboard men—Lead a left jab to the chin. Start slowly and speed up as movement is perfected.
Command—Ready, In! or Ready, Out!

6. Have the class practice cuffing the left lead down.
Inboard men—Hold left arm in extended jab position.
Outboard men—Practice cuffing left lead downward.
Command—Ready, Cuff! or Ready, Strike!

7. Have the class practice cuffing the left lead up.
Inboard men—Hold left arm in extended jab position.
Outboard men—Practice cuffing left lead upward.
Command—Ready, Cuff! or Ready, Strike!

8. Have the class practice cuffing either up or down.

Inboard men—Hold the left arm in extended jab position.

Outboard men—Practice cuffing up or down according to command.

Command—Ready, Up! or Ready, Down! etc.

9. Inboard men—Same as outboard man above.

Outboard men—Lead a slow left jab to the chin.

Command—Ready, Up! or Ready, Down!

10. Have class practice either slipping or cuffing.

Inboard men—Lead slow jab on command.

Outboard men—Practice slipping or cuffing as indicated by command.

Command—Ready, In! (Slip in). Ready, Out! (Slip out). Ready, Up (Cuff up), Ready, Down! (Cuff down).

Defensive Boxing

1. Inboard men—Use only a left jab to the chin.

Outboard men—On defense only, using the inside slip.

2. Inboard men—Use only a left jab to the chin.

Outboard men—On defense only, using the outside slip.

3. Inboard men—Use only a left jab to the chin.

Outboard men—On defense only, slipping to either the inside or outside guard position.

4. Inboard men—Use only a left jab to the chin.

Outboard men—On defense only, cuffing up or down.

5. Inboard men—Use only a left jab to the chin.

Outboard men—On defense only, slipping or culling.

Controlled Boxing

1. Inboard men—Left jab to chin only. Defensive technique. slipping to inside or outside guard position.

Outboard men—Left jab to chin only. Defensive technique, cuffing up or down.

DRILL 10—COVERING AND FOLDING—ROLLING AND WEAVING— THE SNAP AWAY

Technique Drill

1. Explain and demonstrate:
Covering and folding.
Rolling and weaving.
The snap away.

2. Have the class practice covering.
Command—Ready, Cover!

3. Have the class practice folding.
Command—Ready, Fold!

4. Have the class practice rolling.
Command—Ready, Move!

5. Have the class practice the weaving movement.
Command-—One, Two, Three. On One, have class slip to inside, on Two, move to outside guard position, body low; on Three, reassume the on guard position; or on One, have the class slip to the outside guard position; on Two, move to the inside guard position; body kept low; on Three, reassume the on guard position.

6. Have the class practice the snap away.
Command—Ready, Move! or Ready, Strike!

Blocking Drill

1. Inboard men—On command, lead a slow left jab.
Outboard men—Practice covering.
Command—Ready, Strike! or Ready, Cover!

2. Inboard men—On command, lead a slow left jab.
Outboard men—Practice folding under jab.
Command—Ready, Strike! or Ready, Fold!

3. Inboard men—On command, lead a slow left jab.
Outboard men—Practice moving backward with blow.
Command—Ready, Strike! or Ready, move!

4. Inboard men—Hold left arm in extended jab position.
Outboard men—Practice weaving under a jab on command.

Command—Slip to the inside position—One, Two, Three; or slip to the outside position, One, Two, Three! On One, slip to inside guard position; on Two, roll head underneath partner's extended arm to the outside guard position; on Three, reassume the original on guard position; or on One, slip to the outside guard position; on Two, drop head underneath partner's extended left arm and move to the inside guard position; on Three, assume the original on guard position.

5. Inboard men—On command, lead a slow left jab.
Outboard men—Practice the snap away.
Command—Ready, Move! or Ready, Strike!

Defensive Boxing

1. Inboard men—Use only the left jab to the chin.
Outboard men—On defense only, practicing covering and folding.

2. Inboard men—-Use only the left jab to the chin.
Outboard men—On defense only, practicing the snap away.

Controlled Boxing

1. Inboard men—Left jab to the chin only. Defense is covering and folding.
Outboard men—Left jab to the chin only. Defense is rolling and weaving.

2. Inboard men—Left jab to chin only. Defense is the snap away.
Outboard men—Left jab to chin only. All defensive techniques.

DRILL 11—THE COUNTER ATTACK—THE RETURN JAB AS A COUNTER

Hitting Drill

1. Explain and demonstrate the return jab. In order to teach the timing of the opponent's left jab and to get the "feel" of the movement, practice with a partner. Have partner lead a slow left jab. Catch the left jab in the open right glove and hold. Now as partner retracts his left, drive own left into extension.

2. Inboard men—On command, lead slow left jab, carrying right hand in position of block.
Outboard men—Practice return jab to partner's open glove.
Command—Ready, Strike!

Controlled Boxing

1. Inboard men—Use only the left jab to the chin,
Outboard men—Counter with the return jab only.

DRILL 12—THE INSIDE PARRY AND LEFT JAB TO CHIN—THE OUTSIDE PARRY AND LEFT JAB TO CHIN

Technique Drill

1. Explain and demonstrate:
   — The inside parry and left jab to the chin.
   — The outside parry and left jab to the chin.

2. Have class practice the movement of the inside parry and left jab to the chin.
Command—Ready, Parry! or Ready, Strike!

3. Have class practice the movement of the outside parry, and left jab to the chin.
Command—Ready, Parry, or Ready, Strike!

Hitting Drill

1. Inboard men—Hold the left arm in the extended jab position, the right hand, palm open and in front of chin.
Outboard men—On command, practice parrying to the inside guard position, and countering with a left jab to partner's open glove.
Command—Ready, One—Two.
On One, parry to inside guard position; on Two, counter with left jab to chin.

2. Inboard men—On command, lead a slow left jab. Hold the right hand in position of block.
Outboard men—Parry to the inside guard position and counter with a left jab to partner's open glove.
Command—Ready, Strike!

3. Inboard men—Hold the left arm in the extended jab position; the right hand, palm open, in front of chin.
Outboard men—On command, practice parrying to the outside guard position, and countering with jab to partner's open glove.
Command—Ready, One—Two! Parry on One; counter on Two.

4. Inboard men—On command, lead a slow left jab. Hold the right hand, palm open, in front of chin.
Outboard men—Parry to the inside guard position, and counter with a left jab to partner's open glove.
Command—Ready, Strike!

5. Inboard men—On command, lead a slow left jab. Hold the right hand, palm open, in front of chin.

Outboard men—Parry to either the inside guard or outside guard position, and counter with left jab to the chin.

Command—Ready, One! or Ready, Two! One refers to counter number one, the inside parry and left jab to chin; two, refers to counter number two, the outside parry and left jab to chin.

6. Inboard men—On command, lead a slow left jab. Hold the right hand, palm open and in front of chin.

Outboard men—Practice the return jab, the inside parry and left jab or the outside parry and left jab, on command.

Command—Ready, One! or Ready, Two! or Ready, Three! Counter number three in this case would be the return jab. Mix the counters so that action cannot be anticipated.

Controlled Boxing

1. Inboard men—Use only the left jab to chin.
Outboard men—Counter with the inside parry and left jab to the chin.

2. Inboard men—Use only the left jab to the chin.
Outboard men—Counter with the outside parry and the left jab to chin.

3. Inboard men—Use the left lead and return jab to the chin.
Outboard men—Use the left lead and inside parry and left jab to the chin.

4. Inboard men—Use the left lead and return jab to the chin.
Outboard men—Use the left lead and outside parry and left jab to the chin.

5. Inboard men—Use the left lead and outside parry and left jab to the chin.
Outboard men—Use the left lead and inside parry and left jab to the chin.

Teaching drills for the counters for the left jab are fully described in the section on drills.

DRILL 13—THE LEFT JAB TO THE BODY

Technique Drill

1. Explain and demonstrate the left jab to the body.

2. Have the class practice a left jab to the body.
Command—On guard, Left jab to the body, Ready, Strike! Shorten to—Ready, Strike!

3. Have the class practice lunging one step forward as they jab for the body, recovering immediately.
Command—Ready, Strike!

4. Have the class practice the left jab to the body while using the slow advance.
Command—Ready, Strike! Shorten to—Strike!

Hitting Drills

1. Inboard men—Hold the right glove, palm open in front of the solar plexus.
Outboard men—On command, jab to the body.
Command—Left jab to the body, Ready Strike! Shorten to Ready, Strike!

2. Inboard men—Hold both hands, palm open and toward partner, directly in front of the left and right hip.
Outboard men—On command, jab first to partner's right glove, and then to his left glove. On the first command, jab to the left; on the next command, jab to the right. One command for each blow.
Command—Left jab to body, Ready, Strike!

3. Inboard men—Hold hands in the same position as in the above drill.
Outboard men—On command, jab twice in succession to the body. The first to the left, the second to the right.
Command—Ready, Strike! (Two blows)

Defensive Boxing

1. Inboard men—Use only the left jab to the body.
Outboard men—On defense only.

2. Inboard men—Use only the left jab to the chin.
Outboard men—On defense only.

3. Both men—Use only left jab to face or body.

Controlled Boxing

1. Inboard men—Use only the left jab to the chin
Outboard men—Use only the left jab to the body.

2. Inboard men—Use only the left jab to the chin, and the left jab to the body
Outboard men—Use only the left jab to the body.

3. Both men—Use the left jab to the chin and body.

DRILL 14—DEFENSE FOR THE LEET JAB TO THE BODY

THE ELBOW BLOCK, THE FOREARM BLOCK, THE BRUSH AWAY, THE STEP AWAY

Technique Drill

1. Explain and demonstrate:
    — The elbow block.
    — The forearm block.
    — The brush away.
    — The step away.

2. Have the class practice the movement of the elbow block.
Command—Ready, Turn!

3. Have the class practice the movement of the forearm block.
Command—Ready, Fold!

4. Have the class practice the movement of the brush away.
Command—Ready, Brush!

5. Have the class practice the foot movement of the step away.
Command—Ready, Shift!

6. Have the class practice the complete movement of the step away.
Command—Ready, Shift!

Blocking Drills

1. Inboard men—On command, lead a left jab to the body.
Outboard men—Practice the elbow block.
Command—Ready, Strike!

2. Inboard men—On command, lead a left jab to the body.
Outboard men—Practice the forearm block.
Command—Ready, Strike!

3. Inboard men—On command, lead a left jab to the body.
Outboard men—Practice the brush away.
Command—Ready, Strike !

4. Inboard men—On command, lead left jab to the body.
Outboard men—Practice the step away.
Command—Ready, Strike!

Defensive Boxing

1. Inboard men—Use only the left jab to the body.
Outboard men—On defense only.

2. Inboard men—Use either a left jab to the head or a left jab to the body.
Outboard men—On defense only.

Controlled Boxing

1. Inboard men—Use only the left jab to the body.
Outboard men—Use only the left jab to the chin.

2. Inboard men—Use only the left jab to the chin or body.
Outboard men—Use only the left jab to the body.

DRILL 15—THE COUNTER ATTACK

THE OUTSIDE SLIP AND LEFT JAB TO THE BODY—THE INSIDE SLIP AND LEFT JAB TO THE BODY

Technique Drill

1. Explain and demonstrate:
    — The outside slip and left jab to the body.
    — The inside slip and left jab to the body.

2. Have the class practice the outside slip and left jab to the body.
Command—Ready, Counter! or Ready, Hep!

3. Have the class practice the inside slip and left jab to the solar plexus.
Command—Ready, Counter! or Ready, Hep!

Hitting Drill

1. Inboard men—On command, lead a left jab to the chin. Hold the right hand, palm open, directly in front of the solar plexus.
Outboard men—Practice the outside slip and left jab to the body.
Command—Ready, Strike!

2. Inboard men—On command, lead a left jab to the chin. Hold the right hand, palm open, directly in front of solar plexus.
Outboard men—Practice the inside slip and left jab to the body.
Command—Ready, Strike!

3. Inboard men—As above.
Outboard men—Practice either the inside slip or outside slip and left jab to the body, as indicated by the command.
Command—Ready, In! or Ready, Out! The two commands could be numbered as follows:
Number one—Outside parry and left jab to body.
Number two—Inside parry and left jab to body.
Command—Ready, One! or Ready, Two!

Blocking Drill

1. Inboard men—On command, lead a left jab to chin. Practice the brush away for the left jab to body.
Outboard men—Practice the inside slip and left jab to body.
Command—Ready, Strike!

2. Inboard men—As above.

Outboard men—Practice either the outside or the inside parry and left jab to body.
Command—Ready, Strike!

Controlled Boxing

1. Inboard men—Use only the left jab to chin.
Outboard men—Use only the outside slip and left jab to the body.

2. Inboard men—Use only the left jab to the chin.
Outboard men—Use only the inside slip and left jab to the body.

3. Inboard men—Use only the left jab to the chin.
Outboard men—Use either the inside or outside slip and left jab to the body.
4. Inboard men—Use only the left jab to the chin, and the inside slip and left jab to the body.
Outboard men—Use only the left jab to the chin, and the outside slip and left jab to the body.

5. Both men—Use left jab to chin and either the inside slip or outside slip and left jab to the body.

DRILL 16—COMBINATIONS

THE LEFT JAB TO THE CHIN FOLLOWED BY THE LEFT JAB TO THE BODY—THE LEFT JAB TO THE BODY FOLLOWED BY THE LEFT JAB TO THE CHIN

Technique Drill

1. Explain and demonstrate:
   — The left jab to the chin and the left jab to the body.
   — The left jab to the body and the left jab to the chin.

2. Have the class practice the left jab to the chin and the left jab to the body.
Command—Ready, Jab up! Jab down! or Ready—One—Two!
3. Have the class practice the left jab to the body followed by the left jab to the chin.
Command—Ready, Jab down! Jab up! or Ready, One—Two!

Hitting Drill

1. Inboard men—Hold the left glove directly in front of the left; hip, palm open and toward partner. Hold the right glove in front of right shoulder. palm open and toward partner.
Outboard men—On command, jab high to partner's right glove, then follow with low jab to partner's open left glove.
Command—Ready, Jab up! Jab down! or Ready, One—Two!

2. Inboard men—Hold hands as described above.
Outboard men—On command, jab low to partner's open left glove, then high to partner's right glove.
Command—Reddy, Jab down! Jab up! or Ready, One—Two!

Blocking Drill

1. Inboard men—On command, practice the left jab to the chin followed by the left jab to the body.
Outboard men—Defend by using a catch for partner's left jab to chin, and the brush away with the right hand for partner's left to the body.
Command—Ready, One—Two! On One, jab for chin, on Two, jab for body, or Ready, Strike!

2. Inboard men—On command, practice the left jab to the body, followed by left jab to the chin.
Outboard men—Use a right elbow block for partner's left to body and the parry for partner's left jab.
Command—Ready, One—Two! Jab down on One, Jab up on Two, or Ready, Strike!

3. Inboard men—On command, practice either the left jab to chin or left jab to the body, or the left jab to body and the left jab to the chin.
Outboard men—As above.
Command—Ready Strike!

Defensive Boxing

1. Inboard men—Use only the left jab to the chin and the left jab to the body.
Outboard men—On defense only.

2. Inboard men—Use only the left jab to the body and the left jab to the chin.
Outboard men—On defense only.

3. Inboard men—Use either the left jab to body and the left jab to the chin, or the left jab to the chin and the left jab to the body.
Outboard men—On defense only.

Controlled Boxing

1. Inboard men—Use only the left jab to the chin and the left jab to the body.
Outboard men—Use only the left jab to the chin.

2. Inboard men—Use only the left jab to the body and the left jab to the chin
Outboard men—Use only the left jab to the body.

3. Both men—Left jab to face or body, any sequence or combination.

DRILL 17—COMBINATIONS

THE DOUBLE LEFT JAB TO THE CHIN—THE DOUBLE LEFT JAB TO THE BODY

Technique Drill

1. Explain and demonstrate:
    — The double left jab to the chin.
    — The double left jab to the body.

2. Have the class practice the double left jab to the chin.
Command—Double jab, Ready, Strike!

3. Have the class practice the double left jab to the body.
Command—Double jab to the body, Ready, Strike! Shorten to—Ready, Strike!

Hitting Drill

1. Inboard men—Hold the right glove as a target, palm open, directly in front of the right shoulder.
Outboard men—On command, step in with double left jab to target.
Command—Ready, Strike!

2. Inboard men—Hold both gloves directly in front of left and right shoulders as targets, palms open toward partner.
Outboard men—On command, step in with double left jab to partner's right glove, then to his left glove.
Command—Ready, Strike! Drive a double left jab to partner's right glove. On the next command of Strike! drive a double left jab to partner's left glove.

3. Inboard men—Hold gloves as described above.
Outboard men—On command, drive a double left jab first to partner's open right glove, then to his left.
Command—Ready, Strike!

4. Inboard men—Hold the gloves directly in front of each hip, palm open and toward partner.
Outboard men—On command, drive a double left jab to partner's open right glove.
Command—Ready, Strike!

5. Inboard men—Hold gloves as described above.
Outboard men—On command, drive a double left jab first to partner's right glove, then to his left.
Command—Ready, Strike!

6. Inboard men—Hold right glove, palm open and toward partner, in front of right shoulder; left glove, palm open and toward opponent in front of solar plexus.

Outboard men—On command, drive a double jab to chin, followed by double jab to body.

Command—Ready, Strike! (Double jab to chin) Ready, Strike! (Double jab to body)

7. Inboard men—Hold gloves as described above.

Outboard men—On command, drive a double left jab to body, followed by a double left jab to chin.

Command—Ready, Strike! One command, one double blow. Change so that on command, a double jab is delivered first to the body then to the chin, on one command.

Command—Ready, Strike!

Defensive Boxing

1. Inboard men—Use only the double left jab to the chin.
Outboard men—On defense only.

2. Inboard men—Use only the double left jab to the body.
Outboard men—On defense only.

3. Inboard men—Use double left jab to head or body.
Outboard men—On defense only.

Controlled Boxing

1. Inboard men—Use only the double left jab to the chin.
Outboard men—Use only the double left jab to the body.

2. Inboard men—Use only the double left jab to the head or body.
Outboard men—Use only the double left jab to the head.

3. Both men—Use only the double left jab to the chin.

4. Both men—Use only the double left jab to the body.

5. Both men—Use only the double left jab to the head or body.

DRILL 18—THE LEFT HOOK TO THE CHIN

Technique Drill

1. Explain and demonstrate the left hook to the chin.

2. Have the class practice the left hook to the chin.
Command—Ready, One! or Ready, Pivot! Turn the body to the right, shifting to the right foot.
Command—Ready, Two! Turn away from the left hand which remains stationary, left elbow raised slightly.
Command—Ready, Three! Whip the left arm in an arc to the right shoulder. Now shorten the command to two counts. Ready, One—Two! On One, pivot the body to right, shifting the weight to the right foot, at the same time raising the left elbow to the proper hook position; on Two, whip the left arm to the right shoulder. The final command should be Ready, Strike! Insist that the hip and shoulder turn to the center line before the arm is pulled to the right shoulder. This is a power blow, so demand forceful execution of the blow.

Hitting Drill

1. Inboard men—-Hold the left glove directly off the left shoulder, palm open and turned inward.
Outboard men—On command, hook a hard left to partner's open glove.
Command—Ready, Strike!

2. Inboard men—Hold the left glove in the position described above.
Outboard men—On command, drive two left hooks to partner's open glove
Command—Ready, Strike!

Controlled Boxing

1. Inboard men—Use only the left hook to the chin.
Outboard men—Use only a left jab to the chin.
Both men—Use the left jab to the chin and the left hook to the chin.

DRILL 19—DEFENSE FOR THE LEFT HOOK TO THE CHIN

THE FOREARM BLOCK—THE DUCK—THE STEP BACK—CIRCLING TO THE LEFT

Technique Drill

1. Explain and demonstrate the different forms of defense for the left hook to the chin:
    — The forearm block.
    — Ducking.
    — The step back.
    — Circling to the left.

2. Have class practice the forearm block.
Command—Ready, Block!

3. Have the class practice ducking.
Command—Ready, Duck!

4. Have the class practice the step back.
Command—-Ready, Move! or Ready, Hep!

5. Have the class practice circling to the left.
Command—Ready, Hep!

Blocking Drill

1. Inboard men—On command, hook the left to the chin.
Outboard men—Practice the forearm block.
Command—Ready, Block! or Ready, Strike!

2. Inboard men—On command, lead a left hook to the chin.
Outboard men—Practice ducking under the left hook.
Command—Ready Duck! or Ready, Swing!
3. Inboard men—On command, lead a left hook to the chin.
Outboard men—Practice the step back.
Command—Ready, Move! or Ready, Strike!

4. Inboard men—On command, lead a left hook to the chin.
Outboard men—Practice Circling to the left.
Command—Ready, Move! or Ready, Strike!

Defensive Boxing

1. Inboard men—Use only the left hook to the chin.

Outboard men—On defense; use the forearm block only.

2. Inboard men—Use only the left hook to the chin.
Outboard men—On defense; use the duck only.

3. Inboard men—Use only the left hook to the chin.
Outboard men—On defense; use the step back only.

4. Inboard men—Use only the left hook to chin.
Outboard men—On defense; practice circling to the left, carry the right hand high and in position of guard.

Controlled Boxing

1. Inboard men—Use only the left hook to the chin.
Outboard men—Use only the left jab to the chin.

2. Inboard men—Use only the left hook to the body.
Outboard men—Use only the left jab to the chin.

3. Inboard men—Use only the left jab and the left hook to the chin.
Outboard men—Use only the left jab to the chin and body.

4. Both men—Use only the left hook to the chin.

5. Both men—Use only the left jab to face and body and left hook to the chin.

DRILL 20—THE LEFT HOOK TO THE CHIN AS A COUNTER

THE INSIDE GUARD AND LEFT HOOK TO THE CHIN—THE INSIDE HOOK ON A STRAIGHT RIGHT LEAD—THE CROSS PARRY AND LEFT HOOK TO THE CHIN ON A STRAIGHT RIGHT LEAD

Technique Drill

1 Explain and demonstrate:
— The inside guard and left hook to the chin.
— The inside hook on a straight right lead.
— The cross parry and left hook to the chin on a straight right lead.

2. Have the class practice the movement of the inside guard and left hook to the chin.
Command—Ready, Counter!

3. Have the class practice the movement of the inside hook on a straight right lead.
Command—Ready, Counter!

4. Have the class practice the movement of the cross parry and left hook to the chin on a straight right lead.
Command—Ready, Counter!

Hitting Drill

1. Inboard men—On command, lead a left jab to the chin. Hold the right glove high in front of chin, palm turned outward.
Outboard men—Practice the inside guard and left hook to the chin.
Command—Ready, One—Two! On One, parry to the inside guard position; on Two, counter with a left hook to opponent's chin. Shorten to—Ready, Strike!

2. Inboard men—On command, lead a straight right to the chin. Hold the left hand high in front of chin, palm open and turned toward partner.
Outboard men—Practice the inside left hook to the partner's glove.
Command—Ready, Strike!

3. Inboard men—On command, lead a straight right to the chin. Hold the left hand high in front of chin, palm open and turned toward partner.
Outboard men—Practice the cross parry and the inside left hook to the chin.
Command—Ready, One—Two! On One, perform the cross parry; on Two, hook a left inside to partner's glove.

4. Inboard men—On command, lead a straight left or right to chin. Right hand is held open, palm outward, in front of the face.

Outboard men—Practice any of the three counters, depending on the command.
Command—Ready, One! or Ready, Two! or Ready, Three! One, refers to the inside guard and left hook to chin, on a left lead; Two, refers to the inside hook on a straight right lead; Three, the cross parry and inside hook on a right lead.

Blocking Drill

1. Inboard men—On command, lead a left jab to chin. Block partner's left hook with a right forearm block.
Outboard men—Practice the inside guard and left hook to chin.
Command—Ready, Strike!

2. Inboard men On command, lead a straight right to the chin. Block partner's left hook with a left stop block.
Outboard men—Practice the inside left hook on straight right lead.
Command—Ready, Strike!

3. Inboard men—As above.
Outboard men—Practice the cross parry and left hook to chin.
Command—Ready, Strike!

4. Inboard men—On command, lead either a straight left or a right to the chin. Be ready to block partner's left hook counter.
Outboard men—On command, practice the counter called for.
Command—Ready One! or Ready, Two! or Ready, Three! One, refers to the inside guard and left hook to the chin. Two, refers to the inside hook on straight right lead. Three, refers to the cross parry and left hook on straight right lead.

Controlled Boxing

1. Inboard men—Use only a left jab to the chin.
Outboard men—Use only the inside guard and left hook to the chin.

2. Inboard men—Use only a straight right to the chin.
Outboard men—Use only the inside hook.

3. Inboard men—Use only a straight right to the chin.
Outboard men—Use only the cross parry and left hook to the chin.

DRILL 21—COUNTERS FOR A LEFT HOOK TO THE CHIN

THE LEFT JAB—THE STRAIGHT RIGHT—THE RETURN HOOK TO THE CHIN

Technique Drill

1. Explain and demonstrate the following counters for the left hook to the chin:
   — The left jab.
   — The straight right.
   — The return hook.

2. Have the class practice the movement of countering with a left jab, straight right and return hook.
Command—Ready, Strike!

Hitting Drill

1. Inboard men—On command, lead a left hook to the chin. Hold the right hand, palm open and toward partner, directly in front of the chin.
Outboard men—Practice countering with a left jab to partner's right glove.
Command—Ready, Strike!

2. Inboard men—As above.
Outboard men—Practice countering with a straight right to partner's right glove.
Command—Ready, Strike!

3. Inboard men—As above.
Outboard men—Practice countering with a return left hook.
Command—Ready, Strike!

Blocking Drill

1. Inboard men—On command, lead a left hook to the chin. Use a stop block for left jab to the chin.
Outboard men—Practice the left jab to the chin as a counter.
Command—Ready, Strike!

2. Inboard men—On command, lead a left hook to the chin. Use a stop block for the straight right to the chin.
Outboard men—Practice the straight right to the chin as a counter.
Command—Ready, Strike!

3. Inboard men—On command, lead a left hook to the chin. Use a forearm block for the left hook to the chin.

Outboard men—Practice the return left hook to the chin as a counter.
Command—Ready, Strike!

Controlled Boxing

1. Inboard men—Use only the left hook to the chin.
Outboard men—Counter with the left jab.

2. Inboard men—Use only the left hook to the chin.
Outboard men—Counter with a straight right.

3. Inboard men—Use only the left hook to the chin.
Outboard men—Counter with a return hook.

DRILL 22—COMBINATION BLOWS

USING THE LEFT HOOK TO THE CHIN AND THE LEFT JAB TO HEAD AND BODY—THE JAB, STEP AND HOOK

Technique Drill

1. Explain and demonstrate the jab, step and hook, breaking it down into the following units:
   — The extended arm hook.
   — The jab-hook.
   — The jab-step.
   — The jab-step and hook.

2. Have class practice the extended arm hook.
Command—Ready, Strike!

3. Have class practice the jab—step.
Command—Ready, Jab, Hook! or Ready, One! Two! Jab on One, hook on Two.

4. Have the class practice the jab-step.
Command—Ready, Jab, Step! or Ready, One, Two!

5. Have the class practice the complete movement of the jab-step and hook.
Command—Jab, Step, Hook! or Ready, One! Two! Three!

Hitting Drill

1. Inboard men—Hold the right glove in front of the right shoulder, palm open and turned outward toward the opponent. Hold the left hand directly off the left shoulder, palm open and turned inward.
Outboard men—On command, lead a left jab to partner's right glove and left hook to partner's left glove.
Command—Ready, One, Two! Jab on One, hook on Two! Shorten to Ready, Strike!

Blocking Drill

1. Inboard men—On command, practice the left jab to the chin, and the left hook to the chin.
Outboard men—Be ready to block the left jab with a stop block, and the left hook with a forearm block.
Command—Ready, One, Two! Shorten to Ready, Strike!

Defensive Boxing

1. Inboard men—Use only the jab, step and hook.
Outboard men—On defense only.

DRILL 23—COMBINATION BLOWS CONTINUED

THE LEFT JAB TO THE BODY AND THE LEFT HOOK TO THE CHIN

Technique Drill

1. Explain and demonstrate:
    — The left jab to the body and the left hook to the chin.

2. Have the class practice the left jab to the body and the left hook to the chin
Command—Ready, Down, Up! or Ready, One, Two!

Hitting Drill

1. Inboard men—Hold the right hand in front of the solar plexus, palm open and toward partner; hold glove directly off the left shoulder, palm open and turned inward.
Outboard men—On command, jab to the partner's open right hand, and hook the left to partner's open left glove.
Command—Ready, One, Two! or Down, Up!

Blocking Drill

1. Inboard men—On command, practice the left jab to the body, and the left hook to the chin.
Outboard men—Be ready to block the left jab to the body with a brush away, and the left hook to the chin with a forearm block.
Command—Ready, One, Two! On One, jab; on Two hook. Shorten to Ready, Strike!

Defensive Boxing

1. Inboard men—Use only the left jab to the body, and the left hook to the chin.
Outboard men—On defense only.

Controlled Boxing

1. Inboard men—Use Only the left jab to the chin.
Outboard men—Use only the left jab to the body and the left hook to the chin.

DRILL 24—COMBINAATIONS CONTINUED

THE LEFT JAB TO THE CHIN, THE LEFT JAB TO THE BODY AND THE LEFT HOOK TO THE CHIN

Technique Drill

1. Explain and demonstrate:
The left jab to the chin, the left jab to the body and the left hook to the chin.

2. Have the class practice the above technique.
Command—Ready, One, Two, Three! On One, jab to the chin; on Two, jab to the body; on Three, hook to the chin.

Hitting Drill

1. Inboard men—Hold the left glove in front of the chin, palm open toward partner; hold the right hand directly in front of the solar plexus, palm open toward partner.
Outboard men—On command, jab to the chin, then to the body, following with a left hook to the chin.
Command—Ready, One, Two, Three!

Blocking Drill

1. Inboard men—On command, practice the left jab to the chin, the left jab to the body, following with a left hook to the chin.
Outboard men—Be ready to block the left jab to the chin with a stop block, the left jab to the body with a cross brush, and the left hook to the chin with the forearm block.
Command—Ready, One, Two, Three! Shorten to Ready, Strike!

Defensive Boxing

1. Inboard men—Use only the left jab to body and left hook to the chin.
Outboard men—On defense only.

2. Inboard men—Use the left jab to chin or body and the left hook to the chin.
Outboard men—On defense only.

Controlled Boxing

1. Inboard men—Use only the left hook to the chin.
Outboard men—Use only the left jab to the body.

2. Inboard men—Use only the left jab to body and the left hook to the chin.
Outboard men—Use only the left jab to head or body.

3. Inboard men—Use the left jab to head or body and left hook to chin.
Outboard men—Use only the left hook to the chin.

DRILL 25—THE LEFT UPPERCUT TO THE BODY

Technique Drill

1. Explain and demonstrate the left uppercut to the body.

2. Have the class practice the left uppercut to the body.
Command—Ready, One, Two, Three! On One, drop directly to the left; on Two, pivot to right so left hand, palm up, is directly at the midline of the body; on Three, straighten the knees, lift the trunk upward, and whip the left hand, palm up, to opponent's solar plexus.

Hitting Drill

1. Inboard men—Hold the open left glove, palm turned downward, directly in front of the left hip.
Outboard men—On command, whip a left uppercut to partner's open left glove.
Command—Ready, Strike!

2. Inboard men—Hold both gloves, palm downward and open off the left and right hips respectively.
Outboard men—on command, whip a left uppercut to partner's left glove, then follow with a left uppercut to his right glove. One uppercut on each command.
Command—Ready, Strike! Ready, Strike!

3. Inboard men—Hold gloves as described above.
Outboard men—On command, whip the left uppercuts in succession, first to partner's left glove, then to his right glove.
Command—Ready, Strike! (Two blows)

Defensive Boxing

1. Inboard men—Use only the left uppercut to the body.
Outboard men—On defense only.

Controlled Boxing

1. Inboard men—Use only a left jab to the chin.
Outboard men—Use only a left uppercut to the body.

2. Inboard men—Use only a left hook to chin.
Outboard men—Use only a left uppercut to the body.

3. Inboard men—Use only a left jab to the body.
Outboard men—Use only a left uppercut to the body.

4. Both men—Use only the left uppercut to the body.

DRILL 26—DEFENSE FOR LEFT UPPERCUT TO BODY
THE BRUSH AWAY—THE FOREARM BLOCK—THE STEP BACK

Technique Drill

1. Explain and demonstrate:
    — The brush away.
    — The forearm block.
    — The step back.

2. Have class practice the brush away.
Command—Ready, Brush! or Ready, Hep!

3. Have the class practice the forearm block.
Command—Ready, Block! or Ready, Hep!

4. Have the class practice the step back.
Command—Ready, Move! or Ready, Hep!

Blocking Drill

1. Inboard men—On command, lead a left uppercut to the body.
Outboard men—Practice the brush away defense.
Command—Ready, Strike! or Ready, Brush!

2. Inboard men—On command, lead a left uppercut to the body.
Outboard men—Practice the forearm block.
Command—Ready, Strike! or Ready, Brush!

3. Inboard men—On command, lead a left uppercut to body.
Outboard men—Practice the step back.
Command—Ready, Strike! Ready, Move! or Ready, Step!

Defensive Boxing

1. Inboard men—Use only left uppercut to body.
Outboard men—On defense; use the brush away only.

2. Inboard men—Use only the left uppercut to the body.
Outboard men—On defense; use the forearm block only.

3. Inboard men—Use only the left uppercut to the body.
Outboard men—Use the stop block only.

Controlled Boxing

1. Inboard men—Use only the left jab to the chin.
Outboard men—Use only the left uppercut to the body.

2. Both men—Use only the left uppercut to the body.

DRILL 27—THE LEFT UPPERCUT TO THE BODY AS A COUNTER

THE OUTSIDE PARRY AND LEFT UPPERCUT TO THE SOLAR PLEXUS ON A LEFT JAB TO THE CHIN—THE INSIDE GUARD AND LEFT UPPERCUT TO THE LIVER ON A LEET JAB TO THE CHIN—THE CROSS PARRY AND LEFT UPPERCUT TO THE LIVER ON A STRAIGHT RIGHT LEAD

Technique Drill

1. Explain and demonstrate:
    — The outside parry and left uppercut to the solar plexus on a left jab.
    — The inside guard and left uppercut to the liver on a left jab to the chin.
    — The cross parry and left uppercut to the liver on a straight right lead.

2. Have the class practice the movement of the outside parry and left uppercut to the solar plexus.
Command—Ready, One, Two! Parry on One; uppercut on Two. Shorten to—Ready, Strike!

3. Have the class practice the movement of the inside guard and left uppercut to the liver.
Command—Ready, One, Two! Guard on One; uppercut on Two. Shorten to—Ready, Strike!

4. Have the class practice the cross parry and left uppercut to the liver on a straight right lead.
Command—Ready, One, Two! Cross parry on One; uppercut on Two. Shorten to—Ready, Strike!

Hitting Drill

1. Inboard men—On command, lead a left jab to the chin. Hold the right glove, palm open and downward, directly in front of the solar plexus.
Outboard men—Practice the outside parry and left uppercut to the solar plexus.
Command—Ready, One, Two! One, parry; on Two, counter with left uppercut to solar plexus. Shorten to—Ready, Strike!

2. Inboard men—On command, lead a left jab to the chin. Hold the right glove, palm open and downward, directly in front of the solar plexus.
Outboard men—Practice the inside guard and left uppercut to the liver.
Command—Ready, One, Two! On One, guard to the inside; on Two, counter with left uppercut. Shorten to—Ready, Strike!

3. Inboard men—On command, lead a straight right to the chin. Hold the left hand, glove open, palm turned downward, directly in front of the solar plexus.

Outboard men—Practice the cross parry and left uppercut to the liver.

Command—Ready, One, Two! On One, cross parry; on Two, counter with a left uppercut to partner's open glove. Shorten to Ready, Strike!

4. Inboard men—On command, lead a left jab or a straight right to the chin. Hold the hand opposite from that of the lead directly in front of the solar plexus, palm downward and open.

Outboard men—Practice any of the three counters using the left hook to the body.

Command—Ready, One! or Ready, Two! or Ready, Three! One, refers to the outside parry and left uppercut to the solar plexus on a left lead; Two, refers to the inside guard and left uppercut to liver on a left lead; Three, refers to the cross parry and left uppercut to the liver on a straight right lead.

Blocking Drill

1. Inboard men—On command, lead a left jab to the chin. Be ready to block opponent's left uppercut counter, using a right brush away.

Outboard men—Practice the outside parry and left uppercut to the solar plexus.

Command—Ready, Strike!

2. Inboard men—As above.

Outboard men—Practice the inside guard and left uppercut to the liver.

Command—Ready, Strike!

3. Inboard men—On command, lead a straight right to the chin. Be ready to block opponent's left uppercut counter with the left brush away.

Outboard men—Practice the cross parry and left uppercut to the liver.

Command—Ready, Strike!

Controlled Boxing

1. Inboard men—Use only the left jab to the chin.

Outboard men—Use only the outside parry and left uppercut to the solar plexus, right and left steps.

2. Inboard men—Use only the left jab to the chin.

Outboard men—Use only the inside guard and left uppercut to the liver.

3. Inboard men—Use only the straight right to the chin.

Outboard men—Use only the cross parry and left uppercut to the liver.

DRILL 28—THE COUNTER BLOWS FOR THE LEFT UPPERCUT TO THE BODY

THE LEFT JAB—THE STRAIGHT RIGHT—THE RIGHT HOOK—THE LEFT UPPERCUT

Technique Drill

1. Explain and demonstrate the blows listed above which are used as counters for the left uppercut to the body.

2. Have the class practice the movements of countering with a left jab, a straight right, right hook and a left uppercut.
Command—Ready, Strike!

Hitting Drill

1. Inboard men—On command, lead a left uppercut to the body. Hold the right glove directly in front of the chin, open toward opponent.
Outboard men—Practice countering with a left jab to the partner's open right glove.
Command—Ready, Strike!

2. Inboard men—On command, lead a left uppercut to the body. Hold the right glove directly in front of the chin, palm open and toward opponent.
Outboard men—Practice countering with a straight right to partner's open right glove.
Command—Ready, Strike!

3. Inboard men—As above.
Outboard men—Practice countering with a right hook to partner's open right glove.
Command—Ready, Strike!

4. Inboard men—On command, lead a left uppercut to the body. Hold the right glove directly in front of solar plexus, palm open and downward.
Outboard men—Practice countering with a left uppercut to partner's open right glove.
Command—Ready, Strike!

Blocking Drill

1. Inboard men—On command, lead a left uppercut to the body. Use a stop block for the opponent's counter.
Outboard men—Practice countering with left jab to chin.
Command—Ready, Strike!

2. Inboard men—On command, lead a left uppercut to the body.

Outboard men—Practice countering with a straight right to the chin.
Command—Ready, Strike!

3. Inboard men—On command, lead a left uppercut to the body. Be ready to cross block the opponent's counter blow.
Outboard men—Practice countering with a right hook to the chin.
Command—Ready, Strike!

4. Inboard men—On command, lead a left uppercut to the body. Use the brush away defense on opponent's counter.
Outboard men—Practice countering with a left uppercut to the body.
Command—Ready, Strike!

Controlled Boxing

1. Inboard men—Use only the left uppercut to the body.
Outboard men—Counter with left jab to the chin.

2. Inboard men—Use only the left uppercut to the body.
Outboard men—Counter with straight right to the chin.

3. Inboard men—Use only the left uppercut to the body.
Outboard men—Counter with the right hook to the chin.

4. Inboard men—Use only a left uppercut to the body.
Outboard men—Counter with a left uppercut to the body.

DRILL 29—LEFT JAB AND LEFT UPPERCUT COMBINATION; LEFT UPPERCUT AND LEFT JAB COMBINATION

Technique Drill

1. Explain and demonstrate:
   — The left jab to the chin and the left uppercut to the body.
   — The left uppercut to the body and left jab to the chin.

2. Have class practice the left jab to the chin and the left uppercut to the body.
Command—Ready, One, Two! Jab on One; uppercut to the body on Two.

3. Have class practice the left uppercut to the body and left jab to the chin.
Command—Ready, One, Two! Jab on One; uppercut to the body on Two.

Hitting Drill

1. Inboard men—Hold the right glove high, palm open, directly in front of the right shoulder. Hold the left glove, palm open, directly in front of the solar plexus.
Outboard men—On command, jab to the chin and then drive a left uppercut to the solar plexus.
Command—Ready, One, Two! On One, jab; on Two, drive a left uppercut to the solar plexus.

2. Inboard men—Hold hands in same position as described above.
Outboard men—On command, drive a left uppercut to the solar plexus, followed by a left jab to the chin.
Command—Ready, One, Two! On One, uppercut; on Two, jab to the chin.

Defensive Boxing

1. Inboard men—Use only the left jab to the chin, and the left uppercut to the body. Use any sequence or combination.
Outboard men—On defense only.

Controlled Boxing

1. Inboard men—Use only the left jab to the chin.
Outboard men—Use only the left uppercut to the body.

2. Both men—Use only the left jab to the chin and the left uppercut to the body.

DRILL 30—THE LEFT HOOK TO THE CHIN AND THE LEFT UPPERCUT TO THE BODY COMBINATION—THE LEFT UPPERCUT TO THE BODY AND THE LEET HOOK TO THE CHIN COMBINATION

Technique Drill

1. Explain and demonstrate:
    — The left hook to the chin and the left uppercut to the body.
    — The left uppercut to the body and the left hook to the chin.

2. Have the class practice the left hook to the chin, and left uppercut to body.
Command—Ready, One, Two! Hook on One; uppercut on Two.

3. Explain and demonstrate the left uppercut to the body and left hook to the chin.
Command—Ready, One, Two! Uppercut on One, hook on Two.

Hitting Drill

1. Inboard men—Hold the right arm high and in position of forearm block; left glove, palm open and down, directly in front of the solar plexus.
Outboard men—On command, hook a left to the chin, and follow with left uppercut to the body.
Command—Ready, One, Two! Hook on One; uppercut on Two.

Blocking Drill

1. Inboard men—On command, hook to chin, then drive left uppercut to the body.
Outboard men—Use right glove to brush opponent's left uppercut outward, and then use forearm block to stop the left hook.
Command—Ready, One, Two! On One, hook; on Two, uppercut.

2. Inboard men—On command, drive a left uppercut to the chin, then follow with left hook to chin.
Outboard men—Use right glove to brush opponent's left uppercut outward and then use forearm block to stop the left hook.
Command—Ready, One, Two! On One, uppercut; on Two, hook.

Defensive Boxing

1. Inboard men—Use only the left hook to the chin and the left uppercut to the body.
Outboard men—On defense only.

Controlled Boxing
1. Inboard men—Use only the left hook to the chin.
Outboard men—Use only the left uppercut to the body.
2. Both men—Use only the left hook to the chin, and the left uppercut to the body.

DRILL 31—THE JAB-HOOK AND UPPERCUT COMBINATION—THE JAB-UPPERCUT AND HOOK COMBINATION

Technique Drill

1. Explain and demonstrate:
   — The jab-hook and uppercut.
   — The jab-uppercut and hook.

2. Have class practice the jab-hook and uppercut.
Command—Ready, One, Two, Three! Jab on One; hook on Two; uppercut on Three.

3. Have the class practice the jab-uppercut and hook.
Command—Ready One, Two, Three! Jab on One; uppercut on Two; hook on Three.

Hitting Drill

1. Inboard men—Hold the right glove high and open, in front of the face; hold the left glove, palm open and downward, directly in front of the solar plexus.
Outboard men—On command, jab to chin, hook to chin, then uppercut to body.
Command—Ready, One, Two, Three! On One, jab; on Two, hook; on Three, uppercut.

2. Inboard men—Hold hands as described above.
Outboard men—On command, jab to chin, uppercut to body, then hook to chin.
Command—Ready, One, Two, Three! On One, jab; on Two, uppercut to body; on Three, hook to chin.

Blocking Drill

1. Inboard men—On command, jab to the chin, hook to the chin, then uppercut to the body.
Outboard men—Use the catch for left jab to chin, forearm block for the left I hook, and the brush away for the left uppercut.
Command—Ready, One, Two, Three! On One, jab; on Two, hook; on Three, uppercut.

2. Inboard men—On command, jab to the chin, drive a left uppercut to the body, then hook to the chin.
Outboard men—Use a stop for jab, the right glove to brush the left uppercut outward, then raise the right arm to block the left hook.
Command—Ready, One, Two, Three! On One, jab; on Two, uppercut; on Three, hook.

Defensive Boxing

1. Inboard men—Use only the left jab to the chin, the left hook to the chin and the left uppercut to the body.
Outboard men——On defense only.

Controlled Boxing

1. Inboard men—Use only the left jab to the chin, and the left hook to the chin.
Outboard men—Use only the left jab to the chin, and the left uppercut to body.

2. Inboard men—Use only the left jab to the chin, and the left uppercut to the body.
Outboard men—Use only the left hook to the chin and the left uppercut to the body.

3. Both men—Use only the left jab to the chin, the left hook to the chin and the left uppercut to the body.

DRILL 32—THE STRAIGHT RIGHT TO THE CHIN

Technique Drill

1. Explain and demonstrate the straight right to the chin.

2. Have the class practice the straight right to the chin.
Command—Straight right to the chin, Ready, Strike! Shorten to Ready, Strike!

3. Explain and demonstrate:
   — The advance and straight right.
   — The retreat and straight right.
   — The left step and straight right.
   — The right step and straight right.

4. Have the class practice the slow advance combined with the straight right.
Command—Advance, Strike! or One-Two! On One, step forward with left foot; on Two, move the right foot to position and drive the right hand into extension.
The secret of power and timing in a straight right is in the stepping forward with the right foot, bringing of the right foot to position after the left step has been taken. As right foot is moved forward the right hand is driven into complete extension. The right hand and right foot move together as one.

5. Have the class practice the slow retreat and straight right. As the weight shifts to the right leg momentarily, the right hand is driven into extension.
Command—Retreat, Strike! or One, Two! On One, step back with the right foot; on Two, drive the right arm into extension as the left foot recovers position.

6. Have the class practice the left step and straight right. As the weight shifts to the left foot, drive the right hand into extension.
Command—Left step, Ready, Strike! Ready, Strike! or One, Two! On One, step left; on Two, drive the right hand into extension and move right foot to position.

7. Have the class practice the right step and straight right. As the weight shifts to the straight right leg, drive the right hand into extension.
Command—Right step, Ready, Strike! or One, Two! On One, step with the right foot to the right; on Two, drive the right hand into extension and move left foot to position.

8. Have the class practice the different foot movements while delivering right handed blows.
Command—Advance, Strike! Retreat, Strike! Left step, Strike! Right step, Strike!

Hitting Drill

1. Inboard men—Hold the right glove open, directly in front of the right shoulder, palm open toward partner.
Outboard men—On command, drive a straight right to partner's glove.
Command—Ready, Strike!

2. Inboard men—As above.
Outboard men—Step in and drive a right hand to partner's glove. Be sure to move in with the right foot.
Command—Ready, Strike!

Controlled Boxing

1. Inboard men—Use only a straight right to the chin.
Outboard men—Use only a left jab to the chin.

2. Inboard men—Use only a straight right to the chin.
Outboard men—Use only a left hook to the chin.

3. Inboard men—Use only a left jab to the body.
Outboard men—Use only a straight right to the chin.

4. Inboard men—Use only a left uppercut to the body.
Outboard men—Use only a straight right to the chin.

5. Inboard men—Use only a left hook to the chin and a straight right to the chin.
Outboard men—Use only a left jab to the chin and a straight right to the chin.

6. Inboard men—Use only a left jab to the chin and a straight right to the chin.
Outboard men—Use only a left uppercut to the body and a straight right to the chin.

7. Both men—Use only a left jab to the chin and a straight right to the chin.

8. Both men—Use only a left jab and a left hook to the chin and a straight right to the chin.

DRILL 33—THE DEFENSE FOR A STRAIGHT RIGHT TO THE CHIN

THE STOP AND THE LEVERAGE BLOCK FOR THE STRAIGHT RIGHT TO THE CHIN

Technique Drill

1. Explain and demonstrate:
— The stop and the leverage guard for the straight right to the chin.

2. Have the class practice the movement of the stop.
Command—Ready, Strike!

3. Have class practice the movement of the leverage guard for the straight right to the chin.
Command—Ready, Block! or Ready, Guard!

Blocking Drill

1. Inboard men—On command, lead straight right to the chin.
Outboard men—Practice the stop for the straight right.
Command—Ready, Strike!

2. Inboard men—On command, lead a straight right to chin.
Outboard men—Practice the leverage guard.
Command—Ready, Strike! Have men work at close proximity in this drill.

Defensive Boxing

1. Inboard men—Use a straight right to the chin.
Outboard men—On defense only.

2. Inboard men—Use a straight left and right to the chin.
Outboard men—On defense only.

3. Inboard men—Use a straight left and right to the chin and a left hook to the chin.

4. Inboard men—Use a straight left and right to the chin, left hook to the chin, and a left jab to the body.

Controlled Boxing

1. Inboard men—Use only a left jab to the chin.
Outboard men—Use only a straight right to the chin.
2. Inboard men—Use only a left and right to the chin.
Outboard men—Use only a left jab to the body and a straight right to the chin.

DRILL 34—DEFENSE CONTINUED

THE INSIDE PARRY—THE OUTSIDE PARRY—THE CROSS PARRY

Technique Drill

1. Explain and demonstrate:
    — The inside parry.
    — The outside parry.
    — The cross parry.

2. Have class practice the movement for the inside parry.
Command—Ready, Parry! or Ready, Hep!

3. Have class practice the movement for the cross parry.
Command—Ready, Parry!

Blocking Drill

1. Inboard men—On command, lead a straight right to the chin.
Outboard men—Practice the inside parry.
Command—Ready, Parry; or Ready, Strike!

2. Inboard men—On command, lead a straight right to chin.
Outboard men—Practice the outside parry.
Command—Ready, Parry! or Ready, Strike!

3. Inboard men—On command, lead a straight right to the chin.
Outboard men—Practice the cross parry.
Command—Ready, Parry! or Ready, Strike!

4. Inboard men—On command, lead straight right to chin.
Outboard men—Practice the inside parry on one, the outside parry on two, and the cross parry on three, all on command.
Command—Ready, One, two, three; or One, three two! or Three, one, two!

Defensive Boxing

1. Inboard men—Use only the straight right to the chin.
Outboard men—On defense only, use the inside parry.

2. Inboard men—Use only a straight right to the chin.
Outboard men—On defense only. Use the outside parry.

3. Inboard men—Use only a straight right to chin.

Outboard men—On defense only. Use the cross parry.

Controlled Boxing

1. Inboard men—Use only the left uppercut to the body.
Outboard men—Use only the straight right to the chin.

2. Both men—Use only the straight right to the chin.

DRILL 35—DEFENSE CONTINUED

THE SHOULDER BLOCK—SLIPPING INSIDE ON A STRAIGHT RIGHT LEAD—SLIPPING OUTSIDE ON A STRAGHT RIGHT LEAD

Technique Drill

1. Explain and demonstrate:
    — The shoulder block.
    — Slipping to the inside guard position.
    — Slipping to the outside guard position.

2. Have the class practice the movement of the shoulder block.
Command—Ready! Black! or Ready, Hep!

3. Have the class practice the movement of slipping to the inside guard position.
Command—Ready, Slip! or Ready, Hep!

4. Have the class practice the movement of slipping to the outside guard position.
Command—Ready, Slip! or Ready, Hep!

Blocking Drill

1. Inboard men—On command, lead a straight right to the chin.
Outboard men—Practice the shoulder block.
Command—Ready, Strike!

2. Inboard men—On command, lead a straight right to the chin.
Outboard men—Practice slipping to the inside guard position.
Command—Ready, Strike! or Ready, Slip!

3. Inboard men—On command, lead a straight right to the chin.
Outboard men—Practice slipping to the outside guard position.
Command—Ready, Strike!

4. Inboard men—On command, lead a straight right to the chin.
Outboard men—Practice the shoulder block on one, the inside slip on two, and the outside slip on three. All on command.
Command—Ready! One, two, three! or Three, two, one! or Two, one, three!

Defensive Boxing

1. Inboard men—Use only a straight right to the chin.
Outboard men—On defense only.

Controlled Boxing

1. Inboard men—Use only the left hook to the chin.
Outboard men—Use only the straight right to the chin.

DRILL 36—DEFENSE CONTINUED

THE STEP BACK—CIRCLING AWAY FROM AND CIRCLING INTO A STRAIGHT RIGHT LEAD

Technique Drill

1. Explain and demonstrate:
   — The step back.
   — Circling away from a right lead.
   — Circling into a right lead.

2. Have the class practice the movement of the step back.
Command—Step back, Hep! or Ready, Hep!

3. Have the class practice the movement of circling to the right and away from the right hand.
Command—Ready, Hep! or Ready, Circle!

4. Have the class practice the movement of circling to the left and into a right hand.
Command—Ready, Hep! or Ready, Circle!

Blocking Drill

1. Inboard men—On command, lead a straight right to the chin.
Outboard men—Practice the step back.
Command—Ready, Hep!

2. Inboard men—On command, lead a straight right to the chin.
Outboard men—Practice circling right, away from the right lead.
Command—Ready, Hep!

3. Inboard men—On command, lead a straight right to the chin.
Outboard men—Practice circling to the left or into the opponent's right hand lead.
Command—Ready, Strike! or Ready, Hep! or Ready, Circle!

Defensive Boxing

1. Inboard men—Use only a straight right to the chin.
Outboard men—On defense only.

Controlled Boxing

1. Inboard men—Use only the left uppercut to the body.
Outboard men—Use only the straight right to the chin

DRILL 37—THE STRAIGHT RIGHT TO THE CHIN AS A COUNTER

THE INSIDE STRAIGHT RIGHT TO THE CHIN—THE INSIDE GUARD AND STRAIGHT RIGHT TO CHIN—THE CROSS PARRY AND STRAIGHT RIGHT TO CHIN

Technique Drill

1. Explain and demonstrate:
    — The inside straight right to the chin.
    — The inside guard and straight right to the chin.
    — The cross parry and straight right to the chin.

2. Have the class practice the movement of the inside right to the chin.
Command—Ready, One! Two! On one, shift the weight to left leg and turn hip and shoulder to center line; on two, drive the right hand into extension.

3. Have the class practice the movement of the inside guard and straight right to the chin.
Command—Ready, One! Two! On one, guard to inside; on two, drive a straight right to chin.

4. Have class practice the movement of the cross parry and straight right to chin.
Command—Ready, One! Two! On one, parry to inside and step left with left foot; on two, drive a straight right to chin.

Hitting Drill

1. Inboard men—On command, lead a left jab to the chin. Hold the right glove, palm open and toward partner, directly in front of the chin.
Outboard men—Practice the inside straight right to the chin.
Command—Ready, One! Two! On one, turn the right shoulder to a position inside of left lead; on two, drive right hand to partner's open right glove. Shorten to Ready, Strike!

2. Inboard men—On command, lead a left jab to the chin. Hold the right glove, palm open and toward partner, directly in front of the chin.
Outboard men—Practice the inside guard and straight right to the chin.
Command—Ready, One! Two! On one, guard to the inside position; on two, drive an inside right to partner's glove. Shorten to—Ready, Strike!

3. Inboard men—As described above.
Outboard men—Practice the cross parry and straight right to the chin.

Command——Ready, One! Two! On one, cross parry; on two, drive a straight right to the chin. Shorten to Ready, Strike!

Blocking Drill

1. Inboard men—On command, lead a left jab to the chin. Be ready to block opponent's right counter with a right hand stop block.
Outboard men—Practice the inside straight right to chin.
Command—Ready, Strike!

2. Inboard men—On command, lead a jab to the chin. Be ready to block opponent's right counter with a right hand stop block.
Outboard men—Practice the inside guard and straight right to chin.
Command—Ready, Strike!

3. Inboard men—As described above.
Outboard men—Practice the cross parry and straight right to chin.
Command—Ready, Strike!

Controlled Boxing

1. Inboard men—Use only a left jab to the chin.
Outboard men—Counter with the inside straight right to chin.

2. Inboard men—Use only a left jab to the chin.
Outboard men—Use only the inside guard and straight right to chin.

3. Inboard men—Use only the left jab to the chin.
Outboard men—Use only the cross parry and straight right to the chin.

DRILL 38—THE STRAIGHT RIGHT TO THE CHIN AS A COUNTER

THE OUTSIDE SLIP AND STRAIGHT RIGHT TO THE CHIN ON A LEET LEAD—THE OUTSIDE PARRY AND STRAIGHT RIGHT TO CHIN ON A RIGHT LEAD—THE INSIDE PARRY AND STRAIGHT RIGHT TO CHIN ON A RIGHT LEAD

Technique Drill

1. Explain and demonstrate:
    — The outside slip and straight right to the chin on a left lead.
    — Outside parry and straight right to the chin on a right lead.
    — Inside parry and straight right to the chin on a right lead.

2. Have the class practice the movement of the outside slip and straight right to chin.
Command—Ready, Strike!

3. Have class practice the movement of the outside parry and straight right to chin on a right lead.
Command—Ready, Strike!

4. Have class practice the movement for the inside parry and straight right to the chin on a right lead.
Command—Ready, Strike!

Hitting Drill

1. Inboard men—On command, lead a left jab to the chin, Hold the right glove directly in front of chin, palm open and toward partner.
Outboard men—Practice the outside slip and straight right to the chin.
Command—Ready, Strike!

2. Inboard men—On command, lead a straight right to chin. Hold the left glove directly in front of chin, palm open toward partner.
Outboard men—Practice the outside parry and straight right to chin.
Command—Ready, Strike!

3. Inboard men—As described above.
Outboard men—Practice the inside parry and straight right to chin.
Command—Ready, Strike!

4. Inboard men—On command, lead either a straight left or right to the chin. Hold the glove hand not used, directly in front of the chin, palm open and turned toward opponent.

Outboard men—Practice the counter as indicated by command.

Command—Ready, One! or Ready, Two! or Ready, Three! One, refers to the outside stop and straight right to chin on a left lead; two, refers to the outside parry and straight right to chin; three, refers to the inside parry and straight right to the chin.

Blocking Drill

1. Inboard men—On command, lead left jab. Use a stop block for the right hand counter.
Outboard men—Practice the outside slip and straight right to the chin.
Command—Ready, Strike!

2. Inboard men—On command, lead a straight right to the chin. Use the leverage block for the opponent's right counter.
Outboard men—Practice the outside parry and straight right to chin.
Command—Ready, Strike!

3. Inboard men—as described above.
Outboard men—Practice the inside parry and straight right to chin.
Command—Ready, Strike!

Controlled Boxing

1. Inboard men—Use only a left jab to the chin.
Outboard men—Slip to the outside and counter with straight right to chin

2. Inboard men—Use only a straight right to the chin.
Outboard men—Parry to the outside and counter with a right to the chin.

DRILL 39—COUNTER BLOWS FOR THE STRAIGHT RIGHT TO THE CHIN

THE LEFT JAB—THE INSIDE LEFT HOOK—THE STRAIGHT RIGHT TO THE BODY

Technique Drill

1. Explain and demonstrate the following counters for a straight right to the chin.
   — The left jab.
   — The inside hook.
   — The straight right to the body.

2. Have class practice the movements of countering with a left jab to chin, the inside hook to the chin; the straight right to the body.
Command—Ready, Strike!

Hitting Drill

1. Inboard men—On command, lead a straight right to the chin. Hold the left hand directly in front of the chin, palm open toward partner.
Outboard men—Practice countering with a left jab to the chin to partner's open glove.
Command—Ready, Strike!

2. Inboard men—On command, lead a straight right to chin. Hold the left hand directly in front of chin, palm open toward partner.
Outboard men—Practice countering with an inside left hook to chin.
Command—Ready, Strike!

3. Inboard men—On command, lead a straight right to chin. Hold the left glove, palm open and turned outward, directly in front of the solar plexus.
Outboard men—Practice countering with a straight right to the body.
Command—Ready, Strike!

Blocking Drill

1. Inboard men—On command, lead a straight right to the chin. Use a stop block for partner's left counter blow.
Outboard men—Practice countering with a left jab to the chin.
Command—Ready, Strike!

2. Inboard men—On command, lead a straight right to the chin. Block partner's left with a right hand stop block.
Outboard men—Practice countering with an inside left hook to chin.
Command—Ready, Strike!

3. Inboard men—On command, lead a straight right to the chin.

Outboard men—Counter as indicated by command.

Command—Ready, one! Ready, two! Ready, three; One refers to the left jab; two refers to the inside hook; three refers to the straight right to the body.

Controlled Boxing

1 Inboard men—Use only a straight right to the chin.

Outboard men—Counter with a left jab to the chin.

2. Inboard men—As described above.

Outboard men—Counter with a left hook to the chin.

3. Inboard men—As described above.

Outboard men—Counter with a straight right to the body.

DRILL 40—COMBINATIONS USING THE LEFT JAB AND LEFT HOOK TO THE CHIN

LEFT UPPERCUT T0 BODY AND STRAIGHT RIGHT TO CHIN—THE ONE-TWO TO THE CHIN

Technique Drill

1. Explain and demonstrate the one-two to the chin.

2. Have the class practice the one-two to the chin.
Teach the foot step of the one-two. Hands remain in the on guard position without movement. Class should concentrate on the proper movement of right foot to position after the left step.
Command—Ready, One! Two! On one, step forward with the left foot; on two, follow with right foot to position.

3. Have the class practice the left jab while advancing, Right hand remains in position of guard.
Command—Ready, one-two!

4. Have the class practice the movement of the one-two.
Command—One! Two! On one, jab left arm into extension, and move right foot to position; on two drive the right arm into extension as right foot moves to position.

Hitting Drill

1. Inboard men—Hold the right glove in front of the right shoulder, palm open toward partner.
Outboard men—On command, drive the one-two to partner's right glove.
Command—Ready, One-two !

2. Inboard men—Hold right glove in front of right shoulder, palm open toward partner; left hand in front of left shoulder, palm open toward partner.
Outboard men—On command, drive a one-two to opponent's right glove. On next command, drive a one-two to opponent's left glove.
Command—Ready, Strike! Ready, Strike! or One-two! One-two!

3. Inboard men—Hold hands as described above.
Outboard men—On command, drive a one-two first to the opponent's right glove and follow immediately with a one-two to opponent's left glove.
Command—Ready, Strike!

Blocking Drill

1. Inboard men—On command, drive a one-two to the chin.
Outboard men—As opponent leads the jab, execute a stop block with right hand and use the leverage guard for opponent's right.
Command—One! Two!

Defensive Boxing

1. Inboard men—Use only a one-two to the chin.
Outboard men—On defense only.

Controlled Boxing

1. Inboard men—Use only a one-two to the chin.
Outboard men—Use only a jab-hook to chin.

DRILL 41—COMB1NATIONS CONTINUED

THE JAB-CROSS AND HOOK TO THE CHIN—THE JAB-CROSS AND UPPERCUT TO THE BODY

Technique Drill

1. Explain and demonstrate:
    — The jab-cross and hook.
    — The jab-cross and uppercut.

2. Have the class practice the triples.
Command—One, two, three! Means the jab-cross and hook; or One, two four! Means the jab-cross and uppercut.

Hitting Drill

1. Inboard men—Hold the right hand in front of right shoulder, palm open toward partner. Hold the left hand off the left shoulder, palm turned inward.
Outboard men—On command practice the jab-cross to partner's right glove; the left hook to partner's left glove.
Command—One, two, three!

2. Inboard men—Hold the right hand in front of the right shoulder, palm open toward partner; left hand, palm downward, directly in front of the solar plexus.
Outboard men—On command, drive a one-two to the opponent's right glove, and a left uppercut to opponent's left glove.
Command—Ready, One, two three!

Blocking Drill

1. Inboard men—On command, execute a jab, cross and hook to the chin.
Outboard men—Practice a stop for left jab with the right hand, the leverage guard with the left hand for the opponent's right lead, and the forearm block for opponent's left hook.
Command—Ready, one, two, three!

2. Inboard men—On command, execute the jab, cross and uppercut combination.
Outboard men—Practice a stop for left jab, the leverage guard for the straight right and the brush away for right uppercut to the body.
Command—Ready, One, two three!

Defensive Boxing

1. Inboard men—Use only a left jab, straight right, and left hook to chin

Outboard men—On defense only.

2. Inboard men—Use only a left jab, straight right to chin and left uppercut to body.
Outboard men—Defense only.

Controlled Boxing

1. Inboard men—Use only the jab, cross and hook to chin.
Outboard men—Use only the jab, cross and uppercut to the body.

DRILL 42—COMBINATIONS CONTINUED

THE JAB-HOOK AND CROSS TO CHIN—THE JAB-HOOK AND RIGHT UPPERCUT TO BODY

Technique Drill

1. Explain and demonstrate:
    — The jab-hook and cross.
    — The jab-hook and right uppercut to the body.

2. Have the class practice the two triples.
Command—Ready, one, two, three! Is the jab-hook and cross; one, two, four!
Is the jab-hook and right uppercut.

Hitting Drill

1. Inboard men—Hold the right glove directly in front of right shoulder, palm open
and toward partner. Hold the left hand directly off the left shoulder, palm open, glove
turned inward.
Outboard men—On command, practice the jab-hook and cross to chin.
Command—Ready, One, two, three! On one, jab the left to opponent's right glove; on
two, hook the left to opponent's left glove; on three, cross the right to opponent's right
glove.

2. Inboard men—Hold the right glove in manner described above. Hold the left glove,
palm open and downward, directly in front of the solar plexus.
Outboard men—On command, practice the jab-hook and uppercut.
Command—Ready, One, two, three! On one, jab the left to the opponent's right glove;
on two, hook the left to opponent's right glove; on three, drive a left uppercut to the
opponent's left glove.

Blocking Drill

1. Inboard men—On command, practice the jab-hook and cross to the chin.
Outboard men—Use a stop for the left jab with the right hand; use the forearm block
to block the left hook, and the leverage block with left arm to block straight right to
the chin.
Command—Ready, One, two, three!

2. Inboard men—On command, lead a jab-hook and straight right.
Outboard men—Use the forearm block to block the left hook and a brush with the left
hand to block the right uppercut to the body.
Command—Ready, One, two, three!
Defensive Boxing

1. Inboard men—Use only the jab-hook and cross to the chin.
Outboard men—On defense only.

2. Inboard men—Use only the jab-hook to the chin, and the right uppercut to the body.
Outboard men—On defense only.

Controlled Boxing

1. Inboard men—Use only the jab-hook and cross to chin.
Outboard men—Use only the jab-hook and right uppercut to the body.

DRILL 43—COMBINATIONS CONTINUED

THE STRAIGHT HIGH-LOW—THE HIGH-LOW AND CROSS—THE LOW-HIGH AND THE UPPERCUT

Technique Drill

1. Explain and demonstrate:
   — The straight high-low.
   — The high-low and cross.
   — The low-high and uppercut.

2. Have the class practice the straight high-low.
Command—Ready, One, two!

3. Have the class practice the high-low and cross.
Command—Ready, One, two, three!

4. Have class practice the low-high and uppercut.
Command—Ready, One, two, three!

Hitting Drill

1. Inboard men—Hold the right hand high, palm open toward partner, just off the right shoulder. Hold the left hand, palm open and turned downward in front of solar plexus.
Outboard men—On command, practice the straight high-low.
Command—Ready. One, two! or Up, Down!

2. Inboard men—Hold the right hand just off the right shoulder, palm open toward opponent. Hold the left hand in front of solar plexus, palm open and turned inward.
Outboard men—On command, practice the high-low and cross.
Command—Ready, One, two, three! On one, hook high; on two, uppercut: on three, straight right to chin.

3. Inboard men—Hold hands as described above.
Outboard men—On command, practice the low-high and uppercut.
Command—Ready, One, two, three! On one, hook low; on two, hook high; on three, drive a right uppercut to the solar plexus.

Blocking Drill

1. Inboard men—On command, lead a left jab to the chin and a straight right to the body.

Outboard men—Use a stop with the right glove to block left jab; use a left brush to block the straight line to the body.
Command—Ready, One, two!

2. Inboard men—On command, practice the high, low and cross.
Outboard men—Use the right forearm block to block the left hook, the right elbow block to block left uppercut to body and either a stop or a leverage guard with the right hand to block the right to the chin.
Command—Ready, One, two, three!

3. Inboard men—On command, practice the low, high and uppercut.
Outboard men—Block the left uppercut to the body with the right elbow block; the left hook to the chin with right forearm block; and the left uppercut to the body with the left brush away.
Command—Ready, One, two, three! On one, lead a left uppercut to the body; on two hook a left to the chin; on three execute a right uppercut to the solar plexus.

Defensive Boxing

1. Inboard men—Use only the straight high-low.
Outboard men—On defense only.

2. Inboard men—Use only a left hook to chin; left uppercut to the solar plexus, and a right to the chin.
Outboard men—On defense only.

Controlled Boxing

1. Inboard men—Use only the straight high, low.
Outboard men—Use only the high, low and cross.

2. Inboard men—Use only the high, low and cross.
Outboard men—Use only the low, high and uppercut.

DRILL 44—RIGHT HOOK TO THE CHIN

Technique Drill

1. Explain and demonstrate the right hook to the chin.

2. Have class practice the right hook to the chin.
Command—On Guard, Ready, Strike!

3. Explain the coordination of the right hook with the fundamental foot movements; The Advance, The Retreat, The Right Step, The Left Step.

4. Have class practice the right hook and advance. Step with left foot. As the right foot is moved to position, hook the right hand in an arc for the left shoulder.
Command—Ready, Strike!

5. Have class practice the retreat and right hook to the chin. Move one step to the right with the right foot. As the left foot is moved to position, hook the right in an arc for the left shoulder. Carry the left hand high.
Command—Ready, Strike!

6. Have the class practice the right step and right hook to the chin. Step to the right with right foot and quickly move the left foot to position. As the weight shifts to the left leg hook the right hard to the chin.
Command—Ready, Strike!

7. Have class practice the left step and right hook to chin. Step left with the left foot. As the right foot is moved to position, raise the right elbow and hook hard to the left shoulder. Hold the left hand high in position of guard.
Command—Ready, Strike!

8. Now combine the right hook with all of the foot movements.
Command—Advance, Strike! Retreat, Strike! Left step, Strike! Right step, Strike!

Hitting Drill

1. Inboard men—Hold the right hand directly off the right shoulder, palm open and turned inward.
Outboard men—On command, practice the right hook to the chin.
Command—Ready, Strike!
2. Inboard men—Hold both hands directly off the left and right shoulders respectively, palms open and turned inward.
Outboard men—On the first command, drive a left hook to the left glove; on the next command, drive a right hook to the right glove.

Command—Ready, Strike! Ready, Strike!

3. Inboard men—Hold hands as described above.
Outboard men—On command, hook a left to partner's left glove and follow immediately with right hook to partner's right glove.
Command—Ready, Strike! (Two blows.)

4. Inboard men—Hold the right band open, palm down, directly in front of solar plexus. Hold the left hand off left shoulder, palm open and turned inward.
Outboard men—On command, drive a left uppercut to left glove, and the right hook to the right glove.
Command—Ready, Strike! (left uppercut) Ready, Strike! (right hook). One command, one blow.
Command—Ready, Strike! (two blows, left uppercut followed by right hook).

Defensive Boxing

1. Inboard men—Use only a right hook to the chin.
Outboard men—On defense only.

Controlled Boxing

1. Inboard men—Use only the left hook to the chin.
Outboard men—Use only a right hook to chin.

2. Inboard men—Use only a left jab to chin.
Outboard men—Use only a right hook to chin.

3. Inboard men—Use only a straight right to chin.
Outboard men—Use only a right hook to chin.

DRILL 45—THE DEFENSE FOR THE RIGHT HOOK TO CHIN

THE STOP, THE DUCK, THE FOREARM BLOCK, CIRCLIGN TO THE RIGHT, THE STEP BACK

Technique Drill

1. Explain and demonstrate:
    — The stop.
    — The duck.
    — The forearm block.
    — Circling to the right.
    — The step back.

2. Have the class practice the movement of the stop.
Command—Ready, Stop; or Ready, Hep!

3. Have class practice the movement of the duck.
Command—Ready, Duck!

4. Have class practice the movement of the forearm block.
Command—Ready, Block!

5. Have class practice circling to the right.
Command—Ready, Step! or Ready, Strike!

6. Have class practice the-step back.
Command—Ready, Step! or Ready, Strike!

Blocking Drill

1. Inboard men—On command, lead a right hook to the chin.
Outboard men—Practice the stop for the right hook to the chin.
Command—Ready, Strike! or Ready, Stop!

2. Inboard man—On command, lead a right hook to chin.
Outboard men—Practice the duck.
Command—Ready, Strike! or Ready, duck!

3. Inboard men—On command, lead a right hook to the chin.
Outboard men—Practice the forearm block.
Command—Ready, Block! or Ready, Strike!

4. Inboard men—On command, lead a right hook to the chin.

Outboard men—Practice circling to the right.
Command—Ready, move! or Ready, Strike!

5. Inboard men—On command, lead right hook to the chin.
Outboard men—Practice the step back.
Command—Ready, Strike! or Ready, Move!

Defensive Boxing

1. Inboard men—Use a right hook to the chin.
Outboard men—On defense only.

Controlled Boxing

1. Inboard men—Use only a left jab to the chin.
Outboard men—Use only a right hook to the chin.

2. Inboard men—Use only a left hook to the chin.
Outboard men—Use only a right hook to the chin.

DRILL 46—THE RIGHT HOOK AS A COUNTER BLOW

THE RIGHT CROSS—THE INSIDE GUARD AND RIGHT HOOK—THE CROSS PARRY AND RIGHT HOOK

Technique Drill

1. Explain and demonstrate:
    — The right cross.
    — The inside guard and right hook.
    — The cross parry and right hook.

2. Have the class practice the right cross.
Command—Ready, one, two! or Ready, Strike! On one, shift the weight to the left foot and raise right elbow; on two, hook the right to the chin.

3. Have the class practice the inside guard and right hook.
Command—Ready, one, two! or Ready, Strike! On one, step forward and raise the right forearm as if to block; on two, with the elbow and forearm on the same level, drive a right hook to chin.

4. Have the class practice the cross parry and right hook.
Command—Ready, one, two! Later—Ready, Strike!

Hitting Drill

1. Inboard men—On command, lead to left jab to the chin. Hold the right glove as target in front of chin, palm open toward partner.
Outboard men—Practice the right cross.
Command—Ready, Strike!

2. Inboard men—As described above.
Outboard men—Practice the inside guard and right hook to chin.
Command—Ready, Strike!

3. Inboard men—As described above.
Outboard men—Practice the cross parry and right hook to chin.
Command—Ready, Strike!

4. Inboard men—As described above.
Outboard men—Practice the counters as indicated by command.
Command—Ready, one! or Ready, two! or Ready, three! One refers to the right cross; two, to the inside guard and right hook; three, to the cross parry, and right hook.

Blocking Drill

1. Inboard men—On command, lead a left jab to the chin. Use a stop with right hand to block partner's left.
Outboard men—Practice the right cross to the chin.
Command—Ready, Strike!

2. Inboard men—On command, lead a left jab to the chin. Be prepared to block right hook using a stop with the right hand.
Outboard men—Practice the inside guard and right hook to chin.
Command—Ready, Strike!

3. Inboard men—On command, lead a left jab to the chin. Block the opponent's right hook with own right stop.
Command—Ready, Strike!

DRILL 47—COUNTER BLOWS FOR THE RIGHT HOOK TO THE CHIN

THE LEFT JAB—THE LEFT UPPERCUT TO BODY—THE STRAIGHT RIGHT TO BODY—THE LEFT JAB TO THE BODY—THE RETURN RIGHT HOOK TO THE CHIN

Technique Drill

1. Explain and demonstrate the following counters for a right hook to the chin.
   — The Left Jab.
   — The Left Uppercut to Body.
   — The Straight Right to the Body.
   — The Left jab to the Body.
   — The Return Right Hook to the Chin.

2. Have the class practice the left jab as a counter for the right hook.
Command—Ready, Strike!

3. Have class practice the left uppercut to the body as a counter for the right hook to the chin.
Command—Ready, Strike!

4. Have class practice the straight right to the body.
Command—Ready, Strike!

5. Have class practice the left jab to body.
Command—Ready, Strike!

6. Have class practice the return right hook to chin.
Command—Ready, Strike!

Hitting Drill

1. Inboard men—On command, lead a right hook to chin. Hold the left glove directly in front of the chin, palm open toward partner.
Outboard men—Practice countering with a left jab to the chin.
Command—Ready, Strike!

2. Inboard men—On command, lead a right hook to the chin. Hold the left glove, palm open and turned downward, directly in front of the solar plexus.
Outboard men—Practice countering with a left uppercut to the body.
Command—Ready, Strike!

3. Inboard men—On command, lead a right hook to the chin. Hold the left glove, open and toward opponent, directly in front of the solar plexus.

Outboard men—Practice countering with a straight right to the body.
Command—Ready, Strike!

4. Inboard men—As described above.
Outboard men—Practice countering with a left jab to the body.
Command—Ready, Strike!

5. Inboard men—On command, lead right hook to chin. Hold the left forearm ready to block.
Outboard men—Practice countering with the right hook to the chin.
Command—Ready, Strike!

Blocking Drill

1. Inboard men—On command, lead a right took to the chin. Be ready to block left counter with a right stop.
Outboard men—Practice countering with left jab to chin.
Command—Ready, Strike!

2. Inboard men—On command, lead a right hook to chin. Be ready to block the left uppercut with a left cross brush.
Outboard men—Practice countering with a left uppercut to the body.
Command--Ready, Strike!

3. Inboard men—On command, lead a right hook to the chin. Be ready to block the straight right to the body with a left brush away.
Outboard men—-Practice countering with a straight right to the body.
Command—Ready, Strike!

4. Inboard men—On command, lead a right hook to the chin. Be ready to block the left jab to body with a left cross brush.
Outboard men—Practice countering with a left jab to the body.
Command—Ready, Strike!

5. Inboard men—On command, lead a right hook to the chin. Be ready to block the right hook to the chin with a left forearm block.
Outboard men—Counter with return right hook.
Command—Ready, Strike!

Controlled Boxing

1. Inboard men—Use a right hook to the chin.
Outboard men—Counter with a left jab to the chin.

2. Inboard men—Use only a right hook to the chin.
Outboard men—Counter with a left uppercut to the body.

3. Inboard men—Use only a right hook to the chin.
Outboard men—Counter with a straight right to the body.

4. Inboard men—Use only a right hook to the chin.
Outboard men—Counter with a left jab to the body.

5. Inboard men—Use only a right hook to the chin,
Outboard men—Counter with a return right hook to the chin.

DRILL 48—RIGHT HOOK COMBINATIONS

THE LEFT AND RIGHT HOOKS TO THE CHIN—THE LEFT JAB, LEFT HOOK AND RIGHT HOOK TO THE CHIN

Technique Drill

1. Explain and demonstrate:
    — The left hook and the right hook combination.
    — The left jab, left hook and right hook combination.

2. Have class practice the left hook, right hook combination.
Command—Ready, one, two! On one, use the left hook; on two, the right hook. Or Ready, Strike! (Two blows.) The left hook followed by the right hook.

3. Have the class practice the left jab, left hook and right hook combination.
Command—Ready, one, two, three! On one, jab; on two, hook to chin; on three, hook a hard right to the chin. Or Ready, Strike! Three blows in combination.

Hitting Drill

1. Inboard men—Hold both hands shoulder width apart, gloves open and turned inward.
Outboard men—On command, practice the left hook-right hook combination.
Command—Ready, Strike! On one, hook a left to opponent's left glove; on two, hook a right to opponent's right glove.

2. Inboard men—Hold the right hand in front of right shoulder, palm turned outward toward partner. Hold the left hand directly off the left shoulder, palm turned inward.
Outboard men—On command, practice the left jab, right hook combination.
Command—Ready, one, two, three! On one, jab to the opponent's open right glove; on two, hook the left to opponent's left glove; on three, hook right to opponent's right glove. Shorten to Ready, Strike!

Blocking Drill

1. Inboard men—On command practice the left hook, right hook combination to the chin.
Outboard men—Block the left hook using a left forearm block. Block the right hook using a stop with the left hand.
Command—Ready, one, two! Shorten to Ready, Strike!

2. Inboard men—On command, practice the left jab, left hook and right hook combination.
Outboard men—Block the left jab with the right stop; the left hook with the right forearm block and the right hook with the left stop.

Command—Ready, one, two, three!

Defensive Boxing

1. Inboard men—Use only a left hook, right hook combination.
Outboard men—On defense only.

2. Inboard men—Use only a left jab, left hook and right hook combination.
Outboard men—On defense only.

Controlled Boxing

1. Inboard men—Use only the left hook, right hook combination.
Outboard men—Use only the left jab, left hook, right hook combination.

DRILL 49—COMBINATIONS CONTINUED

THE LEFT JAB TO BODY AND RIGHT HOOK TO CHIN—THE UPPERCUT TO THE BODY AND RIGHT HOOK To THE CHIN

Technique Drill

1. Explain and demonstrate:
     — The Left Jab to the Body and Right Hook to Chin.
     — The Left Uppercut to the Body and the Right Hook to the Chin.

2. Have class practice the left jab to the body and the right hook to chin.
Command—Ready, one, two! Jab on one, hook on two. Or Ready, Strike! Blows should be performed in sequence.

3. Have class practice the left uppercut to body and the right hook to Chin.
Command—Ready, one, two! Uppercut on one, hook on two. Or Ready, Strike! Blow performed in sequence.

Hitting Drill

1. Inboard men—Hold the left hand open, palm outward, in front of the solar plexus; hold the right hand off the right shoulder, palm turned inward.
Outboard men—On command, practice the left jab to body and the right hook to the chin.
Command—Ready, one, two!

2. Inboard men—Hold the left hand open, palm turned downward directly in front of the solar plexus; hold the right hand directly off the right shoulder, palm turned inward.
Outboard men—On command, practice the left uppercut to the body, and the right hook to the chin.
Command—Ready, one, two! Shorten to Ready, Strike! The two blows should be performed in sequence.

Blocking Drill

1. Inboard men—On command, practice the left jab to the body and the right hook to chin.
Outboard men—Block the left jab to body with a right brush away, the right hook to the chin with the left stop.
Command—Ready, one, two! Shorten to—Ready, Strike!

2. Inboard men—On command, lead the left uppercut to the body and the right hook to chin.
Outboard men—Block the left uppercut to body with a right brush away and the right hook to the chin with the left stop.

Command—Ready, one, two! Shorten to—Ready, Strike!

Defensive Boxing

1. Inboard men—Use only a left jab to the body and the right hook to the chin. Outboard men—On defense only.

2. Inboard men—Use only a left uppercut to the body, and a right hook to the chin. Outboard men—On defense only.

Controlled Boxing

1. Inboard men—Use only the left jab to the body and the right hook to the chin. Outboard men—Use only the right uppercut to the body and the right hook to the chin.

DRILL 50—COMBINATIONS CONTINUED

THE LEFT HOOK TO THE CHIN, THE LEFT UPPERCUT TO THE BODY AND THE RIGHT HOOK TO THE CHIN—THE LEFT UPPERCUT TO THE BODY, THE RIGHT HOOK TO THE CHIN AND THE LEFT HOOK TO THE CHIN

Technique Drill

1. Explain and demonstrate:
   — The left hook to the chin, the left uppercut to the body and the right hook to chin.
   — The left uppercut to body, the right hook to chin and the left hook to the chin.

2. Have the class practice the left hook to the chin, the left uppercut to the body, and the right hook to the chin.
Command—Ready, one, two, three! On one, hook the left to the chin; on two, the left uppercut to the body; on three, the right hook to the chin. Shorten to—Ready, Strike!

3. Have the class practice the left uppercut to the body, the right hook to the chin, and the left hook to the chin.
Command—Ready, one, two, three! On one, drive a left uppercut to the body; on two, a right hook to the chin; on three, a left hook to the chin.—Shorten to —Ready, Strike!

Hitting Drill

1. Inboard men—Hold the left hand open, palm outward, in front of the chin. Hold the right hand, palm downward, directly in front of the solar plexus.
Outboard men—On command, practice the left hook to the chin, the left uppercut to the body, and the right hook to the chin.
Command—Ready, one, two, three! Shorten to—Ready, Strike! Blows should be performed in sequence.

2. Inboard men—Hold hands as described above.
Outboard men—On command, practice the left uppercut to the body, the right hook to the chin and the left hook to the chin.
Command—Ready, one, two, three! Shorten to—Ready, Strike! Blows should be performed in sequence.

Blocking Drill

1. Inboard men—On command, practice a left hook to the chin, a left uppercut to the body, and a right hook to the chin.
Outboard men—Block the left hook with the right forearm block; the left uppercut with the right brush away; the right hook to the chin with a stop using the left hand.

Command—Ready, one, two, three! Shorten to—Ready, Strike!

2. Inboard men—On command, lead a left uppercut to the body, a right hook to chin and a left hook to chin.
Outboard men—Block the left uppercut to body with right brush away; the right hook to the chin using the stop with the left hand, and left hook to chin using the forearm block.

Defensive Boxing

1. Inboard men—Use only the left hook to the chin, left uppercut to the body and the right hook to the chin in combination.
Outboard men—On defense only.

2. Inboard men—Use the left uppercut to the body, the right hook to the chin, and the left hook to the chin.
Outboard men—On defense only.

Controlled Boxing

1. Inboard men—Use only a left hook to chin, left uppercut to body and right hook to chin in combination.
Outboard men—Use only a left uppercut to the body, right hook to the chin, and the left hook to chin in combination.

DRILL 51—THE STRAIGHT RIGHT TO THE BODY

Technique Drill

1. Explain and demonstrate the straight right to the body.

2. Have the class practice the straight right to the body.
Command—Ready, Strike!

3. Explain and demonstrate stepping in with a straight to the body. Step forward, driving the right hand to the solar plexus. The left hand is held in front of the chin ready for the opponent's counter. Recover the on guard position quickly.

4. Have the class practice stepping in with the straight right to the body.
Command—Straight right to body, Ready, Strike! Recovery must be immediate.

Hitting Drill

1. Inboard men—Hold the right glove directly in front of the solar plexus, palm open and toward opponent.
Outboard men—On command, practice the straight right to the body.
Command—Ready, Strike!

Controlled Boxing

1. Inboard men—Use only the left jab to the chin.
Outboard men—Use only the straight right to the body.

2. Inboard men—Use only the left hook to the chin.
Outboard men—Use only the straight right to the body.

3. Inboard men—Use only the straight right to the chin.
Outboard men—Use only the straight right to the body.

4. Inboard men—Use only the left uppercut to the body.
Outboard men—Use only the straight right to the body.

5. Inboard men—Use only the left hook to the chin.
Outboard men—Use only the straight right to the body.

6. Inboard men—Use only the right hook to the chin.
Outboard men—Use only the straight right to the body.

DRILL 52—THE DEFENSE FOR THE STRAIGHT RIGHT TO THE BODY

THE ELBOW BLOCK—THE FOREARM BLOCK—THE BRUSH OR PARRY—THE STEP AWAY

Technique Drill

1. Explain and demonstrate:
    — The Elbow Block.
    — The Forearm Block.
    — The Brush or Parry.
    — The Step Away.

2. Have the class practice the movement of the elbow block.
Command—Ready, Turn!

3. Have the class practice the movement of the forearm block, on command.
Command—Ready, Block!

4. Have the class practice the movement of the brush or parry.
Command—Ready, Brush!

5. Have the class practice the step away.
Command—Ready, Move!

Blocking Drill

1. Inboard men—On command, lead a straight right to body.
Outboard men—Practice the elbow block.
Command—Ready, Turn! or Ready, Strike!

2. Inboard men—On command, lead a straight right to the body.
Outboard men—Practice the forearm block.
Command—Ready, Strike! or Ready, Block!

3. Inboard men—On command, lead a straight right to the body.
Outboard men—Practice the brush or parry.
Command—Ready, Strike! or Ready, Brush!

4. Inboard men—On command, lead a straight right to the body.
Outboard men—Practice the step away.
Command—Ready, Move! or Ready, Strike!

Defensive Boxing

1. Inboard men—Use a straight right to the body.
Outboard men—On defense only.

Controlled Boxing

1. Inboard men—Use only a left jab to the chin.
Outboard men—Use only a straight right to the body.

DRILL 53—THE STRAIGHT RIGHT TO THE BODY AS A COUNTER BLOW

INSIDE RIGHT TO THE HEART—THE OUTSIDE SLIP AND STRAIGHT RIGHT TO HEART ON A STRAIGHT RIGHT LEAD

Technique Drill

1. Explain and demonstrate:
    — The Inside Right to the Heart.
    — The Outside Slip and Straight Right to the Heart on a Straight Right Lead.

2. Have the class practice the inside right to the heart.
Command—Ready, One, Two! Shorten to Ready, Strike!

3. Have class practice the outside slip and straight right to the heart on a straight right lead.
Command—One, Two! Shorten to Ready, Strike!

Hitting Drill

1. Inboard men—On command, lead a left jab to chin and hold the right hand directly in front of solar plexus, palm open and turned outward.
Outboard men—Practice the inside right to the heart.
Command—Ready, Strike!

2. Inboard men—On command, lead a straight right to chin. Hold the left hand low, palm open and toward opponent, directly in front of the solar plexus.
Outboard men—Practice the outside slip and straight right to heart.
Command—Ready, Strike!

Blocking Drill

1. Inboard men—On command, lead a left jab to the chin. Be ready to block the opponent's right lead with a right hand cross brush.
Outboard men—Practice the inside right to the heart.
Command—Ready, Strike!

Controlled Boxing

1. Inboard men—Use only a left lab to the chin.
Outboard men—Use only a straight right to the heart.

2. Inboard men—Use only a straight right to the chin,
Outboard men—Use only a straight right to the heart.

DRILL 54—COUNTER BLOWS FOR THE STRAIGHT RIGHT TO THE BODY

THE LEFT JAB TO THE CHIN—THE LEFT UPPERCUT TO THE BODY— THE RIGHT UPPERCUT TO THE BODY—THE LEFT HOOK TO THE CHIN

Technique Drill

1. Explain and demonstrate the following counters for the straight right to the body:
    — The Left Jab to the Chin.
    — The Left Uppercut to the Body.
    — The Right Uppercut to the Body.
    — The Left Hook to the Chin.

2. Have class practice the movement of the left jab as a counter for the straight right to the body.
Command—Ready, Strike!

3. Have class practice the left uppercut as a counter for the straight right to body.
Command—Ready, Strike!

4. Have class practice right uppercut to body as a counter for straight right to body.
Command—Ready, Strike!

5. Have class practice the left hook to the chin as a counter for the straight right to the body.
Command—Ready, Strike!

Hitting Drill

1. Inboard men—On command, lead a straight right to the body. Hold left hand. palm open toward opponent, directly in front of the chin.
Outboard men—Practice countering with a left jab to chin.
Command—Ready, Strike!

2. Inboard men—On command, lead a straight right to the body. Hold the left glove directly in front of solar plexus, palm open and downward.
Outboard men—Practice countering with left uppercut to the body.
Command—Ready, Strike!

3. Inboard men—On command, lead a straight right to the body. Hold left hand as described above.
Outboard men—Practice countering with a right uppercut to the body.
Command—Ready, Strike!

4. Inboard men—On command, lead a straight right to body. Hold the left hand directly off the left shoulder, palm open and turned inward.

Outboard men—Practice countering with a left hook to the chin.

Command—Ready, Strike!

Blocking Drill

1. Inboard men—On command, lead a straight right to the body. Be ready to use a stop with the right hand for the counter blow.

Outboard men—Practice countering with a left jab to the body.

Command—Ready, Strike!

2. Inboard men—On command, lead a straight right to body. Block the left uppercut with left forearm block.

Outboard men—Practice countering with a left uppercut to the body.

Command—Ready, Strike!

3. Inboard men—As above. Block the right uppercut with a left forearm block.

Outboard men—Practice countering with a right uppercut to the body.

Command—Ready, Strike!

4. Inboard men—As above. Block the left hook to the chin with a left cross stop.

Outboard men—Practice countering with a left hook to chin.

Command—Ready, Strike!

DRILL 55—COMBINATIONS USING THE STRAIGHT RIGHT TO THE BODY

THE LEFT JAB TO THE CHIN AND THE RIGHT TO THE BODY—THE LEFT HOOK TO THE CHIN AND THE RIGHT TO THE BODY—THE ONE-TWO TO THE BODY

Technique Drill

1. Explain and demonstrate:
    — The Left Jab to the Chin and the Right to the Body.
    — The Left Hook to the Chin and the Right to the Body.
    — The One-Two to the Body.

2. Have the class practice the left jab to the chin and the right to the body.
Command—Ready, One, Two! On one, jab to chin; on two, drive a straight right to the body. Shorten to Ready, Strike! blows being delivered consecutively.

3. Have the class practice the left hook to the chin and straight right to the body.
Command—Ready, One, Two! On one, hook to the chin. On two, drive a straight right to the body.

4. Have the class practice the one-two to the body.
Command—Ready, One, Two! On one, use a left jab to the body. On two, a straight right to the body. Shorten to—Ready, Strike!

Hitting Drill

1. Inboard men—Hold the right hand open toward the partner, directly in front of right shoulder. Hold the left hand open toward partner directly in front of the solar plexus.
Outboard men—On command, practice the left jab to the chin and the straight right to the body.
Command—One, Two! or Ready, Strike!

2. Inboard men—Hold the left hand off the left shoulder, palm turned inward. Hold the right hand open toward the partner directly in front of the solar plexus.
Outboard men—On command, practice left hook to the chin, and straight right to the body.
Command—Ready, Strike!

3. Inboard men—Hold the right glove directly in front of the right hip, open and toward opponent. Hold the left glove directly in front of the left hip, open and toward opponent.
Outboard men—On command, practice the one-two to the body.

Command—Ready, One, Two! or Ready, Strike!

Blocking Drill

1. Inboard men—On command, practice the left jab to the chin and the straight right to the body.
Outboard men—Block the left jab to the chin with a stop block, and the straight right to the body with a left brush away.
Command—Ready, Strike!

2. Inboard men—On command, practice the left hook to the chin and the straight right to the body.
Outboard men—Block the left hook to the chin with a right forearm block; the straight right to the body with a left brush away.
Command—Ready, Strike!

3. Inboard men—On command, practice the one-two to the body.
Outboard men—Block the left to the body with a right brush away and the right to the body with a left brush away.
Command—Ready, Strike!

Defensive Boxing

1. Inboard men—Use only in combination, the left jab to the chin and right to the body.
Outboard men—On defense only.

2. Inboard men—Use only in combination, the left hook to the chin and right to the body.
Outboard men—On defense only.

3. Inboard men—Use only in combination, the one-two to the body.
Outboard men—On defense only.

Controlled Boxing

1. Inboard men—Use only in combination, the left jab to the chin and the right to the body.
Outboard men—Use only in combination, the left hook to the chin, and the right to the body.

2. Inboard men—Use only in combination, the left hook to the chin, and the right to the body.
Outboard men—Use only in combination, the one-two to the body.

DRILL 56—THE RIGHT UPPERCUT TO THE BODY—THE RIGHT UPPERCUT COMBINED WITH FOOTWORK

Technique Drill

1. Explain and demonstrate:
   — The Right Uppercut to the Body.
   — The Right Uppercut to the Body Combined with the Advance, Combined with the Retreat, Combined with the Left Step and the Right Step.

2. Have the class practice the right uppercut to the body.
Command—Ready, One, Two, Three! On one, drop the body directly to the right, forearm parallel to the deck, palm upward; on two, turn the body through to the center line; on three, straighten the body and whip a right uppercut to the solar plexus. Shorten the command to Ready, Strike! Complete movement being performed.

3. Have the class practice the right uppercut and advance.
Command—Advance, Strike!

4. Have the class practice the right uppercut and retreat.
Command—Ready, Strike!

5. Have the class practice the left step and right uppercut.
Command—Ready, Strike!

6. Have the class practice the right uppercut and right step.
Command—Ready, Strike!

7. Have the class practice all foot movements combined with the right uppercut.
Command—Advance, Strike! Retreat, Strike; Left Step, Strike! Right Step, Strike!

Hitting Drill

1. Inboard men—Hold the right glove directly in front of the solar plexus, palm open and downward.
Outboard men—On command, practice the right uppercut to the body.
Command—Ready, Strike!

2. Inboard men—Hold both gloves directly off the left and right hips respectively, palms open and downward.
Outboard men—On command, practice the right uppercut to the body. One blow, one command.

Command—Ready, Strike! Drive the right uppercut to the right glove. On the next command, drive the right uppercut to the left glove.

5. Inboard men—Hold gloves as described above.
Outboard men—On command, practice the left uppercut followed by the right uppercut.
Command—Ready, Strike! Drive the left uppercut to the left glove; on the next command, drive the right uppercut to the right glove. Later, on the command of Ready, Strike!, drive the left uppercut to the left glove, and the right uppercut to the right glove in succession.

Blocking Drill

1. Inboard men—On command, practice the right uppercut to the solar plexus.
Outboard men—Practice blocking the uppercut with the left brush away.
Command—Ready, Strike!

Defensive Boxing

1. Inboard men—Use a right uppercut to the body.
Outboard men—-On defense only.

2. Inboard men—Use both the left and the right uppercuts to the body
Outboard men—On defense only.

3. Inboard men—Use left and right hooks to the chin and left and right uppercuts to the body.
Outboard men—On defense only.
4. Inboard men—Use the left jab to the chin and the right uppercut to the body
Outboard men—On defense only.

5. Inboard men—Use the left hook to the chin and the right uppercut to the body
Outboard men—On defense only.

Controlled Boxing

1. Inboard men—Use only a left jab to the chin.
Outboard men—Use only a right uppercut to the body

2. Inboard men—Use only a straight right to the chin.
Outboard men—Use only a right uppercut to the body

3. Inboard men—Use only a left jab to the body.
Outboard men—Use only a right uppercut to the chin.

4. Inboard men—Use only a left uppercut to the body.
Outboard men—Use only a right uppercut to the body.

5. Inboard men—Use only a right hook to the chin.
Outboard men—Use only a right uppercut to the body.

6. Inboard men—Use only a straight right to the body.
Outboard men—Use only a right uppercut to the body.

DRILL 57—DEFENSE FOR THE RIGHT UPPERCUT TO BODY
THE BRUSH AWAY—THE FOREARM BLOCK—THE STEP BACK

Technique Drill

1 Explain and demonstrate:
— The Brush Away.
— The Forearm Block.
— The Step Back.

2. Have the class practice the movement of the brush away for the right upper cut to the body.
Command—Ready, Brush!

3. Have the class practice the movement of the forearm block.
Command—Ready, Block!

4. Have the class practice the step back.
Command—Ready, Step! or Ready, Move!

Blocking Drill

1. Inboard men—On command, drive a right uppercut to the body.
Outboard men—Practice the brush away.
Command—Ready, Strike!

2. Inboard men—On command, drive a right uppercut to the body.
Outboard men—Practice the forearm block.
Command-—Ready, Strike!

3. Inboard men—On command, drive a right uppercut to the body.
Outboard men—Practice the step back.
Command—Ready, Strike!

Defensive Boxing

1. Inboard men—Use a right uppercut to the body.
Outboard men—On defense, using only the brush away.

2. Inboard men—Use a right uppercut to the body.
Outboard men—On defense, using only the forearm block.

3. Inboard men—Use a right uppercut to the body.
Outboard men—On defense, using only the step back.

DRILL 58—THE RIGHT UPPERCUT TO THE BODY AS A COUNTER BLOW

THE INSIDE SLIP AND RIGHT UPPERCUT TO THE BODY—THE CROSS PARRY AND THE RIGHT UPPERCUT TO THE BODY

Technique Drill

1. Explain and demonstrate:
   — The inside slip and right uppercut to the body.
   — The cross parry and right uppercut to the body.

2. Have class practice the inside slip and right uppercut to body.
Command—Ready, One, Two! On one, step forward to the left with the left foot, slipping blow over the right shoulder; on two, drive a right uppercut to the body. — Shorten to Ready, Strike!

3. Have the class practice the cross parry and right uppercut to body.
Command—One, Two! On one, cross parry the opponent's left lead; on two, step forward and drive hard right uppercut to the body.

4. Have class practice the two counters.
Command—Ready, One! or Ready, Two! The inside slip and right uppercut to the body being one; the cross parry and left uppercut to the body being two.

Hitting Drill

1. Inboard men—On command, lead a left jab to the chin. Hold the right hand, palm open and downward, directly in front of the solar plexus.
Outboard men—Practice the inside slip and right uppercut to the body.
Command—Ready, Strike!

2. Inboard men—On command, lead a left jab to the chin. Hold the right hand as described above.
Outboard men—Practice the cross parry and right uppercut to the body.
Command—Ready, Strike!

Blocking Drill

1. Inboard men—On command, lead a left jab to the chin. Be ready to block the opponent's right uppercut with a left brush away.
Outboard men—Practice the inside slip and right uppercut to the body.
Command—Ready, Strike!

2. Inboard men—On command, lead a left jab to the chin. Be ready to block opponent's right uppercut with a left brush away.

Outboard men—Practice the cross parry and right uppercut to the body.
Command—Ready, Strike!

Controlled Boxing

1. Inboard men—Use only a left jab to the chin.
Outboard men—Use only a right uppercut to the body.

2. Inboard men—Use only a straight right to the chin.
Outboard men—Use only a right uppercut to the body.

3. Inboard men—Use only a left hook to the chin.
Outboard men—Use only a right uppercut to the body.

DRILL 59—THE OUTSIDE SLIP AND RIGHT UPPERCUT TO BODY ON A RIGHT LEAD—THE INSIDE PARRY AND RIGHT UPPERCUT TO BODY ON A RIGIIT LEAD

Technique Drill

1. Explain and demonstrate:
    — The Outside Slip and Right Uppercut to Body on a right lead.
    — The Inside Parry and Right Uppercut to Body on a right lead

2. Have the class practice the outside slip and right uppercut to the body.
Command—Ready, Strike!

3. Have class practice the inside parry and right uppercut to body.
Command—Ready, Strike!

Hitting Drill

1. Inboard men—On command, lead a straight right to the chin. Hold the left hand, palm open and downward, directly in front of the solar plexus.
Outboard men—Practice the outside slip and right uppercut to the body.
Command—Rendy, One, Two! On one, step forward and to the left, slip the right lead over right shoulder, right hand dropping alongside of the body. On two, shift the weight to the left foot and drive a right uppercut to the opponent's left glove. Shorten the command to—Ready, Strike! Perform as one movement.

2. Inboard men—On command, lead a straight right to the chin. Hold the left glove, palm open and downward, directly in front of the solar plexus.
Outboard men—Practice the inside parry and right uppercut to the body.
Command—Ready, One, Two! On one, parry to the inside guard position with the left hand and drop the right hand alongside of the body. On two, step forward and whip the right uppercut to solar plexus. The left hand moves to position of guard off the right shoulder.

Blocking Drill

1. Inboard men—On command, lead a straight right to the chin. Be ready to block the opponent's right uppercut to body with the left brush away.
Outboard men—Practice the outside slip and right uppercut to the body.
Command—Ready, Strike!

2. Inboard men—As described above.
Outboard men—Practice the inside stop and right uppercut to the body.
Command—Ready, Strike!
Controlled Boxing

1. Inboard men—Use only a straight right to the chin.
Outboard men—Use only a right uppercut to the body. Try to slip to the outside position for its delivery.

2. Inboard men—Use only a straight right lead to chin.
Outboard men—Use only a right uppercut to the body. Practice parrying to the inside guard position.

DRILL 60—COUNTER BLOWS FOR THE RIGHT UPPERCUT TO THE BODY

THE LEFT JAB TO THE CHIN—THE LEFT HOOK TO THE CHIN—THE RETURN RIGHT UPPERCUT TO THE BODY

Technique Drill

1. Explain and demonstrate the following counter blows:
   — The Left]ab to the Chin.
   — The Left Hook to the Chin.
   — The Return Right Uppercut to the Body.

2. Have Class practice the movements of the left jab, the left hook to the chin and the return right uppercut.
Command—Left jab, Ready Strike!
Left hook, Ready Strike!
Right uppercut, Ready Strike!

Hitting Drill

1. Inboard men—On command, lead a right uppercut to the body. Hold the left glove directly in front of the chin, palm open toward the partner.
Outboard men—Practice countering with a left jab to the chin.
Command—Ready, Strike!

2. Inboard men—On command, lead a right uppercut to the body. Hold the left glove as described above.
Outboard men—Practice countering with a left hook to the chin.
Command—Ready, Strike!

3. Inboard men—On command, lead a right uppercut to body, Hold the left glove directly in front of solar plexus, palm open and downward.
Outboard men—Practice countering with the return right uppercut.
Command—Ready, Strike!

4. Inboard men—On command, lead a right uppercut to the body.
Outboard men—Practice the counter indicated by the command.
Command—Ready, One! or Ready, Two! or Ready, Three! The left jab is one, the left hook to the chin is two, and the return right uppercut is three.

Blocking Drill

1. Inboard men—On command, lead a right uppercut to the body. Block the opponent's counter with a right hand stop block.
Outboard men—Practice countering with a left jab to the chin.

Command—Ready, Strike!

2. Inboard men—On command, lead a right uppercut to the body. Block the opponent's counter with a left stop block.
Command—Ready, Strike!

3. Inboard men—On command, lead a right uppercut to the body. Block the opponent's counter with a left brush away.
Outboard men—Practice countering with a return right uppercut.
Command—Ready, Strike!

Controlled Boxing

1. Inboard men—Use only a right uppercut to the body.
Outboard men—Use only a left jab to the chin.

2. Inboard men—Use only a right uppercut to the body.
Outboard men—Use only a left hook to the chin.

3. Both men—Use only a right uppercut to the body.

DRILL 61—COMBINATIONS USING THE RIGHT UPPERCUT TO THE BODY

THE LEFT JAB AND RIGHT UPPERCUT COMBINATION—THE RIGHT HOOK AND RIGHT UPPERCUT COMBINATION-—THE RIGHT UPPERCUT AND RIGHT HOOK COMBINATION

Technique Drill

1. Explain and demonstrate the following combinations:
   — The left jab and right uppercut.
   — The right hook and right uppercut.
   — The right uppercut and right hook.

2. Have the class practice the left jab and right uppercut combination.
Command—One, Two! On one, execute the left jab, on two, the right uppercut. Shorten to Ready, Strike!

3. Have the Class practice the right hook and right uppercut combination.
Command—One, Two! On one, execute the right hook, on two, the right uppercut. Shorten to Ready, Strike!

4. Have the class practice the right uppercut and right hook combination.
Command—Ready, One, Two! On one, execute the right uppercut, on two, the right hook. Shorten the command to—Ready, Strike!

Hitting Drill

1. Inboard men—Hold the right glove, palm open and toward partner, directly off the right shoulder. Hold the left glove, palm open and turned downward, directly in front of the solar plexus.
Outboard men—On command, practice the left jab and right uppercut combination.
Command— Ready, Strike!

2. Inboard men—Hold the right glove, palm turned inward, directly off the right shoulder. Hold the left glove, palm open and turned downward, directly in front of the solar plexus.
Outboard men—On command, practice the right hook and right uppercut combination.
Command—Ready, Strike!

3. Inboard men—Hold both hands as described above.
Outboard men—On command practice the right uppercut and right hook combination.
Command—Ready, Strike!

Blocking Drill

1. Inboard men—On command, practice the right hook and right uppercut combination.
Outboard men—Practice a stop for the left jab with the right hand, and the brush away for the right uppercut with the left hand.
Command—Ready, One, Two! Shorten the command to—Ready, Strike.

2. Inboard men—On command, practice the right hook and right uppercut combination.
Outboard men—Block the right hook using the stop with the left hand, then brush downward to block the right uppercut.
Command—Ready, One. Two! Shorten to—Ready, Strike!

3. Inboard men—On command, practice the right uppercut and right hook combination.
Outboard men—Block the right uppercut with the left brush' away, then raising left hand use the stop block for the right hook.
Command—Ready, Strike!

Defensive Boxing

1. Inboard men—Use only a left jab and right uppercut combination.
Outboard men—On defense only.

2. Inboard men—Use only the right hook and right uppercut combination.
Outboard men—On defense only.

3. Inboard men—Use only the right uppercut and right hook combination.
Outboard men—On defense only.

Controlled Boxing

1. Inboard men—Use only the left jab and right uppercut combination.
Outboard men—Use only the right hook and right uppercut combination.

2. Inboard men—Use only the right hook and right uppercut combination.
Outboard men—Use only the right uppercut and right hook combination.

3. Inboard men—Use only the right uppercut and right hook combination.
Outboard men—Use only the left jab and right uppercut combination.

DRILL 62—THE LEFT HOOK AND RIGHT UPPERCUT COMBINATION— THE LEFT AND RIGHT UPPERCUT COMBINATION

Technique Drill

1. Explain and demonstrate:
   — The Left Hook and Right Uppercut Combination.
   — The Left and Right Uppercut Combination.

2. Have the class practice the left hook and right uppercut combination.
Command—Ready—One—Two! Hook on One, uppercut on two. Shorten to—Ready, Strike!

3. Have the class practice the left and right uppercut combination.
Command—Ready—On—Two! Use the left uppercut on one, right uppercut on two. Shorten to—Ready, Strike!

Hitting Drill

1. Inboard men—Hold the left hand off the left shoulder, palm open and turned inward; the right hand, palm open and downward, directly in front of the solar plexus.
Outboard men—On command, practice the left hook, right uppercut combination.
Command—Ready—One—Two! On one, hook, on two, uppercut. Shorten to—Ready, Strike!

2. Inboard men—Hold both gloves directly in front of the left and right hip, respectively, palms open and downward.
Outboard men—On command, practice the left and right uppercut combination.
Command—Ready—One—Two! On one, execute the left uppercut. On two, the right uppercut. Shorten to—Ready, Strike!

Blocking Drill

1. Inboard men—On command, practice the left hook and right uppercut combination.
Outboard men—Block the left hook with the right forearm block and the right uppercut with left brush away.
Command—Ready—One—Two! On one, block the left hook. On two, block the left uppercut. Shorten to—Ready, Strike!

2. Inboard men—On command, practice the left and right uppercut combination to the body.
Outboard men—Block the left uppercut with right brush away and the right uppercut with the left brush away.

Command—Ready—One—Two! On one, black the left uppercut; on two, block the right uppercut. Shorten to—Ready, Strike!

Defensive Boxing

1. Inboard men—Use only the left hook and right uppercut combination.
Outboard men—On defense only.

2. Inboard men—Use only the left and right uppercut combination to the body
Outboard men—On defense only.

Controlled Boxing

1. Inboard men—Use only the left hook and right uppercut combination.
Outboard men—Use only the left and right uppercut combination.

DRILL 63—THE LEFT HOOK, RIGHT HOOK AND LEFT UPPERCUT, RIGHT UPPERCUT COMBINATION—THE LEFT HOOK, LEFT UPPERCUT AND RIGHT HOOK, RIGHT UPPERCUT COMBINATION— THE LEFT UPPERCUT, LEFT HOOK AND RIGHT UPPERCUT, RIGHT HOOK COMBINATOION—THE LEFT HOOK, RIGHT UPPERCUT AND LEFT UPPERCUT, RIGHT HOOK COMBINATION

Technique Drill

1. Explain and demonstrate the following combinations:
   — The Left Hook, Right Hook and Left Uppercut, Right Uppercut.
   — The Left Hook, Left Uppercut and Right Hook, Right Uppercut.
   — The Left Uppercut, Left Hook and Right Uppercut, Right Hook.
   — The Left Hook, Right Uppercut and Left Uppercut, Right Hook.

2. Have the class practice the left hook, right hook and left uppercut, right uppercut combination.
Command—Ready One Two Three Four! On one, the left hook; on two, the right hook; one three, the left uppercut; on four, the right uppercut. Shorten the command to—Ready, Strike!

3. Have the class practice the left hook, left uppercut and the right hook, right uppercut.
Command—Ready One Two Three Four! On one, the left hook; on two, the left uppercut; on three, the right hook; on four, the right uppercut. Shorten to—Ready, Strike!

4. Have the class practice the left uppercut, left hook and right uppercut, right hook.
Command Ready—One Two Three Four! On one, left uppercut; on two, left hook; on three, right uppercut; on four, right hook. Shorten to—Ready, Strike!

5. Have the class practice the left hook, right uppercut and left uppercut, right hook.
Command—Ready One Two Three Four! On one, left hook; on two, right uppercut; on three, left uppercut; on four, right hook. Shorten to—Ready, Strike!

Hitting Drill

1. Inboard men—Hold the left hand high and open in front of the chin, palm outward; right hand in front of solar plexus, palm open and downward.
Outboard men—On command, practice the left hook, right hook and left uppercut, right uppercut combination.
Command—Ready One Two Three Four! Shorten to—Ready, Strike!

2. Inboard men—Hold gloves as described above.
Outboard men—On command, practice the left hook, left uppercut, right hook, right uppercut combination.

Command—Ready—One—Two—Three—Four! Shorten to—Ready, Strike!

3. Inboard men—Hold gloves as described above.
Outboard men—On command, practice the left uppercut and left hook, the right uppercut, right hook combination.
Command—Ready One Two Three Four! Shorten to—Ready, Strike!

4. Inboard men—Hold gloves as described above.
Outboard men—On command, practice the left hook, right uppercut and left uppercut, right hook combination.
Command—Ready One Two Three Four! Shorten to—Ready, Strike!

Blocking Drill

1. Inboard men—On command, practice the left hook, right hook and left uppercut, right uppercut combination.
Outboard men—Block the left hook with the right forearm block, the right hook with a left stop block, the left uppercut with the right brush away, and the right uppercut with the left brush away.
Command—Ready One Two Three Four! On one, block the left hook; on two, block the right hook; on three, block the left uppercut ; on four, block the right uppercut.

2. Inboard men—On command, practice the left hook, left uppercut and right hook, right uppercut combination.
Outboard men—Block the left hook with the right forearm block; the left uppercut with right brush away; the right hook using a stop with the left hand and the right uppercut with left brush away.
Command—Ready One Two Three Four! On one, block the left hook; on two, block left uppercut; on three, block the right hook; on four, block the right uppercut. Shorten to—Ready, Strike!

3. Inboard men—On command, practice the left uppercut, left hook and right uppercut, right hook combination.
Outboard men—Block the left uppercut with left brush away; the left hook with the left forearm block; the right uppercut with the left brush and the right hook with a stop with left hand.
Command—Ready One Two Three Four! On one, block the left uppercut; on two, block the left hook; on three, block the right uppercut; on four, block the right hook.
4. Inboard men—On command, practice the left hook, right uppercut and left uppercut, right hook combination.
Outboard men—Block the left hook with the right forearm block, the right uppercut with left brush; the left uppercut with right brush; and the right hook with the forearm block.

Command—Ready One Two Three Four! On one, block the left hook; on two, block the right uppercut; on three, block the left uppercut; on four, block the right hook. Shorten to—Ready, Strike!

Defensive Boxing

1. Inboard men—Use only the left hook, right hook and left uppercut, right uppercut combination.
Outboard men—On defense only.

2. Inboard men—Use only the left hook, left uppercut, right hook, right uppercut combination.
Outboard men—On defense only.

3. Inboard men—Use only the left uppercut, left hook, right uppercut, right hook combination.
Outboard men—On defense only.

4. Inboard men—Use only the left hook, right uppercut, left uppercut, right hook combination.
Outboard men——On defense only.

Controlled Boxing

1. Inboard men—Use only the left hook and right hook combination.
Outboard men—Use only the left uppercut and right uppercut combination.

2. Inboard men—Use only the left hook and left uppercut combination.
Outboard men—use only the right hook and right uppercut combination.

3. Inboard men—Use only the left uppercut and left hook combination.
Outboard men—Use only the right uppercut and right hook combination.

4. Inboard men—Use only the left hook and right uppercut combination.
Outboard men—Use only the left uppercut and right hook combination.

DRILL 64—BODY FEINTS

Technique Drill

1. Explain and demonstrate the following body feints:
   — The arm swing.
   — The knee feint.
   — The body drop.
   — The side bend.

2. Have the class practice the arm swing, as follows: have the class advance forward, using the step of the body to cause a swing of the left arm. Action must be free and cannot be given by command, except the general command for advance.
Command—Ready, Advance! Allow the left arm to swing free.

3. Have the class practice the knee feint. This is best done by having them advance slowly forward, and then on the command of feint, have them bend the knees, as if to strike.
Command—Ready, Feint!

4. Have the class practice the body drop.
Command—Ready, Feint!

5. Have the class practice the side bend.
Command—Ready, Feint!

Defensive Boxing

1. Inboard Men—Practice the body feints.
Outboard men—On defense only.

Controlled Boxing

1. Inboard men—Use only the left jab to the body.
Outboard men—Practice only the body feints.

2. Inboard men—Use only the straight left or right to the chin.
Outboard men—Use only the body feints and a left jab to the chin or body.

3. Both men—Use only the body feints in combination with the left jab.

DRILL 65—THE ARM FEINTS

Technique Drill

1. Explain and demonstrate the following arm feints:
    — The up-down feints, both hands.
    — The draw back feint.
    — The shift feint.
    — The specific arm feints.

2. Have the class practice the up-down feint, using the left hand.
Command—Ready, Feint up! Feint down! Have the men advance slowly forward while teaching the feints.

3. Have the class practice the up-down feints, using the right hand.
Command—Ready, Up ! or Ready, Down! or Feint up! or Feint down!

4. Have the class practice the draw back feint, while shuffling forward.
Command—Ready, Feint!

Defensive Boxing

1. Inboard men—Use only the up-down feints with both the left and the right hand
Outboard men—On defense only.

2. Inboard men—Use either the draw-back feint or the shift feint.
Outboard men—On defense only.

DRILL 66—THE SAFETY CLINCH THE BICEPS HOLD; THE DOUBLE LOCK; ARM ENCIRCLEMENT; SPINNING OUT OF A CLINCH

Technique Drill

1. Explain and demonstrate:
    — The safety clinch.
    — The biceps hold.
    — The double lock.
    — Arm encirclement.
    — Spinning out of a clinch.

2. Have the class practice the safety clinch.
Inboard men—On command, step forward and swing a wide left hook.
Outboard men—Practice the safety clinch.
Command—Ready, Strike! or Ready, Clinch! Have men hold the clinch until the command is given to break.

3. Have the class practice the biceps hold.
Inboard men—On command, lead a wide left swing to the chin.
Outboard men—Practice the biceps hold.
Command—Ready, Clinch! Followed by Ready, Break!

4. Have the class practice the double lock.
Inboard men—On command, lead a wide left hook.
Outboard men—Practice the double lock.
Command—Ready, Swing! or Ready, Clinch! Followed by Ready, Break!

5. Have the class practice the arm encirclement clinch.
Inboard men—On command, lead a wide left swing to the chin.
Outboard men—Practice arm encirclement.
Command—Ready, Clinch, or Ready, Swing! Followed by Ready, Break!

6. Have the class practice the safety clinch.
Inboard men—On command, swing a wide left hook to the chin.
Outboard men—Practice the safety clinch.
Command—Ready, Swing! or Ready, Break! On breaking, spin the opponent out of the clinch, either to the right or to the left.

Defensive Boxing

1. Inboard men—Practice the left jab to the chin.
Outboard men—On defense only, making use of the clinch.

DRILL 67—INFIGHTING TECHNIQUE; SHIFTING WITH THE OPPONENT; SHIFTING THE ATTACK TO THE HEAD

Technique Drill

1. Explain and demonstrate:
   — Infighting technique.
   — Shifting with the opponent.
   — Shifting the attack to the head.

2. Have the class practice the infighting technique.
Command—Ready, Begin! Have men drive both hands to body, until the command of Ready, Stop!

3. Have the class practice shifting with an opponent.
Inboard men—As the opponent leads a left, drive a short right uppercut inside.
Outboard men—Drive left and right uppercuts to body.
Command—Ready, Strike!

4. Have class practice shifting the attack to the head.
Inboard men—On command, lead a slow left jab, allowing partner to obtain the inside position. When partner starts driving uppercuts to the body, drop the arms to protect the body.
Outboard men—On opponent's left lead, slip to the inside position, and start the body attack. As the partner drops his hands to block the body blows, shift the attack to the head by driving the right hand to the opponent's right shoulder and spinning him into a left hook; or by driving a left arm to the opponent's left shoulder and spinning him into a right hook.
Command—Ready, Strike!

Controlled Boxing

1. Inboard men—Use only a left jab to the chin.
Outboard men—Practice only infighting.

2. Inboard men—Practice only infighting.
Outboard men—Practice only outfighting.

SPECIAL HITTING DRILL

1. Inboard men—Hold the right glove directly in front of right shoulder, palm open and outward toward partner.

Outboard men—On command, practice the left jab to the chin.

Command—Ready, Strike!

2. Inboard men—Hold both gloves directly in front of the left and right shoulders, respectively, palms open toward the partner.

Outboard men—On command, practice the left jab to the chin.

Command—Ready, Strike! Jab to partner's left glove. On the next command of strike, jab to the partner's left glove. Later, on the command of strike, jab first to the partner's right glove and follow immediately with a jab to the partner's left glove.

3. Inboard men—Hold the right glove directly in front of the right shoulder.

Outboard men—On command, practice the straight right to the chin.

Command—Ready, Strike!

4. Inboard men—Hold the right glove, palm open toward partner, directly in front of the right shoulder.

Outboard men—On command, practice the one-two to the chin.

Command—Ready, Strike!

5. Inboard men—Hold the left glove, palm open and turned inward directly off the left shoulder.

Outboard men—On command, practice the left hook.

Command—Ready, Strike!

6. Inboard men—Hold the left glove as described above.

Outboard men—On command, practice the double hook.

Command—Ready, Strike! Two left hooks in succession.

7. Inboard men—Hold the right glove, palm turned inward, directly off the right shoulder.

Outboard men—On command, practice the right hook.

Command—Ready, Strike!

8. Inboard men—Hold both gloves, palms open and turned inward, shoulder width apart.

Outboard men—On command, practice the left and right hooks.

Command—Ready—One—Two! On one, hook the left to the partner's left glove; on two, hook the right to the partner's right glove. One command for each blow. Shorten the command to—Ready, Strike! One command, two blows, the left hook followed immediately by the right hook.

9. Inboard men—Hold the left glove, palm open and downward, directly in front of the left hip.

Outboard men—On command, practice the left uppercut.

Command—Ready, Strike!

10. Inboard men—Hold the right glove, palm open and downward, directly in front of the left hip.

Outboard men—On command, practice the right uppercut.

Command—Ready, Strike!

11. Inboard men—Hold both hand, palms open and downward, directly in front of the left and right hips respectively.

Outboard men—On command, practice the left and right uppercut.

Command—Ready—One—Two! On one, drive the left uppercut to the left glove; on two, the right uppercut to the right glove. One command, one blow. Shorten the command to—Ready, Strike! The left uppercut is followed immediately by the right uppercut. One command for two blows.

12. Inboard men—Hold the left hand shoulder high, palm open and turned inward. Hold the right glove palm turned downward, directly in front of the solar plexus.

Outboard men—On command, practice the left hook to the chin and left uppercut to the body.

Command—One, Two! On one, hook a left to the chin; on two, drive a right uppercut to the body. Shorten the command to—Ready, Strike! Two blows on one command.

APPENDIX II

Lesson Plans

The thirty consecutive lesson plans herein developed are for the guidance of boxing instructors sewing in the Naval Aviation Physical Training Program at the various schools and bases concerned with flight training.

The lesson plans are listed progressively from the simple to the complex, from those consisting of a few simple drills, to those encompassing the more complex and difficult drills.

Directives will be sent from time to time indicating which lessons are to be used to form the syllabus at

The U. S. Naval Pre-Flight School
Primary Flight Training
Intermediate Flight Training

Boxing at the present time is not a part of the instructional program for:

The Flight Preparatory Schools
The War Training Service Schools
Operational Flight Training

Use of the lesson plan: Before attempting to teach boxing the instructor should be familiar with Chapter IV, giving special study to the lesson plan, sample lesson plan, and suggested time allotment.

The lesson plans that follow indicate by percentage the time that should be devoted to each phase of the lesson. This is a suggested allotment only, and will vary according to size of class, facilities, length of period, stage of development, and experience of the instructor. However, in all cases, it indicate: the emphasis and stress to be given and the proper relation of subject matter being taught. The page reference following the name of each lesson refers to the pages in the text where the techniques embodied in the lesson are discussed. The page reference opposite each drill indicates where the complete description of the drill may be found.

THE PROGRAM OF BOXING AT THE WAR TRAINING SCHOOLS

Here too, because flight training has started, and because specialists are not available for its teaching boxing is not included in the program of sports, either instructional or for the sports program period.

THE PROGRAM OF BOXING FOR THE U. S. NAVY PRE-FLIGHT SCHOOLS

Rough body contact sports which call for the utmost in courage, give and take and the will to win, are the core of the Pre-Flight School Athletic Program.

Boxing is one of the basic sports in which each cadet receives a specified number of lessons. The fundamentals of offense and defense are combined in natural relationship and are presented in logical order.

Class Organization and Procedure

Boxing at the Pre-Flight School should be a rugged military sport. Commands should be military; discipline absolute. Any infraction should be given immediate attention through the medium of extra work.

Goldbricking should not be allowed. Inattention, lack of cooperation, poor attitude, the inability to "take it"; all such traits should be recognized as early as possible, and action taken to correct.

A definite lesson plan, utilizing every minute of time, must be followed. Drills should be carried on at "top" speed.

The first day a class reports, explain what is wanted and expected, explain the marking and grading system. Demonstrate the formation to be used. The class is always expected to "fall in" on reporting.

Always space men by having them come to position in double arm order, both arms raised sidewards so there are only a few inches between the finger tips.

A special alertness drill, mixed in with regular commands, is a very effective method of keeping the cadets on their "toes." Any time the command "Hit the deck" is given, the entire class must assume the prone position on the deck, heads inward and toward the instructor. Have the class return to the upright position on the command of "Ready, up!"

An example of the commands used in an alertness drill are as follows:

"Arms up!" (Double arm order)

"Steady, hit the deck!"

"Everybody up!"

"On guard, hep!"

"Steady, front!"

"On guard, hep!"

"Hit the deck!" etc.

The last part of each instructional period should be given over to defensive, controlled and regular boxing, full protective gear being worn.

During actual boxing, use one minute rounds, fifteen seconds between rounds. On completion of each round, have the cadets return to formation on the double, arms spread. Have the cadets change partners each round. Have the inboard cadet rotate one man to either the right of left, outboard cadet standing fast. If a double file formation is used, the end cadet of the inboard file should circle around and take his place at the opposite end of the file.

After fighting the men hard for one minute call "time!" "Everybody in! Come in with arms up!" Men then return to formation with arms spread to a double arm interval position. Rotate the men, give them instructions as to what technique to use the next round, and then call "time ready, box!"

The Sports Program

The purpose of the sports program is to give each cadet the opportunity to face an opponent in the ring alone, and to test his prowess against that of other cadets.

Many cadets have never been struck with a glove or fist in their lives. Actually, they are afraid of the idea of being hit. The first time they receive a hard blow they are prone to believe that they are hurt. After receiving a few such blows, they suddenly realize they are unhurt and still able to fight. That is the most important moment of their entire training period. It is the time when the cadet loses his fear of physical force. From then on, while a cadet may not always win, he will fight with a new intensity became he is no longer afraid.

The sports program places the cadet on his own. In boxing there are no blockers out in front to help, no time out, no substitutes ready to take one's place. One is entirely on his own, alone to face whatever may come. It is an experience that every cadet should have. It builds confidence and faith that is of an inestimable value in combat flying.

The Sports Program Organization

Two days are designated as competitive days. One day being used to fight intra-squadron matches to determine the squadron team, and the other day to fight the inter-squadron mattber. The intra-squadron or trial bouts should be held early in the week; inter-squadron matches the latter part of the week. It is the practice in some of the Pre-Flight Schools to hold intra-squadron or trial bouts on Tuesday, and inter-squadron matches on Thursday. The other three days of the week are designated as practice days. On such days each squadron is worked out by it: own coach in preparation for either the intra-squadron bouts, or the squadron bouts.

On the competitive days, an auxiliary program should supplement competition for those men who are not boxing. Two types of programs can be used. The first is mass boxing instruction for all cadets not competing, the other, a special physical development program.

In either case, a coach or an instructor should be assigned to take care of the non-competitor. Either regular fundamentals or advanced work can be used for the mass instruction drills.

The special development program should consist of running, pushups and situps. During the time of the sports program, 10 laps (2 1/2 miles), 100 pushups and 100 situps should be given. The work can be split over the entire sports program period. This will allow the group to watch some of the fights.

At the beginning of the period, all non-competitors run three laps (three quarters of a mile). On finishing they do fifty pushups and fifty situps. They are then at liberty to watch the squadron bouts until midway during the period when the same workout exactly is repeated. At the end of the period, all cadet: whether they competed or not, are given four laps (one mile).

To further supplement the program, one day a week can occasionally be set aside for a special road work program. It consists of a five mile jog, stopping midway for fifteen minutes of special calisthenics. The whole workout should take less than sixty minutes. During the run, have the men run forward, backward, skip, hop, play leapfrog, run knees high, feet wide apart, do the duck waddle, etc. The cadets enjoy such a program. It should be made informal and full of fun.

THE PROGRAM OF BOXING FOR PRIMARY FLIGHT TRAINING

Here boxing is designed to take advantage of the background of experience already developed. Once fundamentals have been learned and a degree of defensive skill developed, the counter attack is the next logical step.

The counter attack calls for speed, timing, precision, and lends itself well to the mind-eye coordination so necessary to flying.

The sports program should include boxing only as a recreational sport. Supervision should be provided. Stress should be placed on the use of the boxing facilities for training or conditioning purposes.

THE PROGRAM OF BOXING FOR INTERMEDIATE FLIGHT TRAINING

The final stage in the teaching of boxing is now reached. It consists of teaching consecutive action through series punching or combination blows.

The rhythm and speed of the blows, and the natural shifting of weight from one leg to another, combine to give a feeling of power and accomplishment which adds interest and motivates the workouts.

All drills require the use of complete protective gear. Recreational, but not competitive boxing, should be a part of the sports program. Opportunity should be given for men to work out under supervision.

INTRODUCING BOXING IN HIGH SCHOOL OR COLLEGE

If you are the physical education teacher or coach at a school with the problem of starting a boxing program at your institution, why not start with a flourish by organizing a novice boxing tournament. It is a time-tested idea for developing boxing interest that has met with an ever enthusiastic response.

First of all the support of the sports department of the school paper should be enlisted. An enthusiastic reporter may write of the advantages of boxing, the chance to learn how to box and defend one's self under some expert teaching, and the chance to become a CHAMPION.

The rules of the tournament are simple. Merely eliminate anyone who has had a considerable amount of experience, hence everyone is starting from scratch. Draw up a weight schedule, and let the students sign up for their class. Fraternity and living center competition will spur a number of candidates to report. All of this can be duly reported to maintain interest by an embryo newspaperman under your direction.

A month before the tourney is to be held the candidates should report for training and instruction. At this time a 15-minute briefing on the advantages of boxing together with an explanation and use of the equipment they are about to use will start them on their way. Too, the boxers should be informed of their training schedule for the next month. This schedule should not only put them in top-notch physical condition for their big tournament chance, but should also teach them the fundamentals of boxing.

Informing the neophytes that only by Constant repetition does one gain perfection, the following daily schedule is recommended:

    a) Shadow Box—two rounds
    b) Skip Rope—two rounds
    c) Speed Bag—two rounds
    d) Heavy Bag—two rounds
    e) Stomach Exercises—six minutes
    f) Road work—one mile, alternately sprinting and walking.

The lesson plans in this manual should be followed rigidly, for it is a mistake to give a novice too much or too little instruction at one time; too little will cause him to lose interest while too much will bring discouragement. Each new lesson should be preceded by a review of the material covered in previous workouts.

As soon as you feel that a boy has mastered the fundamentals sufficiently well to protect himself and that his physical condition justifies, ring work should be added to the daily training schedule. When ring work is started, contestants should be evenly matched so as not to discourage the novices.

Inexpensive awards, suitable for the occasion of crowning champions, will stimulate interest in the tourney. A simple scoring system, employed at college meets, should be adapted for tournament purposes. The selection of judges and referee from among the school's faculty preferably who have had previous boxing experience will help keep expenses to a minimum.

Decisions are based upon points. Points are scored for each round. The winner of the round should receive ten points, while his opponent should get a smaller number of points in proportion to his showing. Points are awarded for clean hits, well-delivered partial hits, defense and ability to counter-attack, aggressiveness, and generalship. Total points, at the end of three rounds, govern the decision. Hence, as under the intercollegiate rules, it is possible for a contestant to win only one round while losing two, but still win the fight. The score card in such a case might be as follows:

Name	Points			
	1st Rd.	2nd Rd.	3rd Rd.	Total
Smith	10	10	6	26
Jones	9	9	10	28

OFFICIATING

The officials for a Boxing Tournament shall consist of a referee, two judges, a timekeeper, a director of bouts, an announcer, and a physician. For dual meets between colleges, the two judges can be eliminated with the referee determining the winner. In dual meets, a draw decision can be given but in a tournament bout, a winner must be named.

The referee is the chief official and shall have general supervision over the bouts. The judges shall be stationed at opposite sides of the ring.

The duties of a referee are very much the same whether the bout is collegiate, amateur, or professional. The main difference is in scoring the contest. All officials should know the rules governing the match.

The decisions of the referee and judges shall be based primarily on effectiveness, taking into account the following points:

1. A clean, forceful hit, landed above the belt should be credited in proportion to its damaging effect.

2. Aggressiveness—credits should be awarded to the contestant who sustains the action of a round by the greatest number of skilled attacks.

3. Defensive work is relatively important and credits should be given for blocking a blow or cleverly avoiding a blow and counter attacking.

4. Credits should be awarded where ring generalship is conspicuous. This comprises such points as the ability to quickly grasp and take advantage of every opportunity offered; the capacity to cope with all situations which may arise; to foresee and neutralize an opponent's method of attack; to force an opponent to adapt to a style of boxing at which he is not particularly skillful.

5. A contestant should be given credit for sportsman-like actions in the ring, close adherence to the spirit as well as the letter of the rules and for refraining from taking technical advantage of situations unfair to an opponent.

In collegiate boxing, ten points are awarded the winner of the round, or to each opponent in case a round is even. A proportionate number of points less than ten is awarded the contestant who loses a round. The total point score at the end of three rounds determines the winner on each official's scorecard. Each official shall clearly write the name of the winner on his card before it is turned over to the announcer. An exception is made to this rule in dual meets in which draw decisions may be rendered.

In professional boxing, referees and judges will mark their cards at the end of each round, W-L-E. meaning win; "L" meaning lose; meaning even; the round to be given by the officials to the man who in their opinion, 'showed superiority over his opponent in that particular round, At the conclusion of the contest, the boxer winning the greater number of rounds shall be declared the winner.

LESSON 1—POSITION, MOVEMENT AND HITTING POWER
(Page 51)

	Page	Time Allotment
Muster		
Mass Instruction		25%
Drill 1—The on-guard position	221	
Drill 2—The slow advance and the slow retreat	222	25%
Drill 3—The left and right steps	223	25%
Drill 5—The waist pivot	226	25%
Dismissal		

LESSON 2—THE LEFT JAB TO THE CHIN AND BLOCKS
(Page 77 and 81)

	Page	Time Allotment
Muster		
Review: The on-guard position, fundamental footwork, the waist pivot. Drills 1, 2, 3, 5		25%
Mass Instruction		
Drill 6—The left jab to the chin	227	25%
Drill 7—The stop	229	25%
Drill 8—The parry	230	
Defensive and Controlled Boxing. Refer to Drills 6, 7, 8		25%
Dismissal		

LESSON 3—THE STRAIGHT RIGHT TO THE CHIN AND BLOCKS
(Pages 133 and 134)

	Page	Time Allotment
Muster		
Review: The left jab to the chin and blocks. Drills 6, 7, 8		22%
Mass Instruction		
Drill 32—The straight right to the chin	270	25%
The Blocks		
Drill 33—The stop	272	30%
Drill 33—The leverage guard	272	
Defensive and Controlled Boxing. Refer to drills 32, 33		23%
Dismissal		

LESSON 4—THE LEFT JAB TO THE BODY AND BLOCKS
(Pages 103 and 104)

	Page	Time Allotment
Muster		
Review The straight right to the chin and blocks. Drills 32, 33		20%
Mass Instruction		
Drill 13—The left jab to the body	239	30%
Drill 51—The straight right to the body	307	

The Blocks: Drill 14 and 52

	Left jab	Straight right	
The elbow block	241	308	
The forearm block	241	308	25%
The brush away	241	308	
The step away	241	308	
Defensive and Controlled Boxing. Refer to drills 14, 52, 53			25%
Dismissal			

LESSON 5—THE LEFT HOOK TO THE CHIN AND BLOCKS
(Pages 111 and 113)

	Page	Time Allotment
Muster		25%
Review The left jab to the body and blocks. Drills 14, 52, 53		
Mass Instruction		
Drill 18—The left hook to the chin	249	30%
The Block:		
Drill 19—The forearm block	250	20%
Defensive and Controlled Boxing. Refer to drills 18, 19.		25%
Dismissal		

LESSON 6—THE UPPERCUTS TO THE BODY
(Pages 124 ; 134)
THE RIGHT HOOK TO THE CHIN
(Page 151)
THE BLOCKS FOR THE UPPERCUTS
(Page 125 ; 173)
THE BLOCKS FOR THE RIGHT HOOK
(Page 134)

	Page	Time Allotment
Muster		
Review The left hook to the chin and blocks. Drills 18,19		23%
Mass Instruction		
Drill 25—The left uppercut to the body	259	
Drill 56—The right uppercut to the body	315	30%
Drill 44—The right hook to the chin	292	
The Blocks:		
Drill 26—For uppercuts, the brush away	260	
Drill 45—For right hook; the forearm block	294	25%
Drill 45—The stop	294	
Defensive and Controlled Boxing. Refer to Drills 25, 26, 44, 45, 56. ·		22%
Dismissal		

LESSON 7—SLIPPING AND DUCKING
(Pages 86 ; 114 ; 136 ; 153)

	Page	Time Allotment
Muster		
Review The uppercut to the body and blocks		
Drills 25, 26		25%
The right hook and blocks. Drill 44.		
Mass Instruction		
Drill 9—Slipping	232	
Drill 35—Slipping	275	25%
Drill 19—The Duck	250; 294	25%
Defensive and Controlled Boxing. Refer to drills 9, 19, 45.		25%
Dismissal		

LESSON 8—FEINTING
(Page 191)

	Page	Time Allotment
Muster		25%
Review Slipping and ducking. Drills 9, 45, 19		
Mass Instruction		
Drill 64—Body feints	332	25%
Drill 65—Arm feints	333	25%
Defensive and Controlled Boxing. Refer to Drills 67, 68.		25%
Dismissal		

LESSON 9—CLINCHING AND INFIGHTING
(Pages 195-199)

	Page	Time Allotment
Muster		20%
Review Feinting. Drills 67, 68		
Mass Instruction		
Drill 66—Clinching	334	25%
Drill 67—Infighting	335	25%
Defensive and Controlled Boxing. Refer to Drills 70, 71		25%
Dismissal		

LESSON 10—ADVANCED FOOTWORK
(Page 57)

	Page	Time Allotment
Muster		20%
Review: Fundamental footwork. Drills 2, 3		
Mass Instruction		
Drill 2—The quick advance and retreat	222	
Drill 3—The step back	223	30%
Drill 3—The step-in, step-out	223	
Drill 4—The quick shift	224	
Drill 4—The drop shift	224	25%
Drill 4—The rear shift	224	
Defensive and Controlled Boxing, Refer to drills 2, 3, 4.		25%
Dismissal		

LESSON 11—ADVANCED DEFENSIVE TECHNIQUES FOR THE LEFT JAB TO CHIN
(Page 81)

	Page	Time Allotment
Muster		25%
Review: The stop block and parry for left jab. Drills 7, 8		
Mass Instruction		
Drill 8—Parrying to the inside guard position on a left jab	230	
Drill 8—Parrying to the outside guard position on a left jab	230	25%
Drill 8—The cross parry on a left jab	230	
Drill 8—Stopping a left jab	230	
Drill 9—Slipping to the inside guard position on a left jab	232	25%
Drill 9—Slipping to the outside guard position on a left jab	232	
Defensive and Controlled Boxing. Refer to Drills 8, 9		25%
Dismissal		

LESSON 12—ADVANCED DEFENSIVE TECHNIQUE FOR THE LEFT JAB TO THE CHIN—CONTINUED
(Page 81)

	Page	Time Allotment
Muster		
Review: Advanced defensive technique as covered in lesson 11, Drills 8, 9		25%
Mass Instruction		
Drill 9—Cuffing on a left jab	232	25%
Drill 10—Covering and folding	234	
Drill 10—Rolling and weaving	234	25%
Drill 10—The snap away	234	
Defensive and Controlled Boxing. Refer to Drills 9, 11		25%
Dismissal		

LESSON 13—ADVANCED DEFENSIVE TECHNIQUE FOR THE STRAIGHT RIGHT TO THE CHIN
(Page 134)

	Page	Time Allotment
Muster		
Review: The stop block and leverage block for the straight right to the chin. Drill 33.		20%
Mass Instruction		
Drill 34—The inside parry on a straight right to chin	273	
Drill 34—The outside parry on a straight right to chin	273	25%
Drill 34—The cross parry on a straight right to chin	273	
Drill 35—The shoulder block	275	
Drill 35—Slipping inside or outside on a straight right lead	275	20%
Drill 36—The step back	277	
Drill 36—Circling away from a straight right lead	277	15%
Drill 36—Circling into a straight right lead	277	
Defensive and Controlled Boxing. Refer to Drills 34, 35, 36		20%
Dismissal		

LESSON 14—THE LEFT JAB AS A COUNTER BLOW
(Page 94)

	Page	Time Allotment
Muster		
Review: The advanced defensive technique for the straight right to the chin. Drills 34, 35, 36		20%
Mass Instruction		
Drill 11—The return left jab	236	20%
Drill 12—The inside parry and left jab to chin	237	20%
Drill 13—The outside parry and left jab to chin	239	20%
Defensive and Controlled Boxing. Refer to Drills 12, 13		20%
Dismissal		

LESSON 15—COUNTERS FOR THE LEFT JAB TO THE CHIN
(Page 96)

	Page	Time Allotment
Muster		
Review: The left jab as a counter blow. Drills 12, 13		20%
Mass Instruction		
Drill 12—The inside parry and left jab to the chin	237	
Drill 12—The outside parry and left jab to the chin	237	15%
Drill 46—The right cross	296	25%
Drill 37—The inside straight right to the chin	278	
Drill 46—The inside guard and right hook to the chin	296	20%
Defensive and Controlled Boxing. Refer to Drills 13, 37, 48		
Dismissal		20%

LESSON 16—COUNTERS FOR THE LEFT JAB TO THE CHIN—CONTINUED
(Page 96)

	Page	Time Allotment
Muster		
Review: Counters for the left jab to the chin. Drills 13, 37, 48.		20%
Mass Instruction		
Drill 53—The inside straight right to the heart	310	15%
Drill 27—The outside parry and left uppercut to solar plexus, left and right steps	262	15%
Drill 27—The inside guard and left uppercut to the liver	262	15%
Drill 46—The cross parry and right hook to the chin	296	15%
Defensive and Controlled Boxing. Refer to Drills 27, 48, 55		20%
Dismissal		

LESSON 17—THE LEFT JAB TO THE BODY AS A COUNTER
(Page 108)
COUNTERS FOR THE LEFT JAB TO THE BODY
(Page 108)

	Page	Time Allotment
Muster		
Review: Counters for the left jab to the chin. Drills 27, 48, 55.		25%
Mass Instruction. *The Left Jab to the Body as a Counter.*		
Drill 15—The outside slip and left jab to the body.	243	30%
Drill 15—The inside slip and left jab to the body	243	
Counters for the Left Jab to the Body		
Drill 27—The inside parry and left uppercut to the solar plexus and left jab to the chin	262	25%
Drill 58—The cross parry and right uppercut to the body	319	
Defensive and Controlled Boxing. Refer to Drills 16, 27, 60		20%
Dismissal		

LESSON 18—THE LEFT HOOK TO THE CHIN AS A COUNTER
(Page 115)
COUNTERS FOR THE LEFT HOOK TO THE CHIN
(Page 116)

	Page	Time Allotment
Muster		20%
Review: Counters for the left jab to the body. Drills 27, 60		
Mass Instruction The Left Hook as a Counter Blow		
Drill 20—The inside guard and left hook to the chin	252	
Drill 27—The inside guard and left uppercut to liver	262	35%
Drill 20—The inside hook on a straight right lead	252	
Counters for the Left Hook to the Chin		
Drill 21—The straight left jab	254	
Drill 21—The straight right to the chin	254	25%
Drill 51—The straight right to the body	307	
Drill 21—The return left hook to the chin	254	
Defensive and Controlled Boxing. Refer to Drills 20, 21, 27, 55		
Dismissal		20%

LESSON 19—THE LEFT UPPERCUT AS A COUNTER
(Page 126)
COUNTERS FOR THE LEFT UPPERCUT TO THE BODY
(Page 127)

	Page	Time Allotment
Muster		20%
Review: The left hook as a counter blow. Drills 20, 27		
Mass Instruction The Left Uppercut as a Counter		
Drill 27—The outside parry and left uppercut to the solar plexus, right and left steps	262	25%
Drill 27—The inside guard and left uppercut to the liver	262	
Drill 27—The cross parry and left uppercut to the liver on a straight right lead	262	10%
Counters for the Left Uppercut to the Body		
Drill 28—The left jab to the chin	264	
Drill 28—The straight right to the chin	264	25%
Drill 28—The right hook to the chin	264	
Drill 28—The left uppercut	264	
Defensive and Controlled Boxing. Refer to Drill 27, 28		20%
Dismissal		

LESSON 20—THE STRAIGHT RIGHT AS A COUNTER
(Page 140)
COUNTERS FOR A STRAIGHT RIGHT TO THE CHIN
(Page 142)

	Page	Time Allotment
Muster		20%
Review: The left uppercut as a counter, Drill 27.		
Mass Instruction *The Straight Right as a Counter*		
Drill 37—The inside right to the chin	278	
Drill 37—The cross parry and straight right to chin	278	30%
Drill 38—The outside parry and straight right to the chin; right lead	280	
Counters for a Straight Right to Chin		
Drill 39—The left jab	282	
Drill 39—The inside left hook	282	30%
Drill 39—The straight right to the body	282	
Defensive and Controlled Boxing. Refer to Drills 37, 38, 39		20%
Dismissal		

LESSON 21—THE RIGHT HOOK AS A COUNTER BLOW
(Page 155)
COUNTERS FOR A RIGHT HOOK TO THE CHIN
(Page 157)

	Page	Time Allotment
Muster		20%
Review: The straight right as a counter blow. Drills 37, 38		
Mass Instruction. *The Right Hook as a Counter Blow*		
Drill 46—The right cross	296	15%
Drill 46—The inside guard and right hook	296	25%
Drill 46—The cross parry and right hook	296	
Counters for a Right Hook to the Chin		
Drill 47—The left jab	298	
Drill 47—The left uppercut to the body	298	20%
Drill 47—The left jab to the body	298	
Drill 47—The return right hook	298	
Defensive and Controlled Boxing. Refer to Drills 48, 49		20%
Dismissal		

LESSON 22—THE STRAIGHT RIGHT TO THE BODY AS A COUNTER BLOW
(Page 167)
COUNTERS FOR A STRAIGHT RIGHT TO THE BODY
(Page 168)

	Page	Time Allotment
Muster		25%
Review: The right hook as a counter blow. Drill 48		
Mass Instruction *The Straight Right to the Body as a Counter Blow*		
Drill 53—The inside right to the heart	310	
Drill 53—The outside slip and straight right to the heart on a straight right lead	310	30%
Counters for a Straight Right to the Body		
Drill 54—The left jab to the chin	311	
Drill 54—The left uppercut to the body	311	
Drill 54—The right uppercut to the body	311	25%
Drill 54—The left hook to the chin	311	
Defensive and Controlled Boxing. Refer to Drills 60, 61, 62		
Dismissal		20%

LESSON 23—THE RIGHT UPPERCUT TO THE BODY AS A COUNTER
BLOW
(Page 176)
COUNTER BLOWS FOR THE RIGHT UPPECUT TO THE BODY
(Page 177)

	Page	Time Allotment
Muster		
Review: The straight right to the body as a counter blow. Drill 55		25%
Mass Instruction. *The Right Uppercut to the Body as a Counter Blow*		
Drill 58—The inside slip and right uppercut to the body	319	
Drill 58—The cross parry and right uppercut to the body	319	30%
Drill 59—The outside slip and right uppercut to the body on a right lead	321	
Counters for the Right Uppercut to the Body		
Drill 60—The left jab	323	
Drill 60—The left jab to the chin	323	25%
Drill 60—The return right uppercut to the body	323	
Defensive and Controlled Boxing. Refer to Drills 60, 61, 62		20%
Dismissal		

LESSON 24—COMBINATION BLOWS USING THE LEFT JAB TO HEAD
OR BODY
(Page 129)

	Page	Time Allotment
Muster		
Review: The right uppercut to the body as a counter blow. Drill 60, 61		20%
Mass Instruction		
Drill 17—The double left jab to the chin	247	15%
Drill 16—The left jab to the chin, followed by the left jab to the body	245	15%
Drill 16—The left jab to the body, followed by the left jab to the chin	245	15%
Drill 17—The double left jab to the body	247	15%
Defensive and Controlled Boxing. Refer to Drills 17, 18		20%
Dismissal		

LESSON 25—COMBINATION BLOWS USING THE LEFT JAB TO HEAD AND BODY, AND THE LEFT HOOK TO CHIN
(Page 120)

	Page	Time Allotment
Muster		20%
Review: Combination blows using the left jab to the head or body. Drill 17, 18		
Mass Instruction		
Drill 22—The jab-step and hook	256	25%
Drill 23—The left jab to the body and the left hook to the chin	257	20%
Drill 24—The left jab to the chin, the left jab to the body, and the left hook to the chin	258	15%
Defensive and Controlled Boxing. Refer to Drills 22, 23, 24		20%
Dismissal		

LESSON 26—COMBINATION BLOWS USING THE LEFT JAB TO HEAD OR BODY, THE LEFT HOOK TO THE CHIN, AND THE LEFT UPPERCUT TO THE BODY
(Page 129)

	Page	Time Allotment
Muster		
Review: Combination blows using the left jab to the head or body. Drills 23, 24		20%
Mass Instruction		
Drill 29—The left jab and left uppercut combination	266	
Drill 30—The left hook to the chin and the left uppercut to the body combination	267	30%
Drill 30—The left uppercut to the body and the left hook to the chin combination	267	
Drill 31—The jab-hook and uppercut combination	268	30%
Drill 31—The jab-uppercut and hook combination	268	
Defensive and Controlled Boxing. Refer to Drills 29, 30, 31		20%
Dismissal		

LESSON 27—COMBINATION BLOWS USING ALL LEFT HAND BLOWS AND
THE STRAIGHT RIGHT TO THE CHIN
(Page 159)

	Page	Time Allotment
Muster		
Review: Combination blows using the left jab to the head or body, the left hook to the chin and the left uppercut to the body. Drill 29, 30, 31		20%
Mass Instruction		
Drill 40—The one-two to the chin	284	15%
Drill 41—The jab-cross and hook to the chin	286	
Drill 41—The jab-cross and uppercut to the body	286	25%
Drill 42—The jab-hook and cross to the chin	288	
Drill 42—The jab-hook and right uppercut to the body	288	
Drill 43—The straight high-low	290	
Drill 43—The high-low and cross	290	20%
Drill 43—The low-high and uppercut	290	
Defensive and Controlled Boxing. Refer to Drills 42, 43, 44, 45		20%
Dismissal		

LESSON 28—COMBINATION BLOWS USING ALL THE LEFT HANDED BLOWS,
AND THE STRAIGHT RIGHT AND RIGHT HOOK TO THE CHIN
(Page 158)

	Page	Time Allotment
Muster		
Review: Combination blows using all left handed blows, and the straight right to the chin. Drills 42, 43, 44, 45		20%
Mass Instruction		
Drill 48—The left hook and right hooks to the chin	301	
Drill 48—The left jab, left hook and right hook to the chin	301	25%
Drill 49—The left jab to the body and the right hook to the chin	303	
Drill 49—The left uppercut to the body and the right hook to the chin	303	
Drill 50—The left hook to the chin, the left uppercut to the body and the right hook to the chin	305	35%
Drill 50—The left uppercut to the body, the right hook to the chin and the left hook to the chin	305	
Defensive and Controlled Boxing. Refer to Drills 50, 51, 52		20%
Dismissal		

LESSON 29—COMBINATION BLOWS USING ALL THE LEFT HANDED BLOWS,
THE STRAIGHT RIGHT AND RIGHT HOOK TO THE CHIN, AND THE
STRAIGHT RIGHT TO THE BODY
(Page 169)

	Page	Time Allotment
Muster		
Review: Combination blows using all the left handed blows, and the straight right and right hook to the chin. Drills 50, 51, 52		20%
Mass Instruction		
Drill 55—The left jab to the chin and the right to the body	313	20%
Drill 55—The left hook to the chin and the right to the body	313	20%
Drill 55—The one-two to the body	313	20%
Defensive and Controlled Boxing. Refer to Drill 57		
Dismissal		20%

LESSON 30—COMBINATION BLOWS USING ALL LEFT HANDED BLOWS AND
ALL RIGHT HANDED BLOWS, INCLUDING THE RIGHT UPPERCUT TO THE
BODY
(Page 180)

	Page	Time Allotment
Muster		
Review: Combination blows using all the left handed blows, the straight right and right hook to the chin and the straight right to the body. Drill 57		20%
Mass Instruction		
Drill 61—The left jab and right uppercut combination	325	
Drill 61—The right hook and right uppercut combination	325	
Drill 61—The right uppercut and right hook combination	325	30%
Drill 62—The left hook and right uppercut combination	327	
Drill 62—The left and right uppercut combination	327	
Drill 63—The left hook, right hook and left uppercut, right uppercut combination	329	
Drill 63—The left hook, let uppercut, and right hook, right uppercut combination	329	
Drill 63—The left uppercut, let hook, and right uppercut, right hook combination	329	30%
Drill 63—The left hook, right uppercut, and left uppercut, right hook combination	329	
Defensive and Controlled Boxing. Refer to Drills 63, 64, 65		
Dismissal		20%

Printed in Great Britain
by Amazon